SIR ROGER TWYSDEN

By the same author

A HISTORY OF KENT

INTRODUCTION TO KENT FEET OF FINES BEFORE 1272

THE CINQUE PORTS (*with R. F. Jessup*)

Sir Roger Twysden, 2nd baronet of Roydon, aged 51

FRANK W. JESSUP

SIR
ROGER TWYSDEN

1597-1672

LONDON
THE CRESSET PRESS

Published in Great Britain by
The Cresset Press 11 Fitzroy Square London W.1
First published in 1965

Printed in Great Britain by
The Camelot Press Ltd., Southampton and London

Preface

One evening about five years ago when I was staying, a rather lonely stranger, in Cambridge, Massachusetts, Professor Sam Thorne of the Harvard Law School bestowed on me quite the most agreeable form of hospitality; he took me home to a family supper. As we sat in his study afterwards he reached down from a bookshelf the copy of Ussher's *Britannicarum Ecclesiarum Antiquitates* which belonged to Sir Roger Twysden, for whom we discovered that we had a common respect and almost affection. Professor Thorne expressed the view that it was high time that Twysden's life was written and his scholarly achievements described. He added that it would not be a difficult task nor occupy many months; and suggested that, as a Kentish man, I ought to undertake it. This book is the consequence.

Twysden is well known to Kentish antiquaries in whose writings he usually appears as a staunch Royalist, romantically suffering for his King. He is also known to constitutional and legal historians, to whom, however, his personal history is probably not familiar. J. M. Kemble's Introduction to the edition of *Certaine Considerations upon the Government of England* which he prepared for the Camden Society in 1849 contains some biographical material largely derived from the Rev. Lambert B. Larking, but neither Kemble's article nor Seccombe's in the *Dictionary of National Biography* deals with Twysden comprehensively. There is much more material about him in the *Family of Twysden and Twisden* (1939), compiled by Sir John Ramskill Twisden, the twelfth and last baronet of Bradbourne, and completed after his death by Lieutenant-Colonel C. H. Dudley Ward, D.S.O., M.C. The justification for this present book is that it attempts to relate Twysden to his contemporary environment, whereas to Sir John Ramskill Twisden he was chiefly interesting as an important link in the history of the family, stretching from the thirteenth century to the twentieth. Anyone working over the material which Sir John used, as inevitably I have, cannot fail to be impressed by his painstaking care and accuracy, worthy indeed of the subject of this biography. This material is considerable in volume consisting mainly of manuscripts in the British Museum, the Kent County Archives Office, Lambeth Palace Library, the Bodleian Library, Maidstone Museum, and the collections of the Kent Archaeological Society. Not without doubt, and in the uncomfortable certainty that Twysden himself would have disapproved of the practice, I have decided to omit footnote references to manuscript sources. The reasons for the omission are twofold: the references would have been so numerous as to be a nuisance to the reader, and they would have given the book an inappropriate appearance of pseudo-scholarship. And, if Sir Roger is still dissatisfied, I shall beg to remind him that this work, unlike his, is not a controversial treatise nor does it aim at proving anything. If it helps to a better understanding of Twysden himself and what it was like to live through England's time of troubles it will have achieved its purpose.

Although the manuscript material is voluminous, certain periods of Twysden's life and certain aspects of his activities are much better evidenced than others, with a resulting want of proportion in this biography. Fortunately the times and the activities which are of greatest interest to us—although not necessarily to him—are those that are most fully documented. It is always possible that more material will turn up, but much I fear disappeared finally during the Civil War. The arrangement of the book will be clear from the list of contents: Part One is a chronological account of the major events in Twysden's life, Part Two deals with his activities in the role of landowner, public man, and scholar, with a final chapter by way of 'character'.

Twysden spent many months, even years, rummaging amongst the public records in conditions of discomfort and difficulty which are almost inconceivable to the pampered twentieth-century scholar. We take for granted not only the warmth and light of libraries and record offices but also the helpful service which their staffs unfailingly give. In expressing my appreciation of the courteous assistance of the staffs of the Bodleian Library, the British Museum, the Honourable Society of Gray's Inn, the Kent County Archives Office, Lambeth Palace Library, the National Portrait Gallery, and the Society of Antiquaries I am not indulging in any mere formality.

The Kent Archaeological Society and the National Portrait Gallery have kindly given permission for the reproduction of the portraits included in this volume. The Twysden portraits remain at Bradbourne, for nearly three centuries the home of the Twisdens and now the headquarters of the East Malling Research Station, and I am indebted to Dr. F. R. Tubbs, C.B.E., the Director of the Station, and to Mr. Yoxall Jones, of the Photographic Section, for their kind co-operation in enabling me to have some of the portraits photographed.

I record also with gratitude the help which I have received from my brother, Ronald Jessup, Dr. Felix Hull and Miss Elizabeth Melling, who were good enough to read the typescript of this book, and also, in various ways, from Wing-Commander W. V. Dumbreck, Mr. Roger Ellis, Mr. L. R. A. Grove, Mr. J. H. Parker Oxspring, Mr. A. N. G. Richards, Dr. Cecil Roth, the Reverend John Sergeant, Mr. H. P. Smith, and Professor S. E. Thorne.

Finally, I am especially grateful to my wife for putting the manuscript into a form fit for the eye of the printer.

F. W. J.

Thame, Oxon.

I should also gratefully [illegible] the help which I have [illegible] from my brother, Robert Jessup, [illegible] Hall and [illegible] Malling, who was good enough to read the [illegible] of this book, and also [illegible] Commander [illegible], Mr. Roger [illegible], Mr. [illegible] Grove, Mr. [illegible] B. [illegible], Mr. [illegible] G. [illegible], Dr. Cecil Roth, the Reverend [illegible], Mr. [illegible] Steer, and [illegible].

Gray's Inn

[illegible]

Contents

Illustrations

(*None of the artists of the portraits is known*)

PART ONE

CHAPTER ONE

Background

'KENTISH COUSINS—the sense of this', according to the collection of Kentish proverbs made by the Rev. Samuel Pegge in the early eighteenth century, 'is much the same [as] . . . cousins germans quite removed. This county being two-thirds of it bounded by the sea and the river, the inhabitants thereof are kept more at home than they are in the inland counties. This confinement naturally produces intermarriages amongst themselves, and a relation once begun is kept alive and diffused from generation to generation. In humane and generous minds, which have always been the characteristic of this people, friendships and familiarities once commenced, are not easily dropped; and one needs not wonder that amongst such, affinities may sometimes be challenged where the lines may be worn out, or that the pleasantry of less considerate aliens should make a byword of such simplicity of manners.'[1]

What was believed to be true of eighteenth-century Kent was even more characteristic of the county community in the seventeenth and earlier centuries. It was a community marked by stability and continuity and bound together by ties of marriage, friendship, and interest. Lambarde, that pioneer county topographer, has misled many subsequent generations by his statement that 'the gentlemen be not heere (throughout) of so ancient stockes as elsewhere, especially in the partes nearer to London, from which citie (as it were from a certeine riche and wealthy seedplot) Courtiers, Lawyers, and Marchants be continually translated, and do become new plants amongst

[1] *Archaeologia Cantiana*, IX (1874), 125.

them'.[1] Some such immigrants there were, Lambarde himself amongst them, but they were few compared with the indigenous gentry, and East Kent and the Weald were little, if at all, affected by this 'translation' from London.

A recent estimate suggests that of the Kentish gentry in the middle of the seventeenth century only one-eighth had come in since the end of Queen Elizabeth's reign, and that three-quarters of their families had been there since before 1500.[2]

This continuity amongst the gentry is shown in the names of the Kentish Knights of the Shire. Between 1500 and 1750 some three dozen families supplied all the County Members, and the same surnames constantly recur. In the Parliament of April, 16 Charles I, the county was represented by a Twysden and a Knatchbull; it was so again in 1 James II and in 8 George I. In 1640, although not in the same Parliament, the Knights of the Shire included Sir Roger Twysden and Sir Edward Dering; rather more than 100 years later (15 and 21 George II) the Knights of the Shire were another Sir Roger Twysden and another Sir Edward Dering. The adjective 'perdurable' which Dr. Simpson has suggested best describes the East Anglian gentry of the sixteenth and seventeenth centuries is equally applicable to the families that owned and governed Kent.[3]

Another characteristic of the county was the manner in which it was ruled by the gentry free from the domination of any single noble family or even by a handful of potentates. Effectively, in the seventeenth century its affairs were in the hands of some fifty families.[4] Seen at a distance of 300 years they are

[1] W. Lambarde, *A Perambulation of Kent* (1576), p. 10.

[2] A. Everitt, *Suffolk and the Great Rebellion 1640–1660* (1960), p. 21. See also Dr. Everitt's article on 'The Community of Kent in 1640' in *The Genealogists' Magazine*, vol. 14, no. 8 (December 1963).

[3] A. Simpson, *The Wealth of the Gentry* (1961), p. 216.

[4] In 1562 Kent had approximately 50 Justices of the Peace when Devon, Norfolk, Suffolk, and Sussex, counties of comparable size, had respectively about 32, 18, 32 and 25 (excluding grandee *ex officio* Justices). B. Osborne, *Justices of the Peace 1361–1848* (1960), pp. 29–30.

The influential families of the seventeenth century included the following (in some cases there were several branches of the same family): Amherst, Aucher, Austen, Baker, Barnham, Boteler, Boys, Brooke, Cheney, Clerke, Culpepper, Dalison, Darell, Dering, Fane (or Vane), Filmer, Finch,

apt to blend into a pattern of deceptive regularity, into an apparently homogeneous class or caste of 'the gentry'. Themselves they were conscious of social gradations that the backward glance evens out. It was typical both of the man and of his time that on more than one public occasion Twysden demurred to act because it was unfitting that he should do so in advance of those of higher degree, and even in his own private memoranda he apologizes for the solecism if he finds himself obliged to copy a document in which names are wrongly ordered. The gentry were a self-conscious class owning the land and ruling the county, but it is misleading to think of them as a uniform group.

In another respect also Kent differed from much of the rest of England in that there was little of that 'attachment by a lesser man to the following of a greater' which, as Dr. Aylmer has pointed out, 'was still so characteristic a feature of English political and social life' during the reigns of the earlier Stuarts.[1] The absence of a county oligarchy in part accounts for the independence of the Kentish gentry, but so, too, does the fact that most of them were more concerned with managing their own county than in playing a part in national affairs. Even a man like Sir Edward Dering, who was connected through his first marriage with the Cecils and through his second with the Villiers, was not prominent at court, acquired only the office of Lieutenant of Dover Castle (which proved an unprofitable investment), and as a Knight of the Shire was scarcely memorable except for the puritanical zeal with which he moved the first reading of the Root and Branch Bill; but perhaps, in any case, Dering was too unpredictable and enigmatical to be employed in any enterprise, even at court.

Between the gentry and the yeomanry, and between the yeomanry and the labourers, the lines of demarcation may

Guildford, Hales, Hardres, Honywood, James, Kemp, Knatchbull, Lennard, Leveson, Livesey, Lovelace, Manwood, Masters, Mayny, Miller, Monins, Moyle, Nevill, Oxinden, Peyton, Rivers, Rycaut, Sackville, St. Leger, Sandys, Scott, Sedley, Selby, Sidney, Sondes, Spencer, Strode, Style, Tufton, Twysden, Walsingham, Weldon, Wootton.

[1] G. W. Aylmer, *The King's Servants: The Civil Service of Charles I, 1625–42* (1961), p. 83.

have been blurred at the edges, but the classification was a substantive one and its rightness scarcely questioned, certainly not amongst the gentry. There is little evidence, on the part of the gentry, of fear of or hostility towards, the labouring class. Their needs were not altogether neglected, they received a sort of book-justice and sometimes rather more, and of maliciously cruel treatment there is no sign. But the assessment of their needs was pitched low and their *raison d'être* was accepted as being to enable the gentle class to exist at a tolerable level of comfort. A letter amongst the correspondence of Henry Oxinden of Barham illustrates the class solidarity that was expected of gentlemen and the way in which the labourer was regarded as subsisting merely in order to serve his master. Writing in 1639 to his namesake, Henry Oxinden of Deane says: 'I spoke to Sir Thomas Palmer that he would not take it ill if you followed the law against his man for stealing your conies, his answere to mee was very colerik and rash and sayd you did him a great discourtesie to take away his man now he had so important and earnest occasions for him, being harvest and hee his picher, but you might prosecute the others now and after harvest hang his man if hee deserved it.'[1]

However, to offset Sir Thomas Palmer's choler we ought to remember the frequent minor acts of charity performed by the seventeenth-century gentry, a few of which are recorded in this volume, and more generally the substantial sums which they gave for the relief of the poor and the promotion of education. In the first forty years of the century charitable bequests made by members of the gentle class in Kent totalled £33,450, of which nearly £15,000 was for the alleviation of the lot of the poor, and £11,000 for establishing and endowing schools and fellowships.[2]

This rapidly growing concern for education was not peculiar to Kent and, indeed, was not so marked there as in Lancashire and Yorkshire, but it is matched by an interest, amongst the gentry, in learning and scholarship. Mr. Laslett has observed that of thirty-five surnames of Justices appearing in the Maid-

[1] *The Oxinden Letters, 1607–1642*, ed. D. Gardiner (1933), p. 152.
[2] W. K. Jordan, *Social Institutions in Kent, 1480–1660* (1961), pp. 146–8.

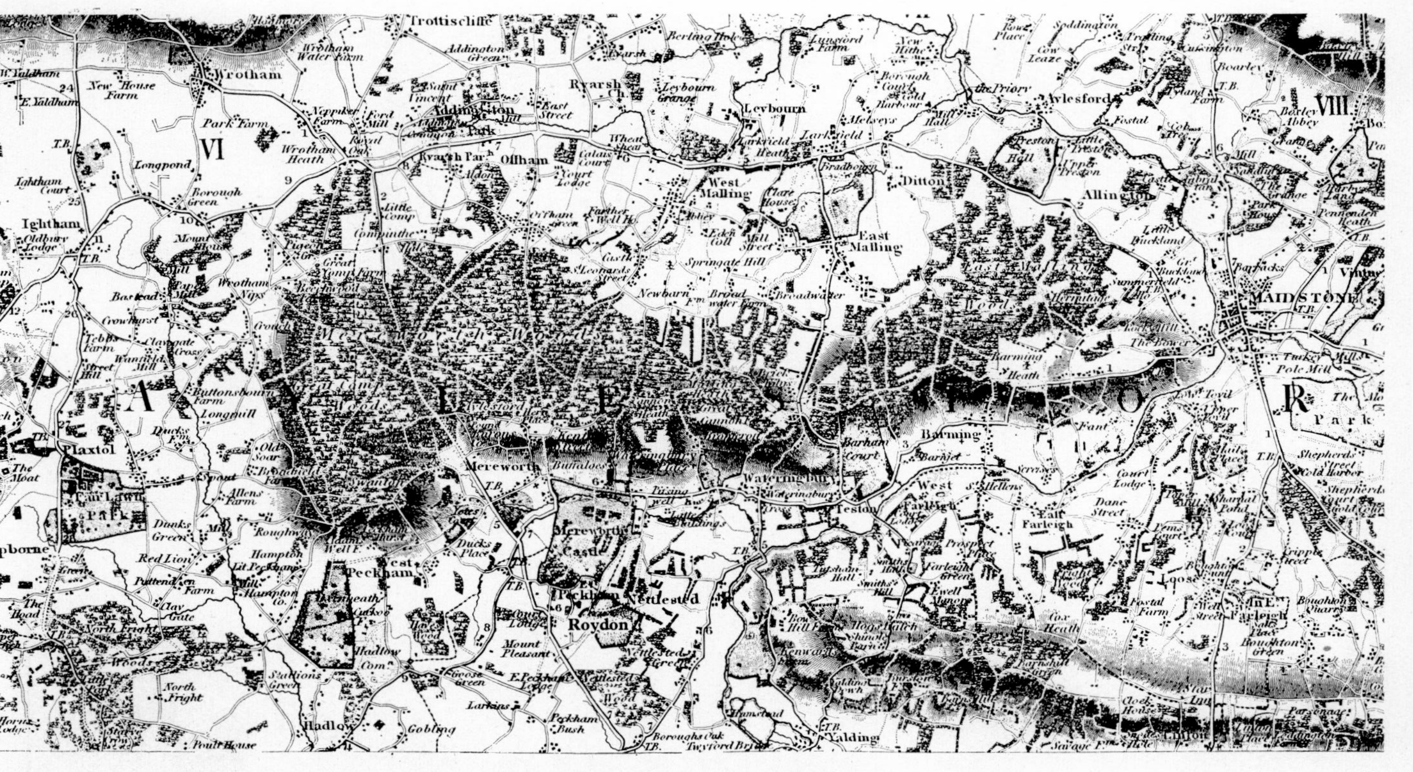

The East Peckham neighbourhood

(Scale approx. $\frac{5}{8}''$ to one mile)

stone Quarter Sessions Book between 1635 and 1642 fifteen belonged to families noted in the *Dictionary of National Biography* for literary achievement.[1] Such an intellectual interest can readily be explained: a gentleman with an estate of £600 per annum could live in comfort and devote his considerable leisure to scholarly pursuits; London, with the court, the Inns of Court, Westminster Hall, and the College of Arms was easily accessible; the Precincts of Canterbury sheltered such men as the Casaubons, Bargrave and Somner; and perhaps there has always been something in the climate or topography of Kent that has induced a high level of civility—Caesar, at least, thought so. The fact that during the reign of the first two Stuarts Kent had more licensed physicians than any other county[2] is to be ascribed to its comparatively advanced state of civilization and prosperity rather than to an unhealthy climate or to an undue valetudinarianism on the part of the inhabitants.

It was into this society that Roger Twysden, the eighth member of the family to bear that name, was born on Sunday, 21 August 1597.

The family, as its name shows, had its origin in the Weald of Kent. There is still a farm called Twysden in Goudhurst parish and a wood of the same name in Sandhurst. It was probably from the Goudhurst *den* that the family took its name. By the fourteenth century it was associated with the manor of Chelmington in Great Chart, and in the fifteenth century Roger Twysden of Great Chart is described in the pardon granted to those who had taken part in Jack Cade's Rebellion as 'gentleman'. Another branch of the family established itself at Wye early in the sixteenth century, and at about the same time William Twysden of Chelmington married Elizabeth, daughter and coheir of Thomas Roydon of Fortune in East Peckham. It was through her that the estate, later known as Roydon, passed to the Twysdens and remained in the family until the nineteenth century. In its continuity and its ramifications within

[1] P. Laslett, 'The Gentry of Kent in 1648', *Cambridge Historical Journal*, IX. 2 (1948).

[2] W. Notestein, *The English People on the eve of Colonization* (1962 edn.), p. 101.

the county the Twysden family is eminently typical of the Kentish gentry.

It was typical also of the interest which men were increasingly taking in history and in the links which bound them to their predecessors that Sir William Twysden, first Baronet, caused a roll to be made exemplifying twenty-three ancient deeds in which a party or witness was named Twysden. They date from 1277, when Adam de Twisden appears as a witness in Sandhurst, to a Writ of Outlawry of 1441 addressed to Roger Twisden, Steward of the Liberty of the Prior of Christ Church, Canterbury. An interest in history and family pride combined in prompting Sir William to go to the expense of preparing this elaborate roll (of which there are copies in the British Museum and in the Kent Archives Office) which he intended should be certified as authentic by Sir Edward Dering, Sir William Segar (Garter King-of-Arms), John Selden, William Le Neve and Thomas Preston, but he died before the certificate could be obtained.

William Twysden who married Elizabeth Roydon about 1540 was the great-grandfather of the Roger Twysden who is the subject of this biography. Amongst the well-known Kentish families with whom the Twysdens and the Roydons had formed marriage-ties in the generation preceding William's were those of Culpepper, Finch and Nevill; one of Elizabeth's sisters married a Catling, another a Darell; Elizabeth herself, as her third husband, married a Golding; of the two children of William and Elizabeth who survived the perils of infancy, one, Roger, married Anne, the daughter of Sir Thomas Wyatt, and the other, Margaret, married a Dering; of the children of Roger and Anne, the eldest son married Anne, the daughter of Sir Moyle Finch and Elizabeth, first Countess of Winchilsea (Roger Twysden being the eldest child of the marriage), the second son married a Lovelace (as his second wife), the second daughter married a Fane, the fifth a Monins and the youngest a Bathurst.

To Twysden this connexion by marriage with a dozen of the leading families in the county was important. He was sharply conscious of those whom he could call 'cousin'—'my very worthy friend and cousin' or 'my noble good friend and cousin' are typical phrases—and he cherished their friendship. With his main seat at East Peckham, his secondary estate in Great Chart and the adjoining parishes (Chelmington remained in the family until Queen Anne's reign), and his grazing lands on Romney Marsh, Twysden came into contact, as neighbour, as tenant, or as landlord, with a good proportion of his fellow gentlemen. He met them again at the Assizes, at Quarter Sessions and at Town Malling where the justices for the South Division of the Lathe of Aylesford usually met. To call this community an oligarchy would be qualitatively unfair and quantitatively inaccurate—it was too large; but it was a close-knit and self-conscious community, thoroughly aware of the common interests which held it together and it might fittingly call itself 'the Kentish family'. The thought that there were another 200,000 men, women and children living in the county, the yeomen, labourers, artisans, their wives and their children, and that they formed no part of 'the family' would not have crossed the minds of the gentry.

East Peckham, the home of the Twysdens for 300 years, is a large and straggling parish on the banks of the Medway, six miles from Tonbridge, eight from Maidstone and five from Town Malling, or West Malling as it is now usually called. The village itself is at the southern end of the parish, where a new church was built in 1842 to serve the needs of the inhabitants who found the parish church of St. Michael, almost three miles from the village and near the northern limits of the parish, inconveniently distant. In the seventeenth century East Peckham was in the Shoreham Deanery, an Archbishop's peculiar, and unfortunately, like other parishes in the Deanery, it does not appear in the Compton census of 1676. From the Hearth Tax assessment of 1664 and from the registers of baptisms it is perhaps a fair guess that the population of the parish was then about 500, probably rather less than it had been in the 1630's.

The property which Thomas Roydon acquired after he had come out of Essex in 1511 to marry the daughter of William Whetenhall of Hextall Court in East Peckham lay near St.

Michael's church, on the north-eastern boundary of the parish, and indeed the estate extended into the adjacent parishes of Nettlestead and Wateringbury. Here Roydon built the house which was at first known as Fortune, and later as Roydon Hall. It was largely reconstructed in the nineteenth century and hardly anything of the original building now remains. It was a sizeable house—Twysden paid 30*s*. tax upon thirty chimneys in 1662[1]—skilfully sited on a rise so that it was protected by the higher ground on the east and north and commanded a view to the west towards Oxenhoath and Hadlow, a landscape without any striking or dramatic quality (except now for that nineteenth-century folly, Hadlow Castle) but one full of quiet interest and peaceful charm. Extensive enough to provide sufficient scope that the eye does not become satiated, but not so extensive as to tempt the mind into extravagant fantasies, it is benevolent, placid and civilized, a combination of nature and man's handwork, the farms and hamlets and fields being set off, but not overwhelmed by, the hills and the woods. No doubt, as Twysden saw it, it was rougher and less neat than it is today, but it cannot have changed a great deal over three centuries. It is a countryside conducive to contentment, not one to breed desperadoes or rebels.

The park of Roydon Hall, on its north side, adjoins the park of Mereworth Castle (the old name has been retained for the Palladian villa built on the site of the castle about 1740) which in the seventeenth century belonged to the Fanes, a family with which the Twysdens were connected by marriage. One branch of the Fanes, or Vanes, was established at Hadlow, three miles away, by 1500, and Sir Henry Vane the elder, Secretary of State and Treasurer during the reign of Charles I, bought Fairlawne on the border of the adjacent parish of Shipbourne in Charles I's reign. It was at Hadlow that that strange man, the younger Henry Vane, who ended his life on the scaffold in 1662, was born in 1613, sixteen years junior to Twysden. To the south-west, not much more than a mile away as the crow flies, stood Hextall Court, the home of the Wheten-

[1] This is his own entry in his estate book, but the tax should have been 2*s*. for every fire-hearth or stove: see 13 & 14 Car. II, c. 10.

halls, another family with whom the Twysdens could challenge cousinship. Twysden held land of the Whetenhalls, and they held land of him, a quite usual arrangement, for tenancy did not necessarily imply social inferiority. In 1527 William Whetenhall was sheriff of the county but the family adhered to the old religion, and although this did not prevent a courteous friendship between them and the Twysdens, it excluded the Whetenhalls from public affairs.

It was a fertile and prosperous part of the county in which the Twysdens lived. Within a radius of half-a-dozen miles of East Peckham there were thirty or more gentle families whom they could claim as neighbours and sometimes also as cousins, relationships which usually led to amity but on occasion might result in discord and uncharitableness.

Twysden's father, William, was born on the 4 April 1566, the eldest son of Roger Twysden of Roydon. He was, according to his son, 'being young . . . somewhat violent in his undertakings, whether it were hawking, hunting, or what else soever. . . . A little impatient, but thereby hurting none but himself.'[1] He graduated, when he was nearly eighteen, at Magdalene College, Cambridge, and was admitted at Gray's Inn in 1584. In 1591 he married Anne, daughter of Sir Moyle Finch of Eastwell and his wife Elizabeth, who was afterwards created Viscountess of Maidstone and Countess of Winchilsea. Anne had been brought up at the Court of Queen Elizabeth, and the wedding was kept at the London house of her grandfather, Sir Thomas Heneage, Vice-Chamberlain of the Queen's Household. His marriage gave William Twysden an entrée to the Court, where he now spent part of his time. In 1592 he was returned as Member of Parliament for Clitheroe and in 1600 for Helston. In 1596–7 he took part in the Island Voyage under the command of the Earl of Essex. He was amongst the band of gentlemen who conducted James I to London on his accession, and on 11 May 1603, at the Charterhouse, the King knighted him for his pains.

During the new reign Sir William Twysden continued to be

[1] In this and other extracts from manuscript sources spelling and punctuation have been modernized.

active in public affairs. He sat in two more Parliaments, as Member for Thetford in 1614 and for Winchelsea in 1627–8 in Charles I's third Parliament. He was a gentleman usher of the Privy Chamber and was amongst the eight Kent baronets in the first creation of 1611 (he then ranked sixty-sixth in the general order and sixth in Kent). When a dispute about precedence arose between the peers and the newly created order Sir William Twysden was one of four baronets chosen to appeal to the King in person against the decision of the Privy Council, an occasion when the impatience which his son noted nearly caused trouble. He was in the Commission of the Peace, although perhaps too busy at Court to take an active part in local affairs, and in 1605 he was appointed by the Lord Lieutenant, Lord Wootton, to be Captain of Light Horse for the Lathe of Aylesford, an office which his father had held in Queen Elizabeth's reign.

The baronetcy cost Sir William Twysden £1,000, a sum which he could ill afford. With a house in London where he spent most of the winter, the Roydon estate, a wife whose mother was a peeress and whose tastes accorded with her mother's rank, and five sons and two daughters to be brought up and provided for, his expenses were heavy and he was forced to borrow money, leaving an encumbered estate to his heir. His London house, in Redcross Street in the parish of St. Giles-without-Cripplegate, was afterwards converted into tenements, but in Sir William's day it was, according to Sir Hugh Cholmley, 'so good a house as few gentlemen in town had the like, and bravely furnished'. Sixty years later, after the Fire of London, it, or its successor, was insured for £160, a sum which scarcely suggests the fine mansion described by Cholmley; perhaps there was a little pardonable exaggeration in his description of his father-in-law's property. However that may be, Sir William Twysden certainly did not make a fortune out of his proximity to the Court, unlike some of his contemporaries such as his neighbour Sir Henry Vane who, beginning official life as carver in the royal household, was able to buy a one-third share in the Subpoena office in 1611 for £8,250 yet had succeeded to an estate worth only £300 a year.

But there was another side to Sir William Twysden besides the man of public affairs, for he was something of a scholar, especially in Hebrew. 'There were but two things worth spending a man's time and study on,' he said towards the end of his life; 'the one is the law of God to teach him the way to Heaven; the other the law of the nation, to direct him how to comport himself in this life and to manage his civil affairs.' He purchased valuable manuscripts and books, was one of the many scholars who borrowed manuscripts from Sir Robert Cotton's magnificent library, and his own library 'he was pleased to make useful to the public'. Those books afterwards formed a cherished, if not much used, part of Twysden's library. Writing of his father, he said '. . . grown to riper years he solely applied himself to learning, and to the best of that kind, to wit to Divinity on which his mind was so wholly set that he took more pleasure in reading the Bible than I should in some well-written History. Indeed his learning lay much in the Hebrew text, in which he had few his equal of any condition what so ever; in Palmistry, Physiognomy and other such like ornaments he had good skill, but especially in Astrology, it is strange what I have known him tell of all these, and he would ever maintain that he had them out of the Sacred Writ.' Unfortunately he has not recorded any examples of the knowledge which Sir William attained to through these strange arts.

His end came about, characteristically, through his impetuosity. Returning to Roydon from London in November 1628, he at once set off to walk to Hythe, forty miles away, and walked so fast that he contracted a fever that would not leave him. At Christmas he was carried to his London house and there he died on 8 January 1629, in his sixty-third year.

CHAPTER TWO

1597–1637

ROGER, THE eldest child of Sir William Twysden and his wife Anne, was born whilst his father was away on the Island Voyage, on Sunday, 21 August 1597, between 2 and 3 o'clock in the afternoon, at the house of his maternal grandfather, Sir Moyle Finch, in the Charterhouse.

Subsequently Lady Twysden bore several more children to her husband. Elizabeth was born at Roydon Hall on 19 August 1600, and became the wife of Sir Hugh Cholmley between whose career and Roger Twysden's there existed, for part of their lives, a parallel manifest to us and presumably also to them. Thomas, born at Roydon Hall on 8 January 1602, lived to become a judge and a baronet, founding the family of Twisden of Bradbourne in East Malling. Anne, born at Roydon on 11 February in the following year, married when she was twenty-seven Sir Christopher Yelverton. Three other sons followed, William (1605), John (1607), and Francis (1609), the two latter being born in London at the house in Redcross Street. William died at the age of thirty-six, unmarried, John became a physician and mathematician, a friend of Samuel Foster, Gresham Professor of Astronomy, and published works on mathematics, the use of dials, fortifications, the truth of the Christian religion, the soundness of the practices followed by the Colleges of Physicians, etc. Francis had a less distinguished career, probably as an attorney, and perhaps it was not only because he became inauspiciously entangled in political affairs in 1648 that his brothers referred to him as 'poor Frank'.

As a family record it is a success story: seven children born, and all of them reared, the two eldest sons both baronets, both daughters married to baronets, and a younger son distinguished as a mathematician and physician.

No doubt the young Twysden, with his brothers and sisters, spent his summers at East Peckham and his winters in London. His father was on sufficiently friendly terms with Alexander Gill the elder, a generous and learned man and High Master of St. Paul's School, to be able to borrow money from him at a good deal below the market rate of interest, and it was to St. Paul's that he sent his son. On 8 November 1614, Twysden, then in his eighteenth year, was entered as a Fellow Commoner at Emmanuel College, Cambridge, at the same time as his brother Thomas, who was only twelve. Sir Walter Mildmay had founded the College for the education of youth 'in all piety and good learning, but especially in sacred and theological learning' and the nature of the theological learning which it taught is indicated by the oath taken by the Fellows in which 'the true religion of Christ' was described as 'contrary to Popery and all other heresies'. The College was well known for its puritanism, which Twysden may not have found to his taste; at least he did not stay to graduate there, and it may be significant that he sent his own sons to Oxford, not to Cambridge. He himself a few years later, probably in the early 1620's, was in Oxford reading in Bodley's Library.

Meanwhile Sir William Twysden exercised his right as a baronet of presenting his eldest son to the King to be knighted. The ceremony took place at Greenwich on 1 June 1620. Sir Roger Twysden, as he now became, was admitted to the Honourable Society of Gray's Inn on 2 February 1623. Membership of one of the Inns of Court was part of a gentlemanly education, suitable for one in Twysden's position although he was never called to the Bar nor practised in the Courts. He entered the Society on almost the same day as its great son and benefactor Francis Bacon retired in disgrace to his chambers there to spend the rest of his life in philosophical speculation and poverty. Another distinguished member of the Society, Sir Henry Yelverton, had also recently been in trouble for having, as Attorney General, shown undue favour to the City of London, but he had been rehabilitated by the end of

1621 and in 1625 he was made an additional Judge of the Common Pleas. It was Yelverton's son, Sir Christopher (who himself had been admitted to Gray's Inn as long ago as 1607), that Twysden's younger sister, Anne, was to marry in 1630.

In 1622 his elder sister, Elizabeth, was married to Sir Hugh Cholmley, son of Sir Richard Cholmley of Whitby. Twysden and Hugh Cholmley were contemporaries at Cambridge, Cholmley being at Jesus College, and both were members of Gray's Inn though Cholmley's admission had taken place in 1618, four years before Twysden's, in spite of the fact that Twysden was three years his senior. However, even if they were contemporaries and acquaintances, it is unlikely that they were intimate. Twysden was a sober young man taking life seriously and inheriting his father's love of book-learning rather than his delight in violent activity; Cholmley, on the other hand, according to his own confession, was at this time given to levity and dissipation, spending the whole of the winter of 1621–2, the winter before his marriage, in gaming at bowling-houses, and other haunts of vice. In middle age he bewailed his wasted opportunity to study the law, a study that could have been useful both in the affairs of the county and in private matters for 'every man that hath but a smattering of the law, though of no fortune or quality, shall be a leader and director to the greatest and best gentlemen on the bench'. Was he thinking, perhaps, of how his brother-in-law had become precisely that?

The marriage of Elizabeth Twysden to Hugh Cholmley took place on 10 December at the church in Milk Street, London. Few were present at the wedding except members of the two families. The marriage was kept at Sir William Twysden's house in Redcross Street, and the couple spent much of their early married life there. Elizabeth's marriage portion was £3,000, of which Sir William paid £2,500 in ready money on the day before the marriage, and the balance of £500 at the end of six months. It was more than his estate could comfortably bear but it was a sum that accorded with the importance of the match, for the Cholmleys were wealthier than the Twysdens. Sir Richard Cholmley settled on his son and daughter-in-law lands to the value of £500 a year, and as much more as after his death would make £2,700, but he had extravagant tastes, including an interest in the philosopher's stone, and by 1627 he was £12,000 in debt. His son threatening to retire abroad, he made over the whole estate to him for ten years, reserving only £400 a year to himself. By the 1650's, thanks to prudent management the settled lands, in spite of all the dislocation and loss caused by the Civil War, were worth more than £3,000 a year. Elizabeth had married well.

Throughout their lives Twysden and Cholmley were to see much of each other and their careers touched at many points. Both sons succeeded to encumbered estates and each inherited vexatious litigation with a troublesome neighbour. They entered public life at much the same time, Cholmley as Member of Parliament for Scarborough in James's last and Charles's first Parliaments, and Twysden as member for Winchelsea in Charles's first and second Parliaments, presumably on the nomination of the Duke of Buckingham, Lord Warden of the Cinque Ports.

In the first session of the Parliament of 1625 Twysden heard increasingly sharp criticism of Arminianism, a debate which no doubt he relished and talked over with his father. Equally interesting was the argument about the legality of the impositions which James had increased by the Book of Rates, and what precedent existed, if any, by which they might be justified. Then, when Parliament was adjourned for a second session to Oxford because of the plague raging in London, the terms of the King's marriage treaty leaked out. For those unpopular provisions and the deception which had been practised by his royal master, Buckingham was believed to be responsible, as well as for the inauspicious promise to Richelieu to lend English ships for use against the Huguenots of la Rochelle. There was plenty here to divide Crown and Parliament, and Twysden heard Sir Edward Coke and Sir John Eliot, amongst others, expressing their doubts and suspicions with a weight of learning and an intensity of oratory that the younger man remembered. It was an eventful initiation into the affairs of the nation.

The King dissolved Parliament on 12 August 1625, as

dissatisfied with it as it was with him and Buckingham. On 6 February 1626, he opened his second Parliament, in which Twysden again sat as a member for Winchelsea. Charles had ingeniously purged his second Parliament in advance, by ensuring the appointment as sheriffs for their counties of the members of his first Parliament who had seemed the sternest critics of the Court party, so that they could not lawfully be returned again. Sir Edward Coke was made sheriff of Buckinghamshire and, although he was elected as Knight of the Shire for Norfolk, he did not take his seat. The danger which Sir John Eliot represented was not realized. He sat for his home constituency of St. Germans and soon was leading the attack against Buckingham. With a Kentish Knight of the Shire, Sir Dudley Digges of Chilham Castle, he acted as one of the managers of the impeachment of the Duke, and the pair of them, for 'some insolent speeches' in the course of the proceedings were consigned to the Tower by the King's order. Especially offensive was Eliot's reference, in his search for precedents, to certain events in the reign of Richard II; it was scarcely tactful to draw attention to that particular regal predecessor, who had been obliged to abdicate the throne. It was during this Parliament that Charles himself told his faithful Commons that 'Parliaments are altogether in my power for their calling, sitting and dissolution; therefore, as I find the fruits of them good or evil, they are to continue or not to be'. Twysden remembered the phrase and critically examined the King's contention many years later when he wrote his treatise on *Certain Considerations on the Government of England*. He was uneasy, too, about the revival of the process of impeachment which, in his opinion, marked an incursion by Parliament into the sphere properly belonging to the judiciary, another subject that he subsequently handled in his treatise. Certainly he served his Parliamentary apprenticeship in anxious and alarming times, in this 'great, warm, and ruffling Parliament' as Whitelocke called it.

Perhaps it was because the times were so stirring and the matters in debate so serious and weighty that the young Twysden did not serve in Charles's third Parliament of 1628–9 but dutifully surrendered his seat to his father. Like Cholmley, he had had his last experience of Parliament until the Short Parliament of 1640.

Cholmley's withdrawal from public life was due at least in part to his father's growing indebtedness. With the current rate on borrowed money at 10 per cent., nearly half the income of the estate was swallowed up in the payment of interest on loans. Lady Twysden, Elizabeth's mother, 'of a passing sweet good-nature' and a generous and sympathetic mother-in-law, would have been willing to come to the assistance of the Cholmleys, but Sir William took a sterner view and would not help—indeed, perhaps could not, for his own debts were burdensome, and probably heavier than his lady knew. It was at this point that Sir Richard made over his assets and his debts to his son. By selling some of the family property in Yorkshire and by careful economy, Cholmley had managed to reduce the debts to about £4,000 by 1632, when his father died.

Until Sir Richard's death the young Cholmleys lived sometimes at Sir William Twysden's house in Redcross Street, sometimes at Roydon Hall. Their first child, who died in infancy, was born in 1624 at the London house and put out to nurse at Wateringbury. William, the second child, was born at Roydon Hall in 1625 and christened in the 'chapel' of the house by the Vicar of the parish. He spent much of his childhood with his grandmother, Lady Anne Twysden, and was no doubt spoiled like any other only grandchild. Even when Sir Richard Cholmley died and Sir Hugh and Elizabeth removed to Whitby (a disastrous removal, for their household things and plate, worth £400 or £500, were sent from London by sea and captured by a Dunkirker) grandmother, daughter and grandson continued to exchange long and frequent visits.

In the meantime, the death of Sir William Twysden in January 1629 left Twysden with the same financial problems as his brother-in-law had been obliged to face. Prudence was not a prominent trait in the character of the Elizabethan and Jacobean gentry. Sir William left a heavily encumbered estate and possibly a financially even more embarrassing relict, a widow who was almost of the nobility, who was notoriously kind and generous, and whose ideas of proper expenditure befitted her mother's station in life rather than her husband's estate. 'She was thrifty, yet very noble in her disposition' as Twysden later wrote in his memorandum book, but her thrift extended only to the minor items, her nobility of disposition to her general style of living.

Sir William was buried at East Peckham on the Sunday following his death, without pomp and at the modest cost of £109 16*s*. 5*d*., of which the major item was £87 14*s*. 0*d*. for blacks for the funeral. The Vicar, Mr. Worrall, demanded the black cloth over the hearse, as his customary due, but Twysden would not surrender it; there was, he maintained, no such custom, and no precedent for Worrall's claim. In itself it was a small incident, but it provides the key to Twysden's character. He hated innovation as much as the Arminians and the Puritans, the Royalists and the Parliamentarians all claimed to hate innovation, but Twysden was more consistent in his detestation of the novel than most of them. However, in 'performing the funeral with as little charge as may be' he was following his father's testamentary instructions, with the unexpected result that some years later he found himself in dispute with the Heralds for improper parsimony.

Sir William made his will only five days before his death, and the painfully written signature is that of a dying man. One of the witnesses was Sir Edward Dering and another Thomas Bates, probably steward of the Roydon Hall estate. Twysden was named as executor and he proved the will in the Prerogative Court of Canterbury on 30 January. There were legacies to the four younger sons: Thomas £100, William £250, John £100, Francis £100, and in addition they were bequeathed jointly 200 acres of land in Romney Marsh. Anne's portion, to be inherited on marriage or at the age of thirty-one, was to be £2,000, with meanwhile an allowance of £100 per annum. To Lady Twysden were left all the goods, plate, jewels, household stuff, coach, and coachhorses, both at the London house and at Roydon Hall, and 'the best of my horses for the maintenance of my breed'—a disposition which suggests that Lady Twysden was a better judge of horses and more interested in the stables than her eldest son. To him Sir William bequeathed his books after Lady Twysden had taken her choice. Finally, he directed that Francis, the youngest son, who was only nineteen, should be maintained by Lady Twysden and by his eldest son, who now succeeded to the estate, subject to the widow's very extensive jointure rights.

When Twysden got in particulars of the estate, he found that the debts were so heavy that the interest on them absorbed a quarter of the income. Not only was he worried about the amount of the debt but also he had doubts, on religious grounds, of the rightness of paying interest on money borrowed. If usury was indeed a sin, was not the payment of interest a sin in the borrower as well as the lender? He searched the scriptures, and thought that the rules against usury to be found in the Old Testament were intended for the Commonwealth of the Jews, not for universal application at all times and to all men; Primitive Christians allowed use for money or goods lent; the prohibitions of the early Councils applied only to the clergy; it was a secular ruler, Charlemagne, who first extended the prohibition to the laity; Aquinas's and Cajetan's answers are not free from ambiguity; and Sir Robert Filmer's little treatise on the subject, which Twysden came upon, gave a reassuring answer; so when Twysden published the tract fifteen years later, he concluded the learned Preface which he contributed to the book with: 'If thou beest a lender and it shall not satisfy thee in receiving profit for the loan of money, I can assure thee that it hath me fully in the paying of it.'

Thus Twysden's religious doubts were set at rest, but to add to his financial problems, Anne Twysden was married on 20 April 1630 to Sir Christopher Yelverton of Easton Mauduit in Northamptonshire. The fact that she was in her twenty-eighth year and that she met Yelverton for the first time less than a month before the wedding suggests that it was an arranged marriage and prompts the ungallant thought that perhaps the lady's portion of £2,000 rather than her person was the attraction. At all events, Twysden had to find the £2,000. Faced with these demands, he took the only sensible course and sold off the outlying Romney Marsh estate, a necessary expedient, but one that to a man like Twysden, who much preferred accumulation to dissipation, was a cause of anxiety—of qualified anxiety, because the Romney Marsh land was unprofitable and he got a good price for it.

Another *damnosa haereditas* that passed to him was a dispute about the right to use a pew on the north side of the south aisle of Great Chart church. The pew went with Chelmington Manor but Sir William Twysden was rarely there, and he lent the pew to Sir Isaac Sedley who, a few years later, claimed it as his own right. Sir William began proceedings in 1621 in the Consistory Court at Canterbury, but when the case was ready for sentence it was removed to the Court of Arches. Thence, in due course, it was removed to the Common Law Courts. Sir Isaac Sedley died, and his son Sir John (of St. Clere) succeeded to the suit, as later Sir Roger inherited the role of plaintiff from his father. Finally, eight years after the suit had been commenced, on 23 March 1629, the jury at Maidstone Assizes found for the plaintiff and the judge awarded the pew to Twysden, with £100 costs. Although he had won the case he had also gained an embittered neighbour, and Sedley's hostile attitude towards him fifteen years later, in his time of troubles, sprang in part from this long and unhappy suit.

The dispute with the Heralds came to a head later. Sir William had directed that his funeral was to cost as little as might be, a quite common form of testamentary instruction, which was sometimes made more precise and explicit as, for example, in the will of Sir Edward Hales of Woodchurch who, dying in 1654, desired to be buried 'without any pomp or ceremonies . . . no vanity of heralds'. This was contrary to the contemporary practice whereby the Heralds assisted at funerals of the aristocracy and gentry and, indeed, devoted much time and labour to the supervision of these important ceremonies—for a fee. The frugal Twysden determined to manage without their help, and perhaps that is what his father meant him to do.

Eight years after the funeral, on 23 January 1637, Grynsted, an officer of the Heralds' Office, came to Roydon Hall and showed Twysden a sealed parchment dated 8 November 1636, summoning him to appear at a Court Marshall, to be held in the Painted Chamber, Westminster, on 28 January to answer

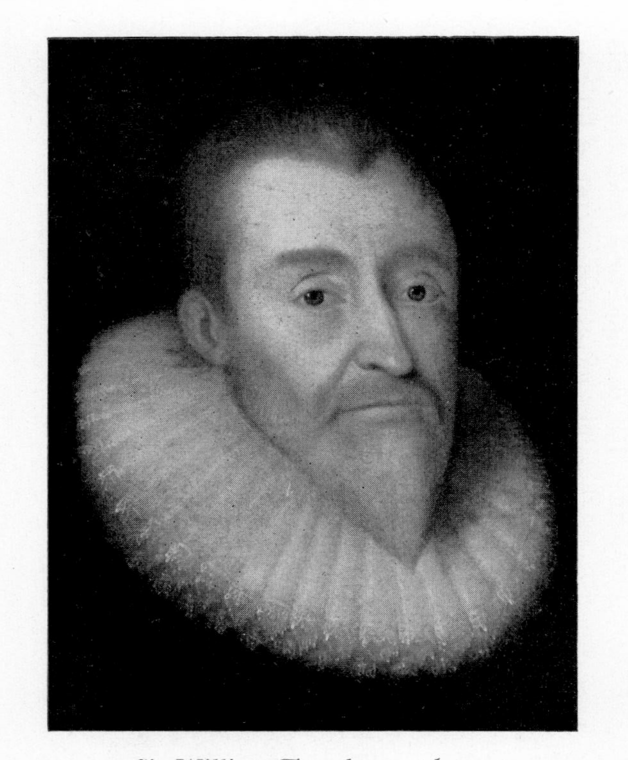

Sir William Twysden, 1st baronet of Roydon

Ann Finch, Lady Twysden

the complaint of the Kings and Officers of Arms for fees unpaid at Sir William's funeral. The Heralds alleged that the privileges which King James had granted to baronets to have 'assistants' at their funerals conferred rights upon the Heralds and that, if the heir chose to have a private funeral, they were entitled to compensation for the loss of the customary fees. It was a difficult point and the Heralds' complaint caused Twysden some anxiety; he decided that he was too unwell to appear at the Court Marshall and got his brother, Frank, to enter an appearance for him. The proceedings were then adjourned until the next Court day, 11 February. In the meantime, Frank met Philipott, Somerset Herald, who, like many of the other sixteenth- and seventeenth-century Heralds, was a Kent man and knew Twysden. In the way of friendship he advised that the fees should be paid and said that Twysden's brother-in-law Yelverton had stood out at first but had finally paid. 'Yes,' replied Frank, 'but was he compelled to pay, or did he pay by way of gratuity?' Philipott repudiated the saucy implication that the Heralds were in need of gratuities, and when Frank contended that if they received fees in every case it would produce an income of £20,000 a year, Philipott would not allow that the figure would amount to more than £3,000 or £4,000.

When the Court sat again on 11 February Somerset reported that Frank Twysden had alleged that the payment made by Yelverton had been by way of alms, which so angered the Court that the young man stood committed for a while. Eventually he was freed, and bound over to appear at the next Court Day, 16 February (each cause that was pending had to come before the court at each session, even if only to be adjourned to the next). Fortunately for him, he had an opportunity of speaking with the Earl Marshall, and explaining away his rash words. He also told Twysden's good friend, Sir Henry Morton, a judge of the Admiralty Court, what he had really said, 'who chid him, whatever he thought, for speaking out'. But Frank was a man of his times; the signal feature of Charles I's reign was that men were no longer willing to hide their thoughts but began to insist on speaking out.

Even after this contretemps had been disposed of the suit did not proceed smoothly. Twysden, warned to appear on 29 April 1637, kept the summons because he thought it contrary to the statute 13 Ric. II, c. 2, in that it did not specify the cause why he had been sent for. Of course he was in no doubt as to the reason, but for Twysden the preservation of freedom was to be found in the meticulous observance of the proper forms of procedure. He was in trouble for not allowing the officer to take the summons back with him, but this soon blew over when Twysden promised to deliver the parchment into Court.

At length, on 28 June, the Court began to hear the merits of the dispute. Dr. Duck, a learned civilian who was the King's Advocate in the Court, argued for the Kings-of-Arms and the Heralds that it had long been the custom that where a burial had not taken place publicly the Heralds had received a composition in lieu of fees, although he had to admit there had been some intermission of the practice towards the end of Elizabeth's reign. For the purpose of avoiding future contention, he alleged, the Commissioners of the Earl Marshalship in 1618 ordered that certificates of death should be entered in the College and appointed set fees to be paid, as was evidenced by divers extant deeds. After dinner Twysden went to Duck and asked to see the deeds. Duck's advice was to try the Heralds' Office so Twysden went off to pursue his inquiry there.

At the Office Twysden could find only an old man, who took him in to Sir John Burroughs, Garter King-of-Arms. Garter received him civilly and repeated Duck's statement, that the nobility had always been subject to have their funerals public. This Twysden did not dispute, but desired to know whether it applied to the *nobilitas major* and *minor* or only the *major*, implying that baronets were only *nobiles minores*, and not to be ranked with the earlier five orders of *majores* ranging from duke down to baron. Garter was obliged to admit that it was only the *nobilitas major*, and gave two examples of the Court of Wards and the Court of Chancery having ordered the payment of the Heralds' funerary fees. Gentlemen, said Garter, had been used to compound for the fees due, but being pressed for evidence that they had been compelled to do so, he could not produce any. This, retorted Twysden, did not then help the Heralds' case, for 'he that gives the least blow to a priest is excommunicated, but he that shoots at him with a gun and misses goes free'.

Although it was not referred to either by Dr. Duck or Garter, a precedent might have been cited from King James's reign when proceedings were brought against the sons of Sir Richard Conquest, Knight, of Bedfordshire for dispensing with the services of an officer of arms at Sir Richard's funeral, and they were ordered to pay £10 to the College of Arms for the benefit of the officer whose turn it was to serve at the funeral. True, there was another, and much more objectionable element in the Conquest case, that a painter-stainer had been engaged to perform functions proper only to a Herald, so the precedent was not on all fours with the Twysden case. Nevertheless, it is surprising that it was not referred to; perhaps no one remembered it. The Earl Marshall's jurisdiction had been uncertain and the proceedings doubtful until by Letters Patent of 1 August 1622 the powers of the court had been authoritatively defined. Even after that, some years elapsed before the proper procedure of the court could be rediscovered, and apart from one case the records do not begin until 1633. Most of the subsequent cases relate to duelling and gave no help either to the Heralds or to Twysden. In truth, the law was uncertain, and whenever the law is uncertain the danger of hateful innovation arises. It was this, as well as a care for money, which made Twysden so obstinate.[1] To his disquiet and annoyance 'a gentleman of the county' told Somerset that Twysden had expressed his willingness to pay the fees, and from the letter of remonstrance, elliptical though it is, which he addressed to Sir Edward Dering on 14 July, it is plain that it was Dering who had set this baseless rumour afoot.

Significantly, there was now a lengthy pause in the proceedings, and it was not until 31 October that Duck gave

[1] For information about the practice of the Court I have drawn on G. D. Squibb, *The High Court of Chivalry* (1959).

Twysden the articles that he was to reply to. The reply was delivered on 18 November, but the Earl Marshall excused Twysden's personal attendance. Apart from the general argument that there was no precedent for the claim, he put forward a special plea: when baronets were first created in 1611 (Sir William Twysden being one of them) the King set out the terms on which he would create a man a baronet, so there was, argued Twysden, a kind of agreement between baronets and the King. The first baronets paid no fee on their creation (that is, they paid no fee to the Heralds: they paid £1,000 apiece to the King); did he, then, intend them to be charged on their death? More especially, could the Commissioners' promulgation of a scale of fees in 1618 bind those who had been created baronet seven years earlier, when no such scale was in force?

There is, so far as I am aware, no record of the determination of the suit. Probably the Heralds were glad to drop the case, for a decision against them would have made it difficult to bluff others into paying funerary fees. Twysden's resistance to the claim, typical of the man, must have surprised them. They expected him to behave like a gentleman; instead he reacted like a baronet with a knowledge of the law and a profound veneration for precedent.

It was qualities such as these, and a patent integrity, which brought Twysden other executorships. Nearly two years after Sir William's death George Chapman died at Roydon Hall on 4 December 1630. He was a servant, or agent, of Twysden, whom he named as his executor. The estate amounted to no more than £70 or so and the legacies were all small, but Twysden dealt with it, and recorded his dealings, with the same meticulous care that he bestowed upon his own financial matters.

When his father died Twysden was in his thirty-second year and still unmarried. The reason was simple: the estate was already so heavily burdened that for it to support another family was out of the question. Even after Sir William's death there was much to be done in reducing the debts—and, in 1630, providing Anne's marriage portion of £2,000—before

Twysden himself could begin to think of marriage. His mother was anxious that he should marry, and he must have seen that a match with a suitable heiress would help to restore the Twysden fortunes. When, finally he took a wife, she brought him comfort and companionship, but little in the way of dowry.

Lady Anne Twysden continued, after Sir William's death, to live in style and liked to have with her a young lady-in-waiting. When, at Michaelmas, 1632, she went off to Fyling Hall in Yorkshire, now the home of the Cholmleys, to spend six months with her daughter and grandchild (only William survived, Richard having died in 1630 and Elizabeth a year later) she took with her Isabella Saunder, the youngest of the three daughters of Sir Nicholas Saunder of Nonsuch in Surrey. Two years later, on 27 January 1635, Twysden married her at 'my mother's jointure house called Roydon Hall'. He was thirty-seven, she thirty-one.

The match seems not to have engendered enthusiasm, and may even have encountered opposition. Lady Anne Twysden was fond of Isabella and must have realized that her son might fall in love with her lady-in-waiting (as her second son, Thomas, did with another of her ladies-in-waiting a few years later). There was no question of Lady Anne having to retire to a dower house on her son's marriage, but perhaps she did not relish the prospect of sharing her house with another woman, or perhaps she regretted that the marriage did nothing to strengthen the Twysden estate. For, by 1635, Sir Nicholas Saunder, who became one of Sir Hugh Myddleton's principal partners in the unsuccessful New River scheme, was seriously embarrassed almost to the verge of ruin, and in no position to provide a handsome marriage portion.

In September 1632, Saunder brought his daughter to East Peckham to accompany Lady Anne Twysden on her visit to Yorkshire, and talking one day with Twysden he related a story which Twysden thought worth recording. It is of sufficient interest in itself, and a sufficiently entertaining illustration of seventeenth-century credulity, to justify an anecdotal digression. It is the tale of the Earl of Arundel's cat (he died in the Tower in 1595). The cat stole a silver cup belonging to its master, which was recovered by the Earl's servant with the aid of a wizard. Going to a clearing in a wood late at night, the servant found there divers creatures forgathered with their thefts. He seized the cup, restored it to his Lordship, and told him of the strange sights he had seen. When the cat came purring about the Earl's legs in the engaging way of cats, he jestingly spoke to her about her naughtiness, whereupon she flew at his throat. Fortunately the Earl was rescued, and the cat was never seen again. A similar tale was told of a Lord Willoughby 'but this,' wrote Twysden, 'coming of so good hands I cannot but believe'. Sir Nicholas had had the story from Lady Arundel herself, 'a virtuous and religious lady in her way' (that is, she adhered to the Roman faith).[1]

The first child of the marriage was born at Lady Anne Twysden's London house a little more than nine months later, on 11 December 1635. The boy was given his paternal grandfather's name, William, and at the baptism which took place privately in the house Sir Nicholas Saunder, Sir Christopher Yelverton, and Lady Anne Twysden stood godparents. On 8 January the baby was brought down in the coach to East Peckham to be put out to nurse. On 15 November 1636 a daughter was born at Roydon Hall, where she was christened Anne by her godparents, the Countess of Winchilsea, Lady Anne Twysden and Francis Finch. On 24 November in the following year another daughter was born at Roydon Hall, and was named Isabella. Three children in thirty-five months was a rate of productivity that was not to be sustained; the fourth child, Frances, was born three years later in 1640, the fifth, Roger, in 1642 and the last, Charles, in 1645. In spite of the difficulties and hardships to come Twysden and his wife succeeded in rearing all six of their children, and they all outlived their parents, a record of survival rare in the seventeenth century.

During the 1630's Twysden's three younger brothers made

[1] Even the scholars of the seventeenth century found a willing suspension of disbelief not hard to achieve. Dugdale, on 24 January 1653, communicated to Twysden, in all seriousness, the scarcely less miraculous story of the pedlar of Swaffham who found two fortunes as the result of a dream.

long visits to the Continent. William went to France in 1631, staying there until 1634. Twysden, who sent him regularly remittances by letters of credit and bills of exchange, asked him to buy books there for the library at Roydon Hall. Frank went to Paris in 1633 and stayed there two years. In June 1638 he went back to Paris and then on to Rome for some months. John went to France early in 1634 with Sir George Stone, and possibly Sir Hugh Cholmley. Whether Twysden himself made the grand tour is uncertain. His knowledge of France and Italy and of the French and Italian languages suggests that he may have done so, but on the other hand shortness of money before his father's death and the multitude of duties which fell to his lot afterwards as head of the family and inheritor of an encumbered estate—duties which he carried out conscientiously whether the business in hand was important or trivial—may have kept him at home.

CHAPTER THREE

1635–1642

BY THE time of his marriage not only were estate matters claiming Twysden's attention, but also he was becoming involved in the government of the county. He was a Justice of the Peace by 1636, and took his duties seriously. He began by keeping a detailed notebook and probably continued the practice so long as he remained in the Commission, although the only notebook for the pre-Restoration period that has survived covers no more than the summer and autumn of 1636. It was a summer when the plague was raging in London, and Twysden and his fellow justices were busy seeing to it that the constables and borsholders were active in apprehending the 'extraordinary confluence of rogues and beggars in streets and highways' by whom the plague was spread.

But other, and even more serious public affairs were engaging his attention. On 20 October 1634, a writ was addressed to the City of London requiring the citizens, at their own expense and within four months, to provide seven men-of-war. Lady Anne Twysden, as owner of the house in Redcross Street, within the City, received a demand for £20. Should she pay it? Twysden advised her not to do so: ship-money levied on the City of London was an innovation and there was no precedent for it, he alleged. However, in March 1635 Lady Anne Twysden paid the sum demanded. Significantly the entry in the book of quit-rents, etc., is in her handwriting, not Twysden's: 'Paid for an unusual sess towards shipping and I think unduly to me made by the city for my house in London £20. 00*s*.'. On the following 4 August the second ship-money writs were sent out, to all counties and towns, inland as well as coastal. Its legality was doubtful, but times were abnormal (they always are) and comfort was to be found in the thought that perhaps it would not happen again. On the other hand, payment would create a precedent rendering any second demand more difficult to resist. In the end, on 25 November, Twysden paid to the sheriff of the county £7 0*s*. 0*d*. as ship-money, for Lady Anne Twysden's land and ability (or wealth), and his ability, in the parish of East Peckham. The amount was not exorbitant; it was the demand itself that was out of the way.

The stirs of the outside world were also affecting the ecclesiastical life of the parish. In 1637 rails were erected around the communion table in East Peckham church by order of Archbishop Laud, an action which caused trouble for the Vicar, Francis Worrall, four years later when a petition was sent by the 'inhabitants' of East Peckham (only five of them signed it) to the House of Commons with the usual Puritan objections to the setting up of the table 'at the east end of the chancel close to the wall, altarwise and railed in, and a new wainscoat made behind it with the picture of angels carved therein'. Twysden's views about these changes are not known; in so far as they could have been represented not as innovations but as a return to the practice of the early Church he would have approved of them. His only recorded comment, characteristically, is that it was done at the expense of the parish, not of the parson, as elsewhere in the Canterbury Diocese. His younger brother, Thomas, more generous or more Puritan, gave the church a new pulpit in the same year.

From his later writings it is clear that Twysden disliked extreme positions in religious as he did in political matters. Presbyterianism and Roman Catholicism, in his opinion, suffered from the same objectionable doctrine, that the Church was to be co-ordinate with, or even superior to, the State. The Calvinists would make the magistracy subordinate to the rule of the Church, wherein 'they follow their private fantasy, which is their general assembly', whilst Catholics would subject the secular power 'to the direction of . . . the Church, which is the Pope'. His rejection of the subordination of State to Church was one respect in which Twysden agreed with Hobbes, although they differed in many others. Twysden, in a notebook not intended for publication, expresses his objection to Presbyterianism in reasonable terms; if it is brought in by law 'it will establish another court, and then every man will exempt himself from punishments by saying he is of another's jurisdiction and the Kingdom will be seldom quiet. . . . No monarch can or will endure tribunals in several parts without a court depending on him to which they are responsible.' The moderate Erastian position held no terrors for him, but to bring in Presbyterianism would involve a strange and fundamental alteration in the law of the land, 'and certainly there is nothing of harder digestion in a nation than *peregrinae leges*, and great tyranny is less, is better borne, than such a change'. With this conservatism goes a fair degree of toleration, especially in the matter of publication. The attempt to control publication, the 'mangling of books' as Twysden calls it, he denounces as 'not letting us find the truth', a practice wherein the Roman Church, with its *Index Expurgatorius*, is at least more open and honest than the followers of Calvin.

Save for such occasional and often oblique references, the great events of the contemporary world find little mention in the memoranda books which Twysden was keeping at this time. In them he entered such details of estate matters or of local administration as he thought might be useful to his heirs and successors. His discussions with his powerful neighbour Sir Henry Vane ranged over the questions of ship-money and the Laudian code but what he wrote down amongst his memoranda was not a record of these conversations but Lady Vane's way of boiling a bullock's cheek, or recipes for mince pies and pancakes, for making sausages or boiling a hen, and several recipes for making ink, with a basis of sack or white wine (it was a beautiful sepia ink and three hundred years have not caused it to fade). He also recorded how to make 'a water to take away heat in the face, an infallible medicine for the biting of a mad dog, an assured medicine for the yellow jaundice', and 'an approved medicine for the stone and gravel in the kidneys' the basis of which was a pot of strong stale beer. This last recipe Twysden had from goodwife Stephens, who had it from a poor woman of Great Chart, who had it from 'a traveller, a kind of soldier'. It is a pity that we cannot know whether the recipe underwent modification during the process of threefold communication and, if so, whether its efficacy was thereby reduced—or perhaps enhanced.

On 26 June 1638 Twysden recorded in his diary (a printed almanac, with little room for additional entries by the possessor) a melancholy domestic accident. Mr. Zachary Scot, who was a guest staying at Roydon Hall, going to wash himself in the pond in the Great Park in front of the house 'was cast away and drowned, he going alone. The next day we borrowed a boat from Mereworth early in the morning, and found his body.'

Four months later another death occurred at Roydon Hall. On Sunday, 23 September, Lady Anne Twysden was taken ill in church and although she wished the sermon done, she would not leave until the service ended. She retired to her room and was well enough the next day to write letters, but she gradually grew worse, and the ministrations neither of Dr. Ramsey of Maidstone nor of Mr. Johannes Hind, the German factotum and counsellor who had been a member of the Twysden household for many years, proved of any use. She received communion on Wednesday, 3 October, and seeing three of her sons, Twysden, Will and Jack at her bedside she besought them to love the Lord Jesus and to love one another. Perhaps with a premonition of the events which were soon to divide the county and the country, she reminded them of 'the tale of the faggot which being bound together is not to be broken but every twig easily by itself'. She died eleven days later, on Sunday, 14 October, at the age of sixty-three.

Lady Anne Twysden was a remarkable woman, who commanded the affection and devotion of her children, her sons-in-law, and, especially, of her daughter-in-law, Isabella. She was well read, and knew Latin, Italian, Spanish and French, but was wise enough to conceal her learning. 'She had,' said Twysden, 'the best way of expressing her mind in writing with the most facility I ever met with in woman.' She was accounted handsome, with an excellent complexion that no painter could ever depict so fair as the original and she retained it until her death. In her latter years she grew so heavy that a childhood lameness became increasingly troublesome, and she could no longer go over the house in person. But 'her mind far outwent her body . . . she was all her life given to much sitting, heavy bred, and bottle-drink-full of meditations.' Although she grew weak of body, her courage remained undiminished and she affirmed that she would rather lie in prison for the rest of her life than pay ship-money, although prudence or her sons' entreaties persuaded her to give up so arduous a course. Above all, she was deeply religious and pious. She would never be in a room with a man, except her husband or, rarely, her sons, unless she had a woman with her, or at least the door open and in sight of her. In a little manuscript handbook she copied passages from the Bible and wrote a number of prayers of her own. Twysden's wife wrote of her 'A more noble, virtuous religious lady this earth bears not. As dearly as her own she loved me, and my love was more to her than I can express.'

By his mother's will, which was made six months before her death, Twysden again found himself acting as executor. Like her husband, Lady Anne Twysden desired that her funeral should be performed with as little charge as it could reasonably be done with, the cost not to exceed £100 in all (in fact it came to £119). With characteristic sagacity she specified in a separate letter who were to receive blacks, and of what value, knowing this to be a matter wherein 'no executor shall ever give content'. Her legacies give some idea of the things she owned and treasured:

> 'To my daughters Cholmley and Yelverton (to whom I have already given most of my jewels) . . . two little cups of gold, like to those in silver I use to drink broth in.
>
> To my eldest son Roger, my gold cup, my gold book set with rubies, which his grandfather Twysden gave me, and my mother's picture set in gold.
>
> To Isabella, wife of Roger, for whom I cannot do as much as she deserves but hope he will, my little gold clock, all my chamber plate, with all my boxes, and contents, of silver, amber, or what else I have not disposed of in my life; and

all the other toys that are usually in the closet next my chamber.

To Mrs. Jane Thomlinson, my little silver striking clock, which I have long worn myself.'

There were pecuniary legacies for the poor of East Peckham (£10), to her four younger sons (£25 each), to Mr. Johannes Hind (£3), and to all the servants; the residue of plate, household stuff, and stock was to go to her executor.

Twysden, now forty-one, at last became the master of Roydon Hall where he had lived since Sir William's death as his mother's dependant. His financial position was still uncomfortable. The marriage of his brother, Thomas, to Mrs. Jane Thomlinson, which took place in the parlour of Roydon Hall on 26 December 1639, was an added expense and this time he had to borrow £500 from his uncle Francis Finch and £200 from his brother, Thomas, all at 7 per cent. interest. The debts were paid off within a year, and at last in full control of the estate and with his liabilities discharged, Twysden could look forward, by 1641, to consolidating his financial position. Given a settled country and another twenty years of life which he could devote to the careful management of his estate, Twysden might fairly expect to die a wealthy man. He began to reduce his expenses by letting (lending he said, but a substantial rent was involved) the London house to Lady Vere in 1641. In more propitious times it might have resulted in a long and profitable tenancy, but by 1642 Lady Vere had quitted.

Before turning to the public affairs in which Twysden was becoming caught up, there is one more family matter that we must mention. On 30 July 1641 his brother William died at Bath. He had been ill for a year or more and had gone to Bath in January, for 'if I recover' he wrote to Twysden 'it must be here'. And to Lady Twysden he confided 'those few hours that I have had without pain I have not passed unpleasantly' amongst the company at Bath. Twysden described him as a man of great learning and wisdom. He travelled much on the Continent meeting many scholars, especially theologians, with whom he kept up a correspondence in which

Twysden also became involved. He remains a shadowy character: perhaps for that reason an attractive one. Naturally he named his eldest brother as his executor, but on this occasion the office was not onerous for William had little to leave and the bequests consisted only of a few small legacies to his brothers and sisters, to a servant and to Johannes Hind.

In public affairs it was the King's attempt to levy impositions on his subjects without authority of Parliament that chiefly engaged the attention of Twysden as of so many of his fellow landowners. With the utmost reluctance and with foreboding, he paid the first ship-money assessed on the county of Kent. The High Sheriff in 1635, to whom fell the task of getting in the money, was Sir George Sondes and Twysden notes that he behaved very reasonably—almost too much so, for he listened to everyone's grievance with the result that he was constantly issuing new and contradictory orders, as many as five, six or seven in the same case. In spite of the consequent confusion, the money came in. Only the Hon. Richard Spencer of Orpington absolutely refused to pay, and to avoid any trouble a friend paid it on his behalf without his knowledge and to his strong resentment when he discovered this well-meant interference in his affairs.

Other men in the county, whilst not standing out as Spencer did, allowed themselves to be distrained rather than make voluntary payment. Twysden was quick to notice the uncertainty whether the constable could give a good title on the sale of distrained goods (as a result of this doubt sometimes no buyer could be found) and he put the question to an unnamed Privy Councillor, almost certainly Sir Henry Vane, Controller of His Majesty's Household. However, he did not get a satisfactory reply, and no one seemed to know whether the failure to give express authority to the constable to warrant the goods distrained was deliberate or due to an oversight. In Kent purchasers came forward so satisfactorily that the county in fact raised £200 more than its quota. The Privy Council graciously told the High Sheriff to give the excess to the Justices so that they might use it for some county purpose, such as the repair of the Boughton highway.

During 1636 there were rumours of another ship-money imposition. Twysden asked his neighbour Sir Henry Vane whether it would be so. Vane replied that there would be more ship-money writs, adding 'Do you think they will not be paid?' 'Indeed I do,' answered Twysden, although as he recorded in his notebook 'I confess my opinion was otherwise'. Vane did not accept Twysden's view, closing the discussion with 'Well, you will be deceived. In East Kent there is not one will refuse, and very few in West Kent.'

However, the opposition was widespread, and Charles thought it wise to reinforce his position by asking the Judges whether he might not, when the kingdom was in danger, demand ship-money of all his subjects, and whether he was not the sole judge of the danger and how it should be avoided. Anxiously men awaited the Judges' reply. If it declared ship-money to be legal, it seemed to put an end to the form of constitutional government, based on the Commons' control of taxation, that had been emerging for centuries, for 'none could expect a Parliament' as Twysden wrote 'but on some necessity not now imaginable'. In these uncertain times strange and sinister interpretations were put upon innocent acts, and men began to say even of Selden's *Mare Clausum* that its true purpose was not, as first thought, to advance the King's claim to dominion over the narrow seas, but to justify ship-money.

The Judges gave their answer, confirming the King's right to levy ship-money and himself to decide, alone, when the kingdom was in danger. The answer was much discussed in the county: 'all concluded that if a kingdom were in danger it ought not to be lost for want of money if it were within it', but some men said that the King was not to be the sole judge of the danger, that being a question of such importance that it must be discussed by a Parliament however 'much to blame' the last Parliament had been 'in their carriages towards His Majesty'. The Judges' answer, argued these men, applied not to time of peace. But in spite of the argument, which continued, most men in Kent paid when they knew that the Judges had given an answer favourable to the King.

As a conscientious magistrate, Twysden went to the next

Assizes at Maidstone, sitting next to Weston, J. on the Bench, and with the other gentlemen in court listened with polite interest to the Judge's charge while he explained the details of certain statutes. It was when he began to speak of ship-money and of the answer given by the Judges to the King's questions that 'the audience (as to that did nigh concern them) did then listen with great diligence, and after the declaration made I did in my conceit, see a kind of dejection in their very looks; some admiring it should here be given in charge, where almost all had already paid the second tax, to acquaint the country with the legality of it'. Twysden himself thought the Judges' answer 'ambiguous' and had no hesitation in expressing his doubts to Weston, J., himself one of the signatories to the answer.

Moreover, it was doubtful whether a mere declaration of the Judges on a reference from the King and not in the course of regular legal proceedings was sufficient to establish the law. Neither Hampden nor Lord Saye and Sele thought so, and did their best to bring to trial actions which they had already commenced. Twysden anxiously watched the delaying tactics on the part of the Crown and followed approvingly Oliver St. John's argument for Hampden, when his case at last came on. By a majority, amongst whom were Weston, J. and Finch, Chief Justice of the Common Pleas, Twysden's distant cousin, the Judges decided in favour of the Crown, but the dissenting judgements of Croke and Hutton were noted down with approbation by Twysden. He himself afterwards claimed, as matter of merit, that he made no payment of ship-money after the first demand, a claim which is supported, negatively, by the absence of any record of payment in his estate accounts. But if he did refuse, presumably he would have been distrained and there is no record that a distress was ever levied against his property; it is inconceivable that he would have failed to record such a proceeding in his notebooks. Probably by making skilful use of the quibbles and delays that were possible to one with his knowledge of constitutional law and procedure, he was able to procrastinate so successfully that the constable never caught up with him.

Ship-money was the most notorious, but not necessarily the most onerous of the impositions under which the people groaned (or some of them did). Twysden made a catalogue of the extraordinary charges levied in Kent after the first ship-money writs. In July 1636, the beacons had to be watched day and night, a great expense to the hundreds they were in; on 30 November 1638 the order was repeated, very unusual for the 'dead of winter', and there were similar commands in September 1639 and September 1640; in February 1639 a sess was levied for supplying the magazines of the county with powder, match and bullet; the following month the trained bands were called out to go north, and the county had to find £1,500 coat and conduct money; in April 1640 the demand for coat and conduct money came to £1,750; all this in addition to the writs for ship-money which were arriving almost annually, the sums laid on Kent being:

October 1635	£8,000
November 1636	£8,000
December 1637	£8,000
January 1638	£2,750
February 1639	£6,400[1]

The traditional impositions, too, were increased in amount. Since the Composition had been settled in 1602 the price of wood and coal had gone up, with a consequent increase of the Composition after 1637 by a groat in the shilling. By 1640 this had become the cause of great complaint in the county.

The taxes were burdensome and vexatious, the method by which they were imposed was disquieting. For eleven years the King had governed without a parliament, and who was to know whether that institution had not ceased to exist? Contemporary trends on the Continent could give no comfort to the English constitutionalist. In France the States-General had last met in 1614; in Spain the Cortes had been suppressed by

[1] Reduced on the County's protest from £8,000 but with a threat that the assessment would revert to the original amount if the money were not paid promptly.

Philip II and in his Kingdom of Naples parliamentary proceedings were a mere formality; elsewhere the Hohenzollerns and the Hapsburgs were demonstrating the redundancy of assemblies. It was with a sense of relief, of a return from an unknown and frightening land to familiar and safe territory, that the country gentry and city merchants heard in February 1640 that Parliament had been summoned to meet on 13 April. It was almost as though after a period of aberration Nature was resuming her accustomed course.

The resulting election of the two Knights of the Shire for Kent, a strange and contentious episode, is described in Chapter Nine. In the event, the two chosen were Twysden and Norton Knatchbull of Mersham Hatch.

As a fellow-member of the House of Commons Twysden again had his brother-in-law Cholmley, who was returned as member for Scarborough. Cholmley had been busily training soldiers for the King's march against the Scots during the previous year, but he refused to pay ship-money and refused with such *éclat* that the whole hundred followed him. Bitterly disappointed at the King's unwisdom in breaking off the Parliament, he made no attempt to conceal his dissatisfaction, and Strafford caused him to be put out of all commissions, namely, the peace, oyer and terminer, the deputy lieutenancy, and the colonelcy, and he was summoned to attend the Council daily for three or four weeks. Back in Yorkshire, Cholmley joined the county gentry at the Assizes in agreeing to address to the Council a complaint of their grievances. He was one of four chosen to draft the petition. The four withdrew to a private room and the work was soon done—very soon, for Cholmley and Sir John Hotham had already written it, and had it in their pockets. It 'did something startle the Council' for it was 'in a pretty high style', but it was nevertheless signed by over 100 of the nobility and gentry. Shortly afterwards, when the King saw Cholmley and Hotham at York, he sharply reproved them, saying 'If you ever meddle or have a hand in any more, I will hang you.'

The Yorkshire episode is not an irrelevant interlude in the Kent story for two years later there was petitioning at the

Maidstone Assizes in which Twysden was involved and of a kind to suggest that he was aware of the role which his brother-in-law had played at York. However, Cholmley's brave show of independence was not Twysden's way; he met trouble squarely when it came, but did not go out of his way to seek it. He was not one of those who 'ambition martyrdom'.

When the King summoned another Parliament in November, 1640 (the Long Parliament, as it became) the Knights of the Shire for Kent were Sir John Culpepper and Sir Edward Dering. Twysden neither wished nor expected to be returned again, for that would have been contrary to the convention of the county. The public office which at this time he was called upon to fill was more burdensome and less dignified. At the Assizes at Maidstone on 23 August 1641 an attempt was made to appoint him Treasurer for the Composition, an attempt which he strenuously resisted, partly because neither he nor his father had ever been a Compounder, but even more because it was a thankless, and sometimes, costly task, as it proved to the gentleman finally appointed, 'who was much troubled to get in his money, and could never get it all in, but . . . was a great loser by it'. Later that year, at the October Quarter Sessions, in spite of his protests, Twysden was appointed to act as Treasurer for 1642. He undertook the office with apprehension and looking back on it in later years, concluded that he had been mistaken in accepting it.

In the House of Commons, in May 1641, Twysden's kinsman and successor as Knight of the Shire, Sir Edward Dering ('a most complete gentleman in all respects, an excellent antiquary' wrote Dugdale, but Henry Oxinden was expressing the more general opinion when he feared lest with his constant turning he 'turn out of his right wits') moved the first reading of the Root and Branch Bill. Until then Parliament had shown itself pretty much of one mind, but as soon as it turned to questions of religion divisions appeared. Six months later, in the debate on the Grand Remonstrance, the rift had become patent. When, on 22 November, the votes on the Remonstrance were counted the Ayes were 159 and the Noes 148. One of the most vehement amongst the minority was Dering's fellow

Knight of the Shire, Culpepper, who sought to enter a protest against the resolution.

The discord between Dering and Culpepper was typical of the growing dissension, although the argument within the county was more moderate and less bitterly contentious than in some other parts of the country. Kent was neither strongly Parliamentarian nor strongly royalist; it was strongly Kentish and wanted nothing so much as to go on conducting its own affairs without outside interference, and particularly without being required to perform the uncomfortable balancing feat of complying at one and the same time with contradictory orders emanating from the King and from Parliament. Twysden leaned somewhat towards the royal side, as being the more legal and, therefore, the safer; as he explained to a Parliamentarian, 'If there should be such a misery as a civil war, such as are for the King will be safer than the others, there being nothing they can *legally* lose.' But the more realistic Parliamentarian replied that if they won 'through a judgement of the Lords on impeachment by the Commons a way will be found to possess the estates of any who oppose them'. The attempt to cling to legality was pathetic and unreal, as pathetic as a pauper's attempt to cling to respectability in the workhouse.

Cholmley, who was taking an active part in affairs at Westminster, found himself in much the same position as Twysden, as worried by the extremists about the King as by the extremists in Parliament. In June 1642 he was appointed by Parliament as one of the four Commissioners to present the Nineteen Propositions to the King. However, he thought the Propositions so unjust and unreasonable that he declined to read them to the King, taking back Charles's message of rejection to Parliament. As Cholmley wrote in his memoirs, in a phrase which sums up also Twysden's view, 'myself desired nothing but that the King might enjoy his just rights as well as the subjects theirs'. It is easy to enunciate the maxim: to define the just rights of the parties has always been the rub. Twysden so misliked the way things were going, and the factions that were developing, that in the early part of 1642 he seriously thought of going abroad until, in some way that could not be foreseen, and at some date that could not be even guessed at, the parties had managed to resolve their differences. To contract out was not a courageous line of conduct, but for a man of his temperament, forced into a position of choosing between alternatives both of which, in their extreme form, he believed to be wrong, it might be the only course compatible with conscience. It was not a course to be taken lightly, without consideration of the cost involved—immediate and perhaps lengthy separation from his family, exile from his beloved estates at East Peckham and Great Chart, abandonment of his position as a county gentleman and as one of the governors of the county. The attainder and execution of Strafford affected him strongly: not that he himself was ever likely to stand in danger of impeachment for anything nearer to high treason than refusal to pay ship-money, but once Parliament had shown such disregard for legal propriety as it had in Strafford's case, there was no illegality it might not perpetrate. The Act of May 1641 against the dissolution of Parliament except with its own consent had also filled Twysden with foreboding. As a precaution, he procured from the Council a pass to go abroad, but put off his going.

Suddenly, in the spring of 1642, he threw off his hesitancy. At Maidstone Assizes on 22 March, he showed that at least with the pen he was a man of action. By that day's work he sealed his own fate and deprived himself of any chance of crossing the sea and escaping from the troubles that were now threatening to slide into civil dissension.

CHAPTER FOUR

March 1642–June 1643

THE HARDENING of political and religious differences throughout the country resulted in a crop of petitions to the House of Commons. Occasionally they were oral, as that of Sir John Culpepper in November 1640, who, presenting the grievances of Kent, said 'Mr. Speaker, I stand not up with the petition in my hand as others have done before me, I have it in my mouth, and in charge from them that sent me hither.' He went on to specify the things that troubled Kent: the increase in the number of Papists, innovations in religion (the position of the altar, bowing, and so on), the expenses of the military preparations, the 'etc.' oath (on which Kent had already submitted some Queries in the preceding July), ship-money and monopolies. More usually petitions were written, like the Petition of the Committee of Kent which proposed the abolition of tithes, and which Spelman thought it necessary to refute, although recognizing that it emanated from an esoteric group and not from the Knights and Gentlemen of the county in common.

For there was no body which could legitimately claim to speak for 'the county of Kent' or the 'Knights and gentlemen' of the shire. A partisan group from the Weald or from Sheppey might, and from time to time did, petition in the name of the county, to the anger of those of their fellow-countymen who held opposite views. It was with these local irritations in their minds, as well as profounder anxieties about the dangerous differences which were developing between King and Parliament and within Parliament, that many of the influential gentry of Kent met for the Spring Assizes at Maidstone on 22 March 1642.

Twysden, as a Justice of the Peace who took his duties seriously, naturally attended the Assizes, to meet his fellow justices, to hear points of the King's policy expounded by the circuit judge, to discuss with him difficult points of law arising from county business or from Quarter Sessions, and perhaps to be consulted by him on the cases coming up for trial. There was a good deal of informality about these exchanges and no wide gulf, social or legal, between the judge of assize and certain of the magistrates.

On Tuesday, 21 March, Twysden went to Maidstone to call on Sir Thomas Mallet, the Judge, at his lodgings during the evening. He fell in with Sir George Strode of Squerryes, Westerham, also going to pay his respects to the Judge, and at the lodgings they met a number of other county justices including Sir John Sedley of St. Clere, Ightham. Afterwards they adjourned together to their inn where all the other justices were at supper, discussing a petition recently delivered to the House of Commons by Sir Michael Livesey. It was a petition protesting against the attempted arrest of the five members during the preceding January, and as with many petitions at this time the initiative came not from the nominal petitioners but from a section of the House itself. A few weeks earlier Twysden had overtaken at Deptford a group of men from Sussex who were on their way to present a petition (probably one similar to Livesey's) to Parliament. Questioned about its tenor and purpose, they had to admit that they knew nothing—they would be told its purport when they got to London. It would be unfair to suppose that Sussex provided England's only brute petitioners; those in Kent were no better, and were a source of embarrassment and irritation to such of the county gentry as happened to hold other views.

And many of them did hold other views. The justices resented Livesey's petition, and at supper there was talk of presenting a counter petition with which the Assize Grand Jury should be associated. After supper the company broke up, Twysden going off with Sir Edward Dering, Sir George Strode and the Hon. Richard Spencer (of Orpington) to Spencer's lodging. Soon afterwards they were joined by Mr. Blount, who subsequently became a strong Parliamentarian. They continued the discussion begun at supper and Twysden suggested some grievances which should be included in the new petition, such as the licence which the Commons took in declaring new and unknown privileges and in ejecting members (of whom Dering was one, the Commons so strongly resenting his collection of speeches against Pym and Hampden that they ordered the book to be burnt, with the result that the price trebled overnight). However, the others feared this might be going too far, and were insistent that the petition must be incapable of giving offence to anyone.

The Assizes began the next day with an ominous change in the usual procedure. It had been customary in Kent for men of small account to be empanelled as grand jurors. The Judge, either of his own accord or prompted by some of his visitors of the previous evening, suggested that Kent might care to do as other counties and empanel a Grand Jury of gentlemen. After some hesitation the suggestion was adopted, and a truly Grand Jury was returned, with the secluded Dering as foreman. To Parliament it must have appeared a suspicious proceeding: so patently suspicious, Twysden afterwards claimed with some subtlety, that it was plain evidence of an innocent intent. In any case, by midday nothing definite had been settled about a petition.

It was evidently discussed at length by the Grand Jury, no doubt at the expense of time spent in considering bills of indictment, and when towards evening Dering and the rest of the grand jurors came to the Judge with a number of true bills, they said that they wished to submit a petition to Parliament provided the Justices of the Peace on the Bench would also join. Mallet, J., said it was none of his business, an attitude which the Commons deemed to be so unsatisfactory that he was afterwards committed to the Tower.

The justices responded more favourably. Indeed they cannot have been surprised at the proposal; to say that the Judge, the Justices of the Peace and the grand jurors were acting in collusion may suggest a more sinister interpretation than the facts warranted, but no doubt they were all well aware of what was in the wind and egged each other on in that kind of quasi-hysteria that sometimes develops when a number of politically-minded men are gathered together. Not only did the justices agree, but Twysden on their behalf suggested what the next steps should be; let the Grand Jury nominate a few justices, and the justices a few grand jurors, who would meet together and draft a paper for submission to them all. The suggestion was adopted and the group, of whom Twysden was one, went off to a private lodging to set about their task.

Did Twysden, as his brother-in-law Cholmley had done at York two years before, go with a draft already in his pocket? There is no proof that he did, but in 1643 the County Committee alleged that he, with Dering, had 'formed and framed' the petition, and probably there were some amongst the Committee who spoke from first-hand knowledge of what had passed. It is at least possible that he had a few 'notes' ready in his pocket. Twysden denied that he drew up the petition, and certainly he did not attend the later session after supper, when it was further discussed, because he was 'that night very ill'. It is unkind, but not altogether unreasonable, to suspect that the illness was brought on by a chance meeting at the Star Inn at supper-time with Blount, who made it plain that he disapproved of the whole proceeding, as no doubt Parliament would also so soon as news of the affair reached Westminster.

The following morning the committee of justices and grand jurors met again at a private house in Maidstone to finish the drafting of the petition. A number of amendments were made, either to reduce the possibility of giving offence, or for the sake of an accuracy that in the circumstances can only be regarded as scholarly to the point of pedantry; for example, in the statement 'Episcopal government has been deduced and dispersed through all the Christian world' it was decided to substitute 'throughout' for 'through all' because it 'was remembered' that Gerundensis had written that some parts of Spain did not admit bishops. It was exactly the kind of erudite accuracy that Twysden would have insisted upon, however apparently unimportant or irrelevant to the matter in hand, and, with the style, is some evidence of his part-authorship.

The next day, Thursday, the petition was submitted to the justices and Grand Jury, sitting openly in Court, and was then still further amended. Finally it was agreed to, as Twysden subsequently wrote, *nemine contradicente*. What he forgot to record was that those grand jurors who misliked the petition withdrew themselves from the Court or were excluded by the others, and they numbered nine out of nineteen. The petition traversed the whole range of contemporary ecclesiastical and political problems, the only unexpected provision being the prayer that the professors of the Civil Law should not find discouragement, a provision which was inserted at the request of Dr. Piers, a civilian who by chance happened to be visiting Kent and seized the opportunity of making propaganda for Doctors' Commons whose strange ways endeared them neither to Parliament nor to the Common lawyers. Since Twysden's participation in the petition was the *fons et origo* of his subsequent tribulations, it deserves in justice to him as well as to his opponents to be set out in full, in spite of its length. In its reasoned conservatism, its insistence upon due process of law and its phraseology, much of it seems to bear traces of Twysden's hand.

'To the honourable house of Commons, the humble Petition of the Gentry, Ministers and Commonalty of the County of Kent, agreed upon at the general Assizes of that county. Most humbly showeth,

That we cannot but take notice how welcome to this honourable house many Petitions have been, which yet came not from an assembled body of any County, as this doth, we do hope to find as gentle and as favourable reception of this as any others have found of their Petitions, our hearts witnessing unto us as good, as peaceable, and as pious purposes as the best. These are therefore the true and the ardent desires of the County.

i. First, you will please to accept our due and hearty thanks for those excellent laws which by his Majesty's grace and goodness you have obtained for us.

ij. Secondly, that all laws against Papists be put in due execution, and accompt taken of their disarming; and that all children of Papists may be brought up in the reformed religion.

iij. Thirdly, that the solemn Liturgy of the Church of England, celebrious by the Piety of holy Bishops and Martyrs who composed it,—established by the supreme law of the land,—attested and approved by the best of all foreign divines; confirmed with subscription of all the Ministry of this land, a Clergy as learned and as able as any in the Christian world, enjoyed, and with an holy love embraced, by the most and best of all the Laity;—that this holy exercise of our religion may by your auctority be enjoyed quiet and free from interruptious storms, prophanations, threats, and force of such men who daily do deprave it, and neglect the use of it in diverse churches, in despite of the laws established.

iiij. Fourthly, that Episcopal government, as ancient in this Island as Christianity itself, deduced and dispersed throughout the Christian world even from the Apostolical time, may be preserved as the most pious, most prudent, and most safe government for the peace of the Church.

v. Fifthly, that all differences concerning religion and Ceremonies may be referred to a lawful, free, national Synod, and, as your Remonstrance promiseth, a General Synod of most grave, learned, pious, and judicious divines, the proper Agents, whose Interests, gifts, and callings may quicken them in that great work, whose choice to be by all the Clergy of the land, because all the Clergy are to be bound by their resolutions; and the determinations of this Synod to bind us all, when you have first formed them into a law; and this we take to be according to the ancient Laws of this land, confirmed by Magna Carta.

vi. Sixthly, that some speedy and good provision may be made, as by his Majesty hath been, and is by all good men desired, against the odious and abominable scandal of schismatical and seditious sermons and pamphlets, and some severe law made against Laymen for daring to arrogate to themselves, and to exercise the holy function of the Ministry, who some of them do sow their impious discontented doctrines even in sacred places, by abuse of sacred

Ordinances, to the advancing of Heresy, schism, prophaness, Libertinism, Anabaptism, Atheism.

vij. Seventhly, that if the coercive power of Ecclesiastical Courts, by way of Excommunication, be already abrogated, or shall be thought fit so to be, that there may be some other power and auctority speedily established for the suppressing of the heinous and now so much abounding sins of Incest, Adultery, Fornication, and other Crimes, and for the recovering of Tithes, Repairing of Churches, Probate of Wills, Church assesses, and providing of Bread and wine for the Communion, and choice of Churchwardens and other officers in the Church, and especially for Ministers who neglect the celebrating of the holy Communion, and of Parishioners for not receiving.

viij. Eighthly, that the professors of that learned faculty of the Civil Law, without which this Kingdom cannot but suffer many inconveniences, may not find discouragement, and so desert their studies and professions.

ix. Ninthly, that honour and profit, the powerful encouragements of industry, learning and piety, may be preserved, without any farther diminution, to the Clergy.

x. Tenthly, that you please sadly to consider the bleeding wounds of our brethren in Ireland, and with speedy succours endeavour to preserve them, whereunto his Majesty hath promised a gracious concurrence.

xj. Eleventhly, that you please to frame an especial law for the regulating the Militia of this kingdom, so that the subject may know how at once to obey both his Majesty and the houses of Parliament, a law whereby may be left to the discretion of governors as little as may be; but that the number of Arms, and what measure of punishment shall be inflicted on offenders, may be expressly set down in the Act, and not left to any arbitrary power; and that, according to the precedents of former laws, the offenders may not be tried out of the County.

xij. Twelfthly, that the precious Liberty of the subject, the Common birth-right of every Englishman, may be, as in all other points preserved entire, so in this also; That no order of either or both houses, not grounded on the Laws of the Land, may be enforced on the subject, until it be fully enacted by Parliament.

xiij. Thirteenthly, that his Majesty's gracious message of the 20th of January last, for the present and future establishment of the privilege of Parliament, the free and quiet enjoying of our estates and fortunes, the Liberties of our persons, the security of the true religion professed, the maintaining of his Majesty's just and royal authority, the establishing of his revenue, may be taken into speedy consideration: the effecting whereof will satisfy the desires of all us his faithful and loving subjects.

xiv. Fourteenth, that all possible care may be taken that the native commodities of the kingdom may have a quick vent; and that clothing and other manufactures may be improved, wherein the livelihood of many thousands do consist; And that trade may be so balanced that the importation do not exceed the exportation, which otherwise will in time prove the consumption of the kingdom.

xv. Fifteenth, that you please to frame some laws concerning depopulations, purveyance, Cart-taking, delays in Justice, Traffic, Fishing on the coast, fulling earth, that our sea Ports may be repaired, and our Magazines renewed.

xvi. Sixteenth, that you please to consider the general poverty that seems to overgrow the Land.

xvij. Lastly, we humbly beseech you to consider the sad condition that we and the whole land are in, if a good understanding be not speedily renewed between his Majesty and the houses of Parliament.

Our hopes are yet above our fears; secure them we beseech you. God direct and bless your consultations for the removing of all distrusts and jealousies, and for renewing that tie of confidence and trust which is the highest happiness between a most gracious Prince, and us his loving people.

And you shall have the daily prayers of your humble Orators the Commons of Kent.'

'This was all publicly read, agreed unto, and concluded, at the Assizes at Maidstone, on the 25 March 1642.'

It was the intention, after the petition had been adopted by the justices and the grand jurors, to send copies of it throughout the county, to invite one gentleman in each division to collect signatures to it (carefully testifying that any copy which he issued was a true copy), and to return the subscribed copies to the Easter Quarter Sessions at Maidstone. Then, on 29 April, accompanied by the gentry of Kent who were to meet at Blackheath, it was to be carried up to the House of Commons, where Augustine Skinner, one of the Knights of the Shire, would be required to present it.

That the petition was controversial Twysden well knew, but as he very fairly said different men have different opinions and the House of Commons exists so that they may be heard. That was, however, not the current orthodoxy. Twysden dined at Fairlawne with Sir Henry Vane, now out of favour with the Court and deprived of all his offices, on the Saturday following the Assizes and it is highly unlikely that Vane failed to warn him that the recent events at Maidstone had been angrily received at Westminster. On the Sunday he went to see his friend and neighbour William James of Ightham (who became a Member of Parliament for Kent in Cromwell's Parliament) and showed him the petition. Twysden was surprised and worried, or at least professed to be so, that a man of such intelligence and integrity as James could think ill of it. Certainly Parliament thought it a pernicious and dangerous document, and acted promptly.

On Monday, 28 March, the House of Commons made an Order for Dering, Strode, Spencer and Twysden (significantly the four who had met at supper on the eve of the Assizes and there had been joined by Blount) to be arrested and brought before the House as delinquents. The House of Lords issued a similar warrant. On the Tuesday the Commons heard from Blount his account of what had passed at the Assizes. On the same day the Commons order was executed, but the Lords were not quite so expeditious, their warrant being served on Twysden on the 30th. Neither warrant specified any cause for their commitment, 'which is what I am sure I have heard enough condemned in others' as Twysden wrote, with an overt reference to Coke's *Institutes* ii, p. 52, para. 4, and a covert reference to Darnel's case.

Early on the 30th Dering came over to East Peckham from Surrenden, and with Twysden set off for London. They had reason for anxiety about their fate; Twysden had an additional husbandly cause for worry, for he left his wife great with child (Roger was born on 26 July) and he had no idea when he might see Roydon Hall or his family again.

Two days later (a wry jest that it was All Fools' Day), they appeared as the prisoners of the Serjeant of the Mace before the House of Commons. Following Spencer and Strode, Twysden knelt at the Bar of the House, confessed that he had subscribed the petition, but denied that he had taken the initiative in it; when he came to the Assizes, he said, it was already table-talk. There were, he added, nearly 2,000 people present when the petition was propounded, the implication being that it was no hole-and-corner affair. If he had offended Parliament, he expressed himself as heartily sorry for it. After brief questioning all four were committed as prisoners to a house in Covent Garden until they could be more closely questioned by an *ad hoc* committee of the Lords and Commons. At their second appearance they were examined upon thirty interrogatories, but all their answers according and showing no criminal activity, the House of Commons, reluctant to release them, was in a quandary. It then determined that they should be required to answer nine interrogatories upon oath, a procedure which conflicted with the principle that no man is obliged to accuse himself and which, when used by the prerogative courts, had angered the Commons. In any case, a committee of the Lords and Commons had no legal power to administer an *ex officio* oath—there was no precedent for it. An attempt to give a show of legality to the proceedings was made by telling each of the four that, in his answers, he was not to incriminate himself; it was hoped that the evidence of the other three would provide sufficient incrimination. However, the further examination revealed nothing more than had emerged in the first inquiry. The Commons then decided that Strode, Spencer and Dering (who had decamped) should be impeached, but the proceedings against Twysden were stayed. Strode and Spencer put in a mollifying answer to their impeachment, and they were all freed on condition of collecting in the copies of the petition which had already been distributed.

Twysden regarded the action of the two Houses as unjust and arbitrary. For Mr. George Peard, a lawyer M.P., to say of the petition that there were things in it not far from treason was absurd. For Parliament to frown upon petitioning when it had itself encouraged their submission showed gross partiality. For his friend and neighbour at Great Chart, Richard Browne, Member for New Romney, to tell him that he, Twysden, did not understand the aim of the petition, a comment that was kindly meant, reflected upon Browne's intellectual grasp rather than Twysden's. He understood the aim of it well enough, and so did the House of Commons; Parliament was arrogating to itself powers beyond those which it had by custom wielded, it was becoming conscious of its power and arbitrary in its exercise; and these were things that the gentry of Kent—or many of them—did not like. Twysden might protest that it was a very innocent petition, with no offence in it, but inwardly he knew better and that he was really playing with fire.

He was at once excluded from the Commissioners for Kent named in the Bill against scandalous ministers in spite of the fact that the lawyer Peard, a severe man, confided to Twysden that he saw very little against him. On 9 April he and Spencer were bailed by Parliament. Twysden was required to enter into a bond for £10,000, and to provide two sureties each for £5,000 that he would surrender within twenty-four hours if ever required to do so by Parliament, that he would not go into any part of Kent, and that he would not move above ten miles from the City of London. The bail was so enormous that Twysden's first inclination was to refuse his freedom on such terms and to remain a prisoner, but reflecting that the whole procedure was illegal and the bonds unenforceable, he decided that it was not too high a price, since unexactable, to pay for liberty. So he got his mother's brother, Francis Finch, and Sir Robert Filmer of East Sutton each to stand surety for £5,000, and with those sureties and his own bond for £10,000 he was released.

Roger Twysden, aged 8

Parliament's manifest displeasure notwithstanding, there were many amongst the Kentish gentry who were still determined to go on with the petition. When they met at Quarter Sessions at Maidstone on 19 April they took the opportunity of collecting more signatures to the petition and on the last day of the month it was carried up to London by a large company. The Sheriff of London closed the bridge to them and would admit them to the City only when they had put off their swords. They took the petition to Westminster, and it was presented by Captain Richard Lovelace and Sir William Boteler, both of whom were promptly committed to prison where they remained for two months.

Twysden, separated from his wife, was in a state of dejection. On 1 May he writes to her from his lodgings in the Inner Temple:

> 'My dear Heart,
>
> I shall assuredly know this week whether I shall come down to thee or thou up to me, for if the Parliament deny me, I am resolved to make my own house ready for you, if you assent to live in town, for thus divided as I now stand I will be no longer. . . . I do infinitely long to be with thee, and till that is will write as much and often as I can.'

And in a post-script he adds

> 'Mr. Trotter sends thee I hope all the King's speeches and letters, which when you have read pray keep clean for me . . . the report only is hereafter they shall be all banished, in respect they carry an infinite mass of treason. . . . Farewell again and again, my own dear heart, whom I never knew what it was to [be] parted from till now.'

He wrote frequently, with concern for his wife and family, their friends and relations, his venison in the park at Roydon Hall, and with comments on public affairs. But suddenly he was assailed by the fear that he might have written too freely of public affairs, for a rumour was abroad that a Commission had been set up to receive information against anyone speaking ill of Parliament, and the mere repetition of the rumour in his last letter might cause him some mischief if the letter were intercepted. Had she received it safely, he asks anxiously? Neither his incautious first letter nor her reply have been preserved, so they may have been amongst the papers removed later when the Parliament men searched Roydon Hall.

On 5 May a counter-petition came up from Kent, much to the liking of Parliament, and on the 10th articles of impeachment were exhibited against Strode and Spencer. By implication Twysden's part in the affair was overlooked and at his request he was given permission on the 12th to return to Kent, the other conditions of his bailment and the security therefor remaining in force. It was a few days before he could get away, but by 17 May he was back in his own home, reunited with his wife and family and firmly resolved to meddle no more with political affairs.

By June men were talking fearfully, but openly, of civil war. Twysden's friend Sir Simonds D'Ewes writing to Richard Dewes on 21 June expressed the feelings of the moderate men on both sides—'by a civil war he [*sc.* the King] will be the greatest loser, whosoever gains, . . . the people slain, his people; the towns and cities burnt, his cities and towns, and the kingdom harrassed, his kingdom. Let your prayers and resolutions be, as mine are, for peace. . . .' That war was the worst evil, worse even than anything that Parliament could do, seems also to have been Clarendon's view, for 'only war itself won by . . . destroying its own enemies, the moderate on both sides.'

Twysden, who disapproved of Parliament's excesses as he had disapproved of ship-money and of Charles's eleven years of government without Parliament, feared and detested the thought of civil war but hoped that economic causes would prevent it. The sinews of war are money; the King was notoriously impecunious and Parliament's resources were such that on 10 June it was driven to the expedient of inviting loans, with interest at 8 per cent., backed by the Public Faith (*publica fides*)—the Public Fraud (*punica fides*) said the wits, for the loans were never repaid. Parliament itself had become a fraud, in Twysden's view, for a minority were exercising power in the name of the whole body and when once they were equipped with arms the sword must become the only arbiter; reason would be found to be on that side which had the bigger battalions.

Prudence dictated that Twysden should remain quietly engaged with his own estate matters at Roydon Hall, eschewing any contact with public affairs, and by nature he was a prudent man. It is, therefore, surprising to find him going to the summer Assizes at Maidstone on 22 July. His attendance he justified to himself on the ground that, in his capacity as a magistrate, he was concerned in a case which was coming on for trial. But he must, too, have been desperately anxious to hear the latest news, and to commiserate with his fellow justices on the disaster towards which they all seemed to be heading with ever increasing speed.

The last Assizes had been the breeding ground of the obnoxious petition; Parliament was determined to have no more commotion of that sort. When the judge, again Mr. Justice Mallet, opened the proceedings he found his court reinforced by a large committee sent down by the House of Commons to prevent 'inconvenience and to use all lawful ways and means to preserve the said County, not only in peace amongst themselves, but in a right understanding of the proceedings of Parliament', with a slighting reference to 'the late dangerous petition'. The committee consisted of fourteen members of Parliament representing Kentish constituencies and the three other committee-men had some connexion with the county. They asked to be seated on the Bench, whether to 'assist' or to supplant the Justices of the Peace was not clear. On the Saturday afternoon, 23 July, their speaker Sir Henry Heyman (M.P. for Hythe) asked the Judge to read out an order made by the House declaring the illegality of the Commissions of Array issued by the King from York on 16 June. Mallet, J. declined to do so, since such powers as he exercised came to him by virtue of the Great Seal, not by an order of the Commons, who had no lawful power to issue commands to the judiciary.

On the following Monday the Committee sought a private

meeting with the Judge. He was reluctant to meet them except in the presence of the Justices of the Peace, although in the end went apart with them to another room. The Committee asked him, first, to give them his best aid in carrying out the orders of the Commons, and, secondly, they repeated their request to be seated on the Bench. His answers were to be put into writing; to both questions he gave a reasoned negative reply. Then the same questions were put to the Justices of the Peace, with the same result. Twysden, with his ever-ready pen, was the draughtsman of the justices' answer. The Committee said that they were unsatisfied with the reply and would repair to the Bench from time to time as they saw fit.

The next day an altercation broke out between the Judge and one of the committee-men, the younger Sir Henry Vane, who wanted to propound 'certain matters of consequence' from the House of Commons. Vane spoke temperately, and had the support of many of the people present in court, but conspicuously not of the gentlemen. His speech was applauded, whilst the Judge was almost shouted down in a disturbance so violent that he threatened to adjourn the court. When the court rose, Twysden was going off to his lodging when a loud shout caused him to return to the Bench. There he found that several young Royalists had brought papers containing instructions to the Knight of the Shire and a petition to the King. It was potentially dangerous stuff and no one could be persuaded to read the papers aloud to the company. Twysden declined, on the gound that it would be improper for him to do so since there were gentlemen of better quality than himself present. Finally a young boy was persuaded to read the papers. The Grand Jury, pressed to support the instructions and petition, said that, *qua* Grand Jury it was none of their affair whatever some of them might think privately. However, it seemed that no one was opposed to the instructions and petition and when Twysden asked whether they were presented by all, everyone cried 'All', and his suggestion that the papers should be read over again was dismissed as unnecessary.

The instructions bade the County's representative tell the Commons that there was no need for their intervention in order to 'preserve' the County in peace, and that the House would be well advised to give His Majesty satisfaction in four specified particulars, including the disbandment of the militia until new legislation had been passed. But Augustine Skinner, the Knight of the Shire to whom the instructions were directed, refused to accept them, and afterwards the paper was thrown to him. The young Royalists, including Sir John Mayny, Rycaut, Sir Edward Filmer, Sir Thomas Boswell, and William Clark (who was killed at Cropredy Bridge) went off to York to join the King, and Twysden returned home.

By now, the end of July, things were in so bad a state that they could hardly be worse. Back at Roydon Hall, alone in his study Twysden must have wondered whether he had acted wisely in becoming involved with yet another petition even though he was not the initiator of it. Careful of his own concerns as he was, there were yet occasions when he could not stand by, a silent witness of grossly illegal proceedings or inequitable conduct. This was one of the occasions when his sense of right triumphed over expediency, when *prudentia* gave way to *justitia*.

The 'Instructions from the County of Kent to Mr. Augustine Skinner' were quickly printed at London and York. Parliament, understandably incensed by the renewed effrontery of the Kentish gentry—and the young gentlemen had certainly couched their paper in forthright, not to say insolent terms—soon put a stop to the London printing and ordered the copies to be destroyed. On 2 August Twysden, Spencer and Strode were ordered to surrender themselves to the House of Commons. Twysden's surety, Francis Finch, fearing to lose his money, sent his man down to East Peckham, post-haste, to urge him to hurry up to London and make his surrender. So, on 5 August, Twysden for the second time was kneeling at the bar of the House. He left Roydon Hall with a heavier heart than ever, for he left behind his wife with the ten-day-old son of whom she had been brought to bed on the 25 July whilst Twysden was away at Maidstone, dangerously compromising himself in anti-Parliamentary activities. Poor lady, her husband was more anxiety than comfort to her at the time of her lying-in, and Parliament's peremptory order must have filled her with dread for his future safety.

The Commons committed Twysden to the Serjeant as a prisoner and he was sent to the Three Tobacco-pipes near Charing Cross, where he was kept for fifteen days with no accusation advanced against him. He was an awkward prisoner, standing stiffly on his rights. His gaoler demanded, as his authorized fee, £1. 6*s*. 8*d*. a day, in addition to the charge for lodging and diet, but Twysden successfully argued that the fee which he had been obliged to pay on the occasion of his first arrest covered the second occasion also. He was offered the chance of going to live at Isleworth at the house of his brother-in-law, Sir Hugh Cholmley, still a supporter of Parliament, but he refused to be so accommodated, stoutly maintaining that his arrest was wrongful. With what breach of the law, he demanded to know, was he charged? The only answer he got was that in these times 'the House could not look at the nice observance of the law'. That might be, he admitted 'with those *qui belli sunt participes*, where the armies lay; but for those who did not at all engage, *contra hos nullum est jus bellicum*', an opinion for which he was able to cite Grotius as authority. *Inter arma leges silent* was not a maxim that had any appeal for him, and perhaps was scarcely yet relevant, for it was a few days later, on 22 August, that Charles raised his standard at Nottingham. One consolation Twysden derived from his incarceration, the chance of friendly and learned discussion with his two fellow-prisoners, Sir Kenelm Digby and Sir Basil Brook. Digby was soon released and Brook was removed to the King's Bench, where, as the prisoner of Lentall, the Speaker's brother, he lived with his man 'as well as at his own home', at a charge of 50*s*. or 60*s*. a week, and was able to keep up his intercourse with Twysden.

If some consolation was to be had from conversation with his fellow-prisoners there was none to be derived from the news from Kent. On 19 August the Parliamentarian forces made a rapid incursion into the county, seizing strong-points such as Dover Castle and Rochester Castle, destroying ungodly furnishings of churches, and visiting the houses of known or suspected

Royalist sympathisers whence arms and armour as well as money and other goods were removed. It was a spoiling raid, ruthlessly and efficiently carried out, frightening those not addicted to Parliament's cause and successfully preventing any possibility of effective Royalist support in Kent. As inevitably happens in such a precautionary and punitive raid, excesses were committed—at Canterbury even Sir Michael Livesey, scarcely an apostle of sweetness and light, felt called upon to apologize to the Dean and Chapter for the behaviour of his men, and at East Sutton the troopers set fire to Sir Robert Filmer's house apparently believing it to be Sir Anthony St. Leger's seat, Wierton Place, about three miles away. Rumours about the terrible conduct of the soldiers spread rapidly through the county. Barely three miles from Roydon Hall, at Barham Court in Teston, Colonel Edwin Sandys' soldiers tortured one of Sir William Boteler's servants by setting fire to some gunpowder which they made him hold in the palm of his hand, a practice which the Colonel justified as being a normal military punishment (and he had some reason for vexation, for the servant when commanded to show the visitors where his master kept his armour and money had led the Colonel into a privy-house).

When next day the news of the Barham Court outrage, which grew more fearful with each retelling, reached Roydon Hall, Lady Twysden sent the children away for safety and, weak as she still was from her recent lying-in, at once took horse for London to take up her abode in the Redcross Street house.

Left alone in his prison without companions now that Digby and Brook had gone, and not permitted even to go to church, Twysden decided to petition the Commons for his release. On 12 September he was bailed again, on condition that he did not go into Kent, a course for which in any case he had no heart. For the present he retired to his house in Red Cross Street, although he advised the Serjeant of the Mace that he was in possession of a pass and would probably go abroad. Indeed, he designed to go with Sir John Finch who unfortunately was killed in falling from his horse, so that plan had to be abandoned. But Twysden did not give up the idea. He entrusted his children to an old and faithful servant and tenant at East Peckham, George Stone, to whom from Lady Day 1643 he leased the land there and at Wateringbury and Yalding at an annual rent of £134. 12*s.* 0*d.* for three years, if Twysden or his heirs should not, in the meantime, return to Roydon Hall. Lady Twysden returned to Kent to live in the mansion house whilst her husband in London went forward with his preparations for leaving England.

These were interrupted by the parish officers who required to know how much he was prepared to give upon the Propositions of the Public Faith as his contribution towards the City's gift to Parliament. He temporized; he had no money, no plate except that which was in use, his wife was away in Kent, he did not know the state of his property there. For two months he heard no more and then received a ticket for £400, for his twentieth part. He protested that as, at best, an involuntary inhabitant of London he was not within the Ordinance, and even if he were all that he had in London was not worth £400, still less twenty times that sum. The officers said that if he gave £200 at once he might appeal as to the balance. He refused. Some months later the officers returned with carts and carried away the whole of the contents of the house, leaving nothing of value behind.

Twysden was met with a similar request for his property at East Peckham. Sir Francis Barnham, M.P. for Maidstone and a supporter of Parliament, with whom Twysden remained on friendly terms however much they might differ on constitutional questions, meeting him at the Temple towards the end of September urged that in his own interests he should give something upon the Propositions. The House of Commons was likely to deal severely with the reluctant, and the county, he warned, was now *de facto* governed by Sir Anthony Weldon and Sir John Sedley, no friends to Twysden.

Again Twysden refused; he stuck upon the point of conscience—he had refused to pay ship-money because he believed it to be an illegal impost, as was this of Parliament, and he must act consistently; the House itself had urged men to protect the liberties of the subject; to force men through fear to part with their property was a total denial of those liberties; the war, if it continued, would prove the ruin both of the Protestant religion and the laws of the land. Besides, if the King got the upper hand and came in as a conqueror (a prospect which Twysden abhorred) he might proceed against all those who had helped Parliament, even under compulsion, for treason under the statute 25 Edward III, St. V, c.2. Barnham thought this an unlikely contingency, and that in any event Coke's maxim *salus populi suprema lex* would prevail against an indictment for treason. But Twysden was not thus easily to be comforted, and on the other side offered another quotation from Coke: '*Optima regula, qua nulla est verior aut firmior in jure, neminam oportet esse sapientiorem legibus.*' He was certainly no Royalist partisan and he thought Charles unreasonable and singularly unwise when, unable to give protection to his people, he threatened the penalties of the Statute of Treasons upon those who gave aid or assistance to the two Houses, even where it was done under duress.

For most men in whatever direction they looked the prospect was foreboding, the future doubtful and uncertain. Some, the perhaps fortunate minority, could believe wholly in the one cause or the other and achieve satisfaction in vigorous action for King or for Parliament. Twysden was not amongst them; all he could see was disregard of the constitutional principles which he held dear and no way out of the slough into which the nation had stumbled. Yet it was still possible for civilized debate to continue between old friends and neighbours, especially in a county such as Kent, where 'ancient amity and good will' persisted among 'men of different opinions in these dividing times', or where, as Clarendon put it 'good fellowship was a vice generally spread over that country'. When Spencer said that a man must fight on one side or the other he would find many in Kent to disagree with him—or in Yorkshire, where the gentry agreed to keep the county neutral, or in the West Country. If friends and kinsmen found sadly that they must differ over King and Parliament yet there was comfort, as Thomas Barrow wrote to Henry Oxinden, in the remembrance that 'we have one Lord, one faith, one baptism'.

It was all very well for men like Twysden and Barnham, Barrow and Oxinden, in the privacy of their closets or their cautiously conducted correspondence, to explore their differences in an unimpassioned way; amongst the men of action, in the seats of power, different attitudes almost inevitably prevailed. In Chapter IX of *Certain Considerations upon the Government of England* Twysden anatomizes the progress of rebellions and civil wars, concluding 'popular stirs many times, if not most, set up the worser sort of the people, the fiercest, cruellest, fullest of fraud'. In saying this he was in part following Tacitus, but also he was drawing on his own unhappy experiences at the hands of the County Committee and especially of its chairman Sir Anthony Weldon.

The County Committee[1] consisted of a group of gentlemen who supported Parliament and who ruled the county with only lax control from Westminster. It grew out of the deputy lieutenancy, was largely self-perpetuating, and it arrogated powers to itself without bothering too precisely whether they had a basis in law, or even the approval of Parliament. As tends to happen in an assembly wherein acute differences prevail, control gradually became centred in the more extreme and more enthusiastic members, in those who were prepared to attend regularly and who were not too nice about the methods they employed. Deterred by these attitudes, the moderate men began to fall away, with the result that the extremists brought in more of their own reliable supporters, so consolidating their position. There was 'a gradual secession of county families and influx of parochial gentry. Equally important . . . the preponderance of indigenous families tended to diminish.'[2]

For six years, from 1642 until 1648, the County Committee was the machinery through which Weldon ruled Kent, just as his henchman Sir John Sedley of St. Clere ruled the southern division of the lathe of Aylesford through the sub-committee (if that is not too precise a term for constitutional relationships

[1] The County Committee of Kent is the subject of an excellent study by Dr. A. M. Everitt, *The County Committee of Kent in the Civil War* (1957).
[2] Op. cit., p. 21.

which were imprecise) which met at the Swan Inn at West Malling.

Weldon and Twysden were acquainted and the relationship, which at one time included a lawsuit, was not an amicable one. Indeed, it is doubtful whether any of Weldon's relationships were amicable. His consciousness of the folly of men, his dislike of cant, the cool detachment with which he surveyed the contemporary scene and the mordant wit with which he expressed his unflattering views made him little liked, at Court or in Parliament. His father was Clerk of the Kitchen to Queen Elizabeth and he himself held the same office at the Court of King James, afterwards being advanced to the Clerkship of the Greencloth. He accompanied the King on his visits to Scotland but he was so scurrilously satirical about the Scots that he was dismissed from Court—with a pension. He amused himself by writing the *Court and Character of King James*[1] in, he said, the space of four days; if he did, he had an enviable turn of speed with the pen. It was not intended for publication ('it treads too near the heels of truth, and these times, to appear in public'), but the manuscript was lent to Lady Elizabeth Sedley of Southfleet, and somehow found its way to the printer. His writing was vigorous, strong, unsentimental, sometimes coarse. Twysden in his *Certain Considerations upon the Government of England* cast doubts upon Coke's historical scholarship, but Weldon's attack upon 'the English Tribonian' was far more trenchant. 'The folly' he wrote 'of that great clerk, though no wise man, Sir Edward Coke', and reflecting upon Coke's partisan attitude in the Overbury murder trial he said 'the good lawyers of those times . . . did believe that Mrs. Turner was directly murdered by my Lord Coke's law, as Overbury was without any law'. He writes about Finch, who led the Judges in finding for the King in the ship-money case, about Strafford, about the bishops, about James and Charles with a Machiavellian sharpness of perception, but without bitterness. He was not a Puritan or a fanatic, but a man without illusions, of a melancholy disposition, expecting his fellows,

[1] It was republished posthumously 'by authority' in 1651, with his later work *The Court of King Charles*.

whether Royalist or Parliamentarian, to behave with egregious lack of wisdom and seldom finding his expectations disappointed.[1] The reaction of his neighbours and acquaintances was an understandable resentment, which served to strengthen further his own indifference and rancour. His qualities, by no means despicable, are easier for us to appreciate after the lapse of 300 years than for his contemporaries who were the unhappy objects of his satirical tongue and pen.

Such was the character of the man who, with Sedley, as Barnham told Twysden 'now ruled all Kent'. Twysden was strongly tempted to carry out the plan he had considered previously and go overseas. However, he decided to wait and see whether the negotiations at Oxford in February 1643 (the 'Treaty of Oxford') offered any prospect of an accommodation between King and Parliament, meanwhile spending a great deal of his time at the Tower in the examination of ancient records, some of which he caused to be transcribed. His taste for antiquity had been formed in discourse with Dering, Somner, Phillipott, and others; now he had the opportunity of indulging it.

The Treaty of Oxford broke down. Sir Christopher Nevill, who was intending to obtain a pass so that he could go from Parliament's quarters to join the King at Oxford, offered to get Twysden's name and his wife's inserted in it. But Twysden saw no good in abandoning his estate to Parliament for he still protested his innocence of any offence known to the law, and he could not neglect the duty of providing for his five small children and a number of old servants. Besides, if he went to Oxford he would be ashamed not to be in the army yet he knew himself unable to endure a soldier's life.

About the same time that the parish officers removed all his belongings from the Redcross Street house, troopers were searching Roydon Hall for arms and other warlike provisions.

[1] Typical of his pungent wit and disillusioned view of his fellow-men is the story of a fortune-teller who professed to foretell the success of amorous intentions, lawful or, more often, otherwise: 'that you may know his skill, he was himself a cuckold, having a very pretty wench to his wife, which would say, she did it to try his skill, but it fared with him as with astrologers, that cannot foresee their own destiny'.

He carefully made a list of what they carried away 'on Wednesday, the . . . of April 1643:

'A saddle.
2 or 3 bits, girths, snaffles, stirrups, and all of that kind they met with.
Nurse, her laced handkerchief.
William Sparks' shirts, 3 bands, 4*s.* 8*d.* in money, a box in silver out of my wife's closet.
Captain Vaughan's two-handed sword.
A glove of mail.
A book and a pair of compasses.
A pair of pistol cases, a comb, and a book or two of Ward's.[1]
A little dagger, two belts and girdles.
2 little books of wax candles.'

The position seemed hopeless. Dejectedly Twysden resumed his preparations for going abroad. On 1 May he gave over house-keeping at Roydon Hall having already leased the land there to George Stone. A fortnight later he sent his eldest son William, then scarcely more than seven years of age, with his tutor, Hamnet Ward, into France. On 9 June Twysden himself set out in the guise of servant to one of a party of Frenchmen and Portuguese with whom he travelled. Their road lay through Bromley, and by a singular ill-chance the County Committee was meeting in the town that day. He hoped to slip by unnoticed in the group of travellers, especially as he was wearing 'a cap of hair which they [*sc.* the members of the Committee] had never seen me in'—a somewhat disingenuous way of recording that he was wearing a wig as disguise.

Unluckily for Twysden, he was recognized, although for some time he denied his identity. To appear thus, trying to pass himself off as a foreigner and a servant before his neighbours and acquaintances, Weldon, Sedley, James, Skinner and the others—never can he have felt such humiliation. The situation appealed to Weldon's sardonic sense of humour; if, as the man alleged, he was not Sir Roger Twysden, then he was a rogue and must be whipped as such. It was impossible to keep

[1] Ward was tutor to Twysden's son.

up the pretence. His sword and watch were taken away and fifteen pounds in money that he had given to a Frenchman believing that with him it would be safe. He was promptly returned to London and brought before the Committee for Accusations as a prisoner. Twysden complained of the way he had been used; they demanded to know what he had given on the Propositions; 'Nothing' was his reply, and at once he was committed to the Counter at Southwark. No reason was given for his imprisonment. Parliament was following again the practice which it had so readily condemned in others.

The *Diurnal* a little later came out with a report that Twysden's offence was that he was carrying intelligence of great importance 'subtly conveyed into nutshells'. It sounds typical of those rumours which his plot-prone and credulous contemporaries so readily accepted. Twysden's explanation was that a physician had given him a little round ball, to be worn as an antidote against infection, and his captors found the supposed preservative contained in a nutshell. He maintained that he did not know what ingredients it contained. Is it possible that it really was a secret letter? But who would have entrusted such an errand to Twysden, for he had given little indication of staunch support for the King's cause? If it were not for the curiously elliptical disavowal by Twysden of any knowledge of the contents of the 'little round ball' one would be inclined to dismiss the rumour as fantastic nonsense.

But, nonsense or not, Twysden was securely back in prison.

CHAPTER FIVE

June 1643–1647

ALMOST AT once Twysden received a visit in the Counter from his kinsman Sir Edward Monins who brought him the news that his estate had been sequestrated since May. The current half-year's rents having already been paid by the tenants could not be touched, but future rents would go into the hands of the Parliamentary receivers, not into Twysden's. It was, protested Twysden, quite illegal: it was contrary to c. 29 of Magna Carta, and to the admirable precepts contained in the Code of Theodosius. They were learned objections, but he must have been naïve if he really thought that now they would carry much weight with the House of Commons, still less with the County Committee.

However, events outside his prison distracted Twysden from dwelling on his own wrongs. On 18 June Hampden was mortally wounded at Chalgrove Field, Newcastle defeated Fairfax on the 30th, Waller's army was worsted near Devizes on 13 July, and Bristol capitulated to Prince Rupert on the 27th. Parliament feared, and Twysden and many others in a like plight hoped, that the King and Newcastle would advance on London. Early in August it was decided to remove the more important prisoners to ships lying in the river, to prevent any possibility of their heading a rising in London and on 12 August Twysden was amongst those who were consigned for safe custody to the *Prosperous Sarah*. It must have been a source of satisfaction to him that 'when I came to the ship I observed none but persons of good quality lodged in it'. It was a small ship, a collier's barque, and the standard of the lodging it provided did not accord with the quality of its guests. Stifled with heat and lack of air, they were kept in an 'unhealthy, uneasy, obscure room'. But it soon became apparent that the King was frittering away his chances by laying siege to Gloucester instead of advancing on London, and after two or three days the prisoners were returned to the Counter. Twysden's indignation at having to pay 20*s*. for his unattractive quarters aboard the *Prosperous Sarah* seems justified.

The immediate excitement over, he turned again to his sequestration. By whose order, he wished to know, was the sequestration made? It was not by the Committee of Lords and Commons at Westminster. He obtained a copy of the Ordinance of 31 March (or 1 April) 1643 against Notorious Delinquents. Was he such a one? Was he one of the named bishops or one of those who had raised arms against Parliament? Had he voluntarily contributed money to support the King's army against Parliament? Had he joined in any oath or act of association against Parliament? Had he imposed, or used force in levying any tax for the maintenance of the war? Obviously not, and counsel whom Lady Twysden consulted suggested that there must be other charges against him which she would not reveal. Then, on 19 August, Parliament issued another Ordinance 'explaining' (but really extending) the former. It now included those who fraudulently conveyed away their goods to avoid payment of any tax, or who kept out of the way so that a tax could not be levied, or who sued such as had yielded obedience to Parliament or were employed by them. This last provision, putting Parliament's adherents and servants beyond the reach of the law, was especially offensive to Twysden's sense of legal propriety.

The order had in fact been made by the Committee for Sequestrations of the County Committee. Twysden, although he could not know it at this time, was only one of 500 delinquents in Kent who were sequestrated, 60 per cent. of the gentry suffering that fate.[1] Most of them were in trouble for their local activities—or passivities—not because they ardently supported the King: 'they were not sufficiently "royalist" to

[1] A. M. Everitt, *Suffolk and the Great Rebellion, 1640–1660* (1960), p. 11.

Sir Roger Twysden, Kt., aged 28

leave the county for Oxford and yet they did not sympathize with Parliament.'[1]

To take on the management of hundreds of estates, to ensure that they were cultivated in a husbandlike manner, to secure the prompt and full payment of all the rents due,[2] was a task for which the County Committee was not equipped. Particularly they failed to manage the woodlands with the loving care that the Kentish gentry lavished on their timber. A good supply of timber was essential to any estate, for house and farm building and repairing, for fences and hop-poles, for firewood. But it was more than a utilitarian product, it was also, in modern terminology, a status symbol. It was even more than that, it was a symbol of continuity, of a man's link with the past and with the future; with his ancestors from whom he had inherited his woods, with his descendants to whom he must leave them, improved, if possible, as a monument to his own care and wisdom.

The essentially conservative attitudes had little attraction for the County Committee-men. From a mixture of spite, ignorance of the art of arboriculture, bad estate management, a desire to convert capital into revenue, and a pressing need for firewood to keep Parliamentarian London warm, there was a rapid felling of wood on sequestrated estates, especially near London. The owner might protest, but the first difficulty was to get any witnesses to come forward, and, secondly, if they did, to get them accepted, for if a man was described as 'malignant' or 'ill affected towards Parliament' his testimony was rejected. Then there would be argument whether the trees were 'timber' as defined by Common Law or local custom, and with questions such as these the trial could be prolonged until, meanwhile, the trees had all been felled and the woodland cleared. In prudent and careful estate-owners such proceedings bred first exasperation, then frustration and

[1] Op. cit., p. 14.

[2] In the unsettled conditions tenants were reluctant to pay their rents, sometimes not knowing whom to pay, and Henry Oxinden, writing to Thomas Denne about October 1644, said that landlords in East Kent had been obliged to abate their tenants' rents by one-third. (*The Oxinden and Peyton Letters*, ed. D. Gardiner (1937), p. 68.)

finally despair, and the nearest they ever got, probably, to sheer hatred of Parliament and its agents.

It was in the autumn or early winter of 1643 that Twysden learned of the felling of those woods at Roydon Hall which the County Committee determined to be coppice. He became more persistent than ever to discover the cause, and test the legality, of his sequestration. His brother Francis solicited the County Committee to know by what law, order or ordinance the sequestration had been made. The result of his importuning was committal to Peterhouse prison on the pretext that he was in criminal correspondence with France, but the charge could not be proved and after a month he was released. On 23 October Twysden wrote a dignified letter to Dyke, the Sequestrator General of Kent, asking the cause of his sequestration. To this there was no answer. On 30 November he wrote to Sir Edward Scott of Scott's Hall, his kinsman and intimate acquaintance, now one of the leading County Committee-men, describing his plight—no income, heavy expenses for his imprisonment, a wife, five children, and a score of servants that looked to him for support—and repeating his question. To this also there was no reply. From Mr. James of Ightham (the Mr. James to whom Twysden had shown the proposed petition of March 1642 and who misliked it) Twysden learned that he had asked the County Committee the reason for his neighbour's sequestration but 'his demand they rather wondered at than answered'. Probably, thought James, it was Twysden's attempted escape whilst he was on bail. But if this was the reason, it did not bring Twysden, as any lawyer must have known, within the Ordinances of March or August; the proper remedy, if he had broken bail, was against the sureties, not sequestration.

Feeling that in James he had a friend on the County Committee Twysden sent his wife down to Knole, to wait upon the Committee and try to secure some relief. By bad luck James was not present that day and the only answer that Lady Twysden received was that if Twysden would admit the sequestration to be just she should be allowed the one-fifth of the estate to which she was entitled under the Ordinance;

otherwise she would be allowed nothing. Sadly she returned to London on 21 December, empty-handed.

Twysden had now been in the Counter for six months, and found it an inconvenient prison, especially in its remoteness from Westminster whither Lady Twysden often went two or three times a day about her husband's business. He petitioned to be removed to a more convenient place, and thanks to the intervention of his brother-in-law Yelverton he was transferred on 23 February 1644 to Lambeth Palace. At first Twysden was somewhat resentful, for this was not the place he would have chosen; afterwards he began to realize the advantages of Lambeth. He was assigned a lodging three floors up, consisting of three rooms and a study, that had formerly been occupied by one of the Archbishop's chaplains, and for this he paid 12*s.* a week (or ought to have paid; after the first six months he struck against the payment of any further rent). He was allowed to receive a visit from his brother Francis, to walk in the garden provided that the keeper was present (but this was an empty privilege for the keeper never had time to accompany him) and to have his own provisions and fuel sent up from Kent. Books he had, or could borrow, and time for reflection and writing. If deprivation of liberty were the only hardship that he suffered these were the conditions that might make it nearly tolerable. But that was not the only adversity to be borne; Twysden's income had ceased, he was on the way to financial ruin, his carefully tended estates were neglected and his timber was being wantonly destroyed.

It was the felling of his woods that goaded Twysden to action again. He put in a petition to the Committee of Lords and Commons for Sequestrations at Westminster, and on 16 February 1644 an Order was made calling upon the County Committee for Sequestrations to certify the cause of Twysden's sequestration, and meanwhile to stop the cutting down of any more trees.

The County Committee's reply was dated 20 February, although Twysden was not allowed to see it until 14 March. Under the hand of Serjeant Wild, then chairman, the Committee answered:

'... although it may very well happen, that in some cases, we can not carry the sequestration and cause in mind, to give a speedy accompt thereof; yet in this case of Sir Roger Twysden's, we could not expect now to be called to an accompt, there being so many concurrent causes even known to all the Parliament....' (these were his part in the March 1642 petition and his attempted flight)... 'Besides all this, he hath been refractory to all proceedings of Parliament.... His holding correspondence, by letters intercepted, both to priests in his own county and strangers abroad, of ill consequence.... If all this together be not sufficient to sequester him ... we confess we understand not how to proceed upon that Ordinance; but shall be very tender hereafter, when such an accompt is required, for so notorious a delinquent of

John Wild'

Even if all this were true, it still did not bring Twysden within a strict construction of the Ordinances and, as he fairly argued (though he was in advance of his age in doing so) since they were penal they ought to be strictly interpreted and their meaning restricted rather than extended. As for his correspondence with strangers abroad, it was true that Twysden, who was intensely interested in ecclesiastical as distinct from religious matters (an interest which was afterwards to bear fruit in *An Historicall Vindication of the Church of England in point of Schism as it stands separated from the Roman, and was reformed 1 Elizabeth*), had endeavoured in 1635 and 1638 to obtain from continental scholars such as Padre Fulgentio and M. de Cordes more information than was available in print about the Council of Trent, with a view to refuting claims of the Roman Catholic church. If it happened that his correspondents were priests, it could not be helped, but what harm could there be in such scholarly intercourse? It was a reasonable enough question, but it was not seasonable.

Meanwhile there was no cessation of the felling of his timber.

When the County Committee's reply came before the Committee of Lords and Commons it was the general opinion that there was no ground disclosed on which he might be sequestrated. They said as much to the County Committee, who were angry at this intervention in their affairs. Sir John Sedley, himself later to fall under the Commons' displeasure, came to Westminster to justify their action; perhaps that lawsuit about the pews at Great Chart still rankled. But however much the members of the County Committee might bluster, the Committee of the Lords and Commons for Sequestrations could scarcely let the matter drop. So on 15 May the Lords and Commons Committee directed an inquiry to be made as to who had authorized the sequestration; an answer was to be given within a month, and meanwhile a stay was to be made of the felling of timber, and 'all persons employed in the service to take notice hereof, at their perils'.

Twysden's affairs, so his friends thought, were beginning to take a favourable turn. The County Committee were being taken to task for their persecution, and a petition which he had submitted to the Commons for his freedom had been referred, on 27 February, for the consideration of the Committee appointed to confer with the Scottish Commissioners. However, the terms on which he might have regained his liberty would have included an admission of the legality of his sequestration and adhering to the Covenant whereby the Scottish divines sought to impose Presbyterianism on England. Neither of these things could Twysden, in conscience, do.

Nor did he fare much better in getting the sequestration removed. On 25 April the Committee of Lords and Commons for supply of the cities of London and Westminster, etc., with wood for Fuel made an order that the felling of wood was to cease, but the Order was so 'explained' on 7 May as to amount to a revocation. The number of committees, the uncertainty as to their respective jurisdictions and their vacillation faced any petitioning prisoner with a veritably Kafkaesque situation.

The Committee of the Lords and Commons followed up their order of 15 May to the County Committee with a private letter expressing the opinion that Twysden was not sequestrable. The County Committee were not thus to be browbeaten by Westminster: on 22 May they replied '. . . his breach of trust to the country hath brought such an odium upon him that it will be a great discouragement to all well affected, to have him unsequestered . . . they conceive, if none of the said crimes were sufficient yet the accumulation of so many are sufficient'. As for the felling of timber, they know nothing about it, and it was not done by their order. His friends, Sir Edward Monins and Sir Thomas Style (of Wateringbury), visiting Twysden in his prison at Lambeth, advised him not to allow his case to to be decided by the County Committee, where a majority would certainly vote against him, however meritorious his claim might be. But Mr. William Say, a Member of Parliament and a lawyer whom Twysden consulted, was equally discouraging about an appeal to the House of Commons; the House, he said, took much more delight to punish than to free any man, and although Twysden, in his opinion, was not within the Ordinance of Sequestration, he bade him not hope for his discharge by the House.

The order of the Lords and Commons Committee suspending the felling of trees was due to expire on 15 June. On the 14th Lady Twysden petitioned that her husband's case should be heard and the Committee forthwith ordered that it should be heard in a week, that the County Committee should present their case at once, and 'in the meantime, that there be a respite of cutting down, felling, or carrying any woods'. Five days later the County Committee made an order to the effect that the order of the Committee of the Lords and Commons was to be interpreted as not extending to woods which had been felled and sold before the last order: they might lawfully be carried away. This was almost open disobedience to the commands of the Lords and Commons Committee and even the County Committee under the notorious Weldon and Sedley would scarcely have ventured on such a course unless they were assured of support by their friends at Westminster. When Lady Twysden complained to the Lords and Commons Committee the only satisfaction that she received was that 'The Committee of Kent would do what they would do'. It was tantamount to an admission that the Commons had no control over the County Committee.

The 21st of June was the date on which the Lords and Commons Committee had peremptorily ordered Twysden's case to be heard. Lady Twysden attended with counsel, but the case was put off until 26 June, then until 3 July, then until 26 July (when a standstill order was made) and then until 21 August. On each date Lady Twysden had to attend with counsel, who had to be feed. Even the standstill order of 26 July did Twysden no good, for on the 30th the County Committee made an order in which they authorized the carrying away of any timber bought or contracted for before 26 July. To Twysden this appeared not as open defiance of the Lords and Commons Committee by the County Committee, but as evidence of collusion between them.

Again Twysden turned his mind to the question, by what show of law or colourable excuse could the County Committee justify his sequestration. His counsel, Heron and Newdigate, were as baffled as he was. Could it be the petition of March 1642? But Twysden had never subscribed it, as such: all he had done was to certify that those which he had distributed were true copies. Was this an offence? His Great Chart neighbour and cousin Richard Browne, M.P. for New Romney, asked the House of Commons to resolve the question, but they declined to do so. It was becoming only too plain that Weldon's Committee had decided 'by power, to effect what, in justice, they came short in'.

Finally, on 21 August, Twysden's petition was heard in the Painted Chamber, which thus continued to witness proceedings that were too extraordinary for the Common Law, with Samuel Browne (who later became a serjeant, a judge of the King's Bench and after the Restoration a judge of the Common Pleas) in the Chair. Twysden's part in the Assizes petition was inquired into: Mr. James admitted that Twysden had commended it to him; Sir John Rivers recalled that Twysden was for the petition but told Sir John that 'he had not wit to understand it'. But the principal witness for the prosecution, if that is not too regular a word to describe irregular proceedings, was Sir John Sedley. He gave a highly coloured account of Twysden's actions at the Assizes, just the kind of evidence that the County Committee needed to bolster up its case. 'Never did I see so good a witness in my life' as a gentleman who was present sarcastically said to Twysden afterwards: 'let us but let him know what we would have him swear to, and it is done immediately.' Heron and Newdigate spoke for Twysden and gave reasons, with which the chairman appeared to agree, why he was not within the Ordinance of Sequestration. Points of difficulty arose and the hearing was adjourned for two days. Selden and Sir Simonds D'Ewes, old friends of Twysden's, and several other members of the Committee of Lords and Commons spoke in his favour, but the result was a foregone conclusion; as the young Sir Henry Vane told Francis Twysden not long afterwards, the Committee would not, for one man's sake, disoblige a whole county. When the Committee came to give its decision Lady Twysden and Twysden's counsel were turned out of the Chamber, although those who represented the County Committee were allowed to remain. Was not this worse, demanded Twysden, than the Star Chamber?—men's estates taken away without themselves or their counsel so much as hearing why. When the order was drawn up it merely stated that the sequestration was to continue, but gave no reasons. Only the Clerk, as a memento for his personal use, jotted down in the margin of the order book that the ground of sequestration was associating in the Kentish petition.

Twysden had now to accept that the sequestration, just or unjust, was real and official. He began to take soundings whether he might be allowed to become tenant of his own estate as some other delinquents had done, but his endeavours came to the knowledge of the County Committee who strongly opposed any such scheme. It would, they said, permit the delinquent to exercise too much influence; it would expose tenants who had been active for Parliament to 'the revenge and spleen of their old, malignant landlord'; it would tend towards neutrality amongst the farmers; and much more in the same strain, some of it sensible, some of it irrelevant or even contradictory. The County Committee knew themselves to be in the wrong and were the more spiteful in consequence. It can hardly have been any other motive than spite that caused them now to have Twysden's few pieces of bedding and household things, of little value, removed from Chelmington.[1]

[1] 2 featherbeds, 2 bolsters, pillow, 3 blankets, 3 tables, 2 cupboards, 2 bedsteads, fire-back, 4 chairs, 1 cushion, 1 curtain, 2 pairs shoes.

He had failed to get the sequestration taken off, he had failed to become the tenant of his own estate; was there anything that could be saved from the wreck? The felling of his trees, especially those near the house, grieved Twysden sorely, and Lady Twysden petitioned the Committee for Sequestrations on 6 September that the land around the mansion house might be included in the fifth part of the estate to which she was entitled. 'Yes, yes,' said Samuel Browne, who again was in the Chair, 'let her have them, she hath had measure hard enough.' So an order was directed to the County Committee, recommending that Lady Twysden's request should be allowed, and she herself, again great with child, took it down to the Committee at Knole on 19 September. Weldon, in the Chair, treated her with hostility and paid scant regard to the order. Others of the Committee, such as Sir Edward Monins, Henry Oxinden, Mr. James of Ightham, and Sir Nicholas Miller of Oxenhoath, were favourably disposed towards Twysden but could not stand up to the vehemence of Weldon. He demanded that she should bring in detailed particulars of the estate, the tenants and their rents, an altogether unreasonable demand for Twysden had been deprived of possession of all the records, as well as all the rents, for the past eighteen months. Unless she produced a rental by Michaelmas, Weldon threatened, she should receive no part of the half-year's rent then due.

On 3 October Lady Twysden once again rejoined her husband, empty-handed except for the order of the Committee of the Lords and Commons which she had, with difficulty, got back from the County Committee.

Even after this setback she did not give up. She presented herself again before the Committee at Westminster, who said they could do no more for her, but advised her yet once more to apply to the County Committee. On 2 November she returned to Kent, this time to the Friars at Aylesford now the headquarters of the County Committee, where she was received with some civility, even being allowed a stool to sit on—not an extravagant courtesy seeing that at this time she was six months pregnant. But still the Committee insisted that she must produce a rental before they could assign to her the one-fifth of the property which was her due.

By inquiring of all the tenants what rents they paid Lady Twysden was able to make up a rental and fortunately it agreed fairly closely with the one in the County Committee's possession. They now ordered that a survey and valuation of the estate should be made, but the order was countermanded the next day; the reason is evident, that on the first day Weldon was absent but present on the second, although the excuse was that Twysden had secreted £10,000 worth of goods at Roydon Hall. This was utterly untrue. His most valuable goods he had sent overseas for safety but they were nearly all lost. Some he had entrusted to friends. A few beds and pieces of household furniture remained at Roydon Hall, but this was all that thirty soldiers who searched the premises had been able to find—understandably enough, for it was all that was there, although Weldon was too passionate in his animus against Twysden to believe it. After a few more days' delay the survey and valuation of the estate was made, and Lady Twysden on 24 December again attended the Committee at Aylesford. The outcome of all these negotiations was a bitter disappointment; on 31 December the Committee ordered only that she should receive one-fifth of the rents and profits of the estate since last Michaelmas—nothing about her share of the rents for the previous eighteen months, nothing about the woods, nothing about the land around the mansion house.

A final plea in January 1645 to the Committee of Lords and Commons brought no relief. Talking with one of the Committee, Lady Twysden was told that they must defend their County Committee against her husband, for they were for them whereas he was against them. What had he done to show it, demanded Lady Twysden? 'We know his thoughts' was the only answer that she was vouchsafed.

As no help was to be had from the County Committee or the Committee of Lords and Commons for Sequestrations, Lady Twysden decided to petition the Committee for supply of London, etc., with Wood for Fuel with one of whose members, Sir Thomas Dawes, M.P. for Herefordshire, Twysden was well acquainted. So on 18 January 1645 she put in her petition to the Committee and he wrote to Dawes, soliciting his support. Whether it was this solicitation, the merits of the case, an aesthetic dislike of defacing the site of a mansion house, class solidarity between county landowners, or a mixture of all these motives that led the Committee to take a sympathetic view cannot be known. At all events, Lady Twysden's petition was granted and on 4 February she was given an order forbidding the felling of any more woods on the estate.

Four days later Lady Twysden went down to Kent, riding pillion behind George Stone, for her lying-in, and armed with her peremptory order prohibiting any more tree-felling. The constant journeying and the worry of the last few months had taken their toll of her health. Her sixth and last child, a boy, was born at Roydon Hall on 6 March, and the next day was christened Charles by Twysden's brothers Thomas and Charles, and Lady Berkeley. For some time she was too weak to move from Roydon Hall and to the end of her life she never fully recovered her strength. Not until 23 May was she well enough to make the journey to London and rejoin her husband at Lambeth.

Twysden, a prisoner in his four rooms at Lambeth, was perforce obliged to leave the handling of his affairs to his brothers, friends, counsel, and above all to his wife. Estate and public responsibilities were removed from him and even family responsibilities he was in no position to do much about. Security, of a kind, he enjoyed, leisure—abundant leisure—and access to books. To one of his scholarly appetites it might be said of such incarceration

> Minds innocent and quiet take
> That for an hermitage.

Undisturbed by minor daily cares he was able to pursue his studies. In 1642 he had been busy at the Tower examining and transcribing ancient records. Whilst at Lambeth, in 1645, he made a careful and critical compilation of the Journals of the Lords and Commons for the whole of Elizabeth's reign (now B. M. Stowe 359) extracted mainly from transcripts lent him by Sir Simonds D'Ewes but using other sources also. He devoted himself to mastering Anglo-Saxon at a time when few men had studied the language (his friend, William Somner, was the greatest Anglo-Saxon scholar of the age). He begged the loan of books as well as of transcripts from his friend Sir Simonds D'Ewes, and in David Sibbald he had an accurate amanuensis, able to make copies of records in which Twysden was interested. In the summer of 1645 he published the *Laws of Henry I*, from the Red Book of the Exchequer, as a supplement to a new edition of Lambarde's *Laws of the Saxon Kings*, to which he added also Selden's edition of the *Laws of William the Conqueror*.

Before this book was in the press he was turning his attention to the history of Parliament. The House of Commons, as he knew from bitter experience, had of recent years acted tyrannically and unconstitutionally, in ways unjustified by any precedent. From the ancient records he assembled a mass of notes on the history of the powers and privileges of Parliament, notes that were eventually expanded and rewritten as *Certain Considerations upon the Government of England*, his most important original work which was not finished until about 1655.

But if Twysden, as a prisoner at Lambeth, was relieved of the minor daily cares that are the lot of the house-keeper, he was still beset by major worries. The peremptory order of 4 February 1645 forbidding the cutting down of more trees was of no more effect than previous orders. The Committee for the Supply of Wood, etc., were persuaded by some of the County Committee to modify their order by another, issued on 13 February, calling merely for a survey to be made of the woods. The destruction went on. Twysden, in despair, got Sir Simonds D'Ewes to petition the Committee for the Supply of Wood again on his behalf, and on 2 April a further order was directed to the County Committee to make a stay. It was of no use; the County Committee were not going to take their orders from a committee in London. The order was produced to Walter Brooke, the purchaser of the woods, who was quite unimpressed when told that the order came from the Committee of the Lords and Commons—he would not be put off with 'fiddle faddle' he said. So the felling continued.

Twysden was not to be deterred. The trees now being felled in Stockenbury Wood were, he alleged, timber trees, and so outside the Ordinance for the felling of non-timber trees for fuel. The Committee for the Supply of Wood resolved on 17 April that the oak was not to be reputed timber, because it grew from the boles where the trees had previously been cut down. They were ignorant of the custom of the county recorded in the Kentish proverb

> T'oak that grows on the father's head
> Is as good Timber as ever was bred.

To refute their view Twysden got four experienced men who knew East Peckham and the custom of the county to certify that the Stockenbury oaks were indeed timber, and armed with this certificate Sir Simonds D'Ewes once again interceded for Twysden with the Committee for Lords and Commons on Sequestrations. On 14 May that Committee resolved to call for some of the Committee for Woods to give an explanation. At the hearing on 30 May Twysden's witnesses testified that at least a thousand oaks growing clear out of the ground, not from any former stock, had been felled. Walter Brooke—he who had described a previous order as 'fiddle-faddle'—objected against Twysden's witnesses that they had been in a recent rising in Kent against Parliament (presumably the rising of July 1643 which spread from Ightham where the Minister refused to comply with the ordinance requiring all clergy to impose upon their parishioners the oath of assistance to the Parliamentary forces), and another witness on his side said that the woods were not of the quality alleged, although when he was questioned he had to admit that he had never seen them, nor indeed had he ever been into Kent. Lady Twysden, who had resumed the role of her husband's solicitrix, came back to Lambeth in the cheerful expectation that at last right would be done. But when the Committee's order was made it denied that there had been any felling of timber trees and simply reiterated that Lady Twysden should have one-fifth share of the woods that remained and of the proceeds of those that had been felled. Privately, some of the members of the Committee admitted that the order did not conform with their decision, but none was willing to raise the matter again. Even D'Ewes, no doubt, felt that he had acted the part of *ombudsman* often enough, and Twysden's continuous importunity, even when transmitted through so wise and temperate an agent as Lady Twysden, must have become a fusty irritant and exasperation to men who were much burdened with the affairs of the country.

Locally, too, there was sheer malice. When walking through Stockenbury Wood that spring Lady Twysden remarked to Walter Brooke's son of a fine growing tree that she hoped it might be left. 'It shall be cut,' he retorted 'because you have prayed it should be allowed to stand', and soon had it down.

At last Twysden confessed himself beaten. What more could he do? His enemies on the County Committee, and now also the agents for the Committee of Woods, *per fas seu nefas* would have what they would and there was none to restrain them. He made no more attempts to preserve his beloved woods.

His personal situation at Lambeth was not so uncomfortable that he was urgent to exchange it for the uncertain and insecure position of an ex-prisoner of Parliament. As far back as August 1644 the Goldsmiths' Hall Committee (of the Treasury for Sequestrations) had sent to Lambeth to inquire about the estate and goods of Sir Rogert Twysden and five other prisoners, and to give them an opportunity to appear before the Committee. Twysden, convinced of the illegality of his sequestration and sanguine at that time that it would soon be taken off, took little notice of the order from Goldsmiths' Hall. However, six months later on 11 March 1645 he was summoned to appear before the Committee, informed that Parliament had set a fine of £3,000 upon him, and courteously invited to discuss the method of payment.

Thus, as Twysden wrote, was Star Chamber moved to the other end of Westminster Hall. Parliament had set the fine upon him, himself unheard and with no attempt to discover how his estate stood—and this to compound a sequestration which was unlawful. What, he asked the Goldsmiths' Hall Committee, was his fault? To the answer, for abetting the Kentish petition, he entered a vigorous denial, but the Committee said it was none of their business. 'We sit here to oppress no man,' said the chairman, Mr. John Ash, 'and for my part I think this gentleman to have had very hard measure. But we can do him no good other than give him time for payment.' The only redress, he added, was by petitioning the House, but it was not proper for any of the Committee to do that on his behalf.

Taking advantage of being out of prison, he sought out his brother-in-law Yelverton, who continued to sit in the Commons until Pride's Purge, and who gave it as his view that the fine would be mitigated if Twysden would confess himself a delinquent. Stiff as ever in his principles, even to his financial disadvantage, he refused. He wished to have a full hearing of his case by the House, and would submit if they decided that he was, indeed, guilty of delinquency. But this, said Yelverton, was impossible; the House was too busy, and in particular was too busy if a petitioner had a hope of being freed from sequestration.

Twysden, with his righteous consciousness of his own innocence and his constant petitioning, applying and importuning, must have been something of a nuisance to his Parliamentarily respectable brother-in-law. The relationship between them seems never to have been so cordial as that between Twysden and his other brother-in-law, Cholmley, even though the temperamental differences which had appeared between the two young men as fellow students at Gray's Inn, Twysden sober, reserved, perhaps a bit dull, Cholmley gay, casual, perhaps a bit of a wastrel, remained until the end of their lives. But, in a quiet way, there was real friendship between Yelverton and Twysden and Yelverton's house at Easton Maudit in Northamptonshire being uncomfortably close to the Royalist garrison at Banbury, it was natural that the Yelvertons, in need of fresh air, should spend the summer of 1645 at Roydon Hall.

Almost on the very day that Lady Yelverton retired to Roydon, 24 July 1645, Cholmley was surrendering Scarborough Castle to the Parliamentary forces. Cholmley, although originally on the side of Parliament, had never supported their cause without reservation, and he had found distasteful his task as one of the four Commissioners of presenting the Nineteen Propositions to the King. He thought that Parliament's conduct lacked candour, and when he was sent in the summer of 1642 to secure Scarborough Castle for Parliament he finally decided to hold it for the King. His wife (who at first disapproved of this *volte face* but afterwards with true wifely complacence praised his conduct) was allowed to join him with their two daughters. The children were sent over to Holland when the siege of the castle began in 1644, but for the whole weary twelve months Lady Cholmley stayed with her husband. By the terms of the surrender he was allowed to join the King or to go overseas. He chose the latter, and went to Holland, leaving Lady Cholmley in England. After a few months in Holland he went on to Paris and spent the winter of 1645/6 at Rouen with little William Twysden, now nearly ten years old, and his uncle Dr. John Twysden. Of course Cholmley was sequestrated, but he had been cautious enough to make over part of his estate to trustees for his son in 1640, so this eased matters.

Yelverton was shocked by the spoliation which he found during his summer at Roydon Hall. When he came back to London in September he urged Twysden to try to find some way of getting his affairs put into order. The only way was by petition to the House of Commons but that was not easy: the Commons could always find time to set or accept a fine but if one of their prisoners petitioned for his case to be heard, they were not at leisure to hear him, because of the press of public affairs. Not until 9 December 1645 could Twysden get his petition before the House, when it was commended to their favourable consideration by his old neighbour at Great Chart, Richard Browne. He argued that being concerned with the Kentish petition did not make a man sequestrable, and spoke to such good purpose that the House ordered Twysden to be bailed and the Committee for Sequestrations to report upon his case. Lady Yelverton herself, kind soul that she was, brought the order to him at Lambeth the next day.

It was an inconvenient moment for Twysden to assume his freedom. He was engaged in a lawsuit about a field he had bought at East Peckham from Robert Kenward and he feared that, once he was out of Lambeth, he might be attached at the suit of the vendor's widow's second husband and promptly landed in another prison. However, he succeeded in compromising the suit, and now all that remained for him to do was to settle his bill with the keeper of the prisoners at Lambeth, Dr. Leighton, who as a good Scottish Presbyterian and author of a book against prelacy (for which he was atrociously punished by the Star Chamber) was deemed a suitable man to have the charge of the Archbishop's house.

Up to 16 August 1644 Twysden had paid 12*s.* a week for his lodging. With some other prisoners he then went to Leighton and said that he could no longer afford to pay so high a rent. Leighton refused to make any abatement so Twysden set about appealing to the Committee for Prisoners, meanwhile paying nothing. The Committee decided the following February that the entrance fee should be 40*s.* (Leighton had claimed that 66*s.* 8*d.* was the proper fee for a baronet) and the weekly charge should be reduced to 8*s.* o*d.* On this basis Twysden now made his final settlement with Leighton, from whom he parted on friendly terms, and on 20 February 1646, almost exactly two years after his removal from the Counter to Lambeth, he went to lodge in St. Anne Street, Westminster. There he stayed for another two years, almost every morning finding him at the door of the House of Commons, putting into the hands of his friends petitions that the House would name a date for the execution of their order of 9 December 1645.

His friend, Selden, whom he met one day, advised him to apply to Goldsmiths' Hall and compound, for there was no other way of getting off. This Twysden was reluctant to do, for the Goldsmiths' Hall Committee could only negotiate about the payment of a fine or composition, and had no power to hear a case on its merits. What Twysden wanted was to be told exactly with what offence he was charged, and proceeded against in a legal way. But he suspected that the House of Commons knew him to be innocent of any breach of law or Parliamentary ordinance, and therefore refused to hear him so that he could continue to be kept out of his estate.

Eventually, despairing of any other way, he waited upon the Chairman of the Goldsmiths' Hall Committee only to find that, because of a technicality, they could not help him; they were authorized to compound for delinquencies committed since the beginning of the war, which was taken to be 20 May 1642, but the Kentish petition, for which Twysden was sequestrated, was agitated in March of that year.

Back he went to Westminster, and saw Samuel Browne, chairman of the Committee for Sequestrations, who seemed surprised that the Goldsmiths' Hall Committee had refused to compound, adding 'I warrant you that they will'—a hint, perhaps that an order would follow from the Commons that they were not to turn money away on account of a technicality.

But for Twysden there was another difficulty, more than a technicality. To be allowed to compound he must take the Scottish Covenant, and that his conscience forbade—unless he were permitted to make his own explanation of how he understood the Covenant, a proviso that the Committee was scarcely likely to welcome. So throughout 1646 and the first half of 1647 he remained in London, conversing with his friends, continuing his study of the ancient records (an occupation involving physical difficulties such as are hard for us to imagine), and hoping that somehow, in a way that no man could foresee, order might yet come out of the constitutional chaos. The Royalists had been defeated in the field but the King was still alive and his existence put into doubtful question the legitimacy of Parliament and all its actions, and the Army, which contained men of honour and tolerance and mercy, was becoming a political force. No obvious solution to the country's perplexities was in sight. All that Twysden and others like him could do was to hang on in the blind hope, unreasoning and unreasonable as nevertheless it must have seemed, that one day things would come right again.

CHAPTER SIX

1647–1660

FOR THE Twysdens, the summer of 1647 saw the beginning of a family reunion. In June Lady Twysden went down to East Peckham with Anne, her second child, who was now nearly eleven. Will, a year older, was still in France and his mother regularly sent him instalments of his yearly allowance of £100. Francis Twysden escorted Lady Cholmley to France in June but was back by August. Jane, the wife of Thomas Twisden, whose practice at the Bar continued to flourish, joined Lady Twysden at Roydon Hall and at last on 5 August Twysden himself returned to the home that he had not seen for five years. But his sequestration was not removed, and it was to be another two years and more before he could resume control of his estate.

He found much changed at East Peckham. His old acquaintance Francis Worrall, the Vicar, had been ejected in 1644, and William Polhill was now in possession of the living. In Nettlestead, the next parish, a new Rector, the Reverend Samuel Deacon, presented by Sir Edward Scott, had been admitted by the Parliamentary Commissioners in March 1647. Hextall Court, the home of his neighbours the Whetenhalls, stood empty: they were Catholics and had withdrawn themselves. Half the trees in Stockenbury Wood had been felled and Prior's Broom, Motewood and Oven's Wood had all been cleared. Twysden was conscious of decay both at Roydon Hall and at Chelmington, which he visited in October, but it must be admitted that the estate accounts show no large expenditure on repairs; perhaps the dilapidations were conspicuous mainly to the fond eye of the owner.

Life at East Peckham began to settle down into something like a normal course. Thomas Twisden's wife had her seventh child there on 17 September 1647 and her eighth on 22 October 1648. They were baptized the new way, without godparents. Old friends began to visit again. In October 1647 Sir John Skiverstone and his son, returning from France, came to see Twysden—if they brought news of Will they must have been doubly welcome guests. There were visits to London, the best way to obtain intelligence of how affairs stood between the King, Parliament, and the Army, for it was imprudent to write about such matters and the rumours that filtered through to remote parishes such as East Peckham were untrustworthy. Nearer home the County Committee had been racked by a violent quarrel between Weldon and Sedley culminating in Sedley's being barred from all offices in State and Commonwealth in April 1647. Weldon did not for long enjoy his triumph for he died in October 1648.

At Christmas 1647 there were riots at Canterbury not so much in support of the King's cause as in protest against the City government and the ordinance declaring Christmas festivities unlawful. For a week or two the mob were in control of the City. Even so far away as East Peckham the riot had repercussions, and the trained bands from the village were amongst those that in January 1648 were called out to quell the rising. It was difficult to foresee where the disturbance would end, and on 21 January 1648 Twysden took his family back to their old lodgings in St. Anne Street, Westminster. If there was going to be trouble in Kent it was better that he, a man known to be obnoxious to Parliament, should be out of the way. However, soon there was trouble in London, for on 9 April the City apprentices rioted because the Mayor forbade them to play at bat, but the soldiers put down the riot, with only a few apprentices killed. In Kent a far more serious disturbance was developing. A special court was set up at Canterbury to deal with the Christmas rioters, but although the Grand Jury had been selected with care it refused to find a true bill and took the opportunity of organizing a petition. It was moderately worded and the main prayer seems unexceptionable, that men should 'for the future be governed and judged by (the English subject's undoubted birthright) the known and established laws of this kingdom'. The violent reaction of the County Committee sparked off an even more violent reaction throughout the county, and there was a general rising under the leadership of the incompetent Earl of Norwich and the inadequate Edward Hales. Fairfax, with 7,000 men of the New Model Army, quickly suppressed the insurgents, one part of the army passing close to East Peckham on its way to Maidstone and Dover. Twysden had done wisely, by removing himself, to prevent any suspicion of contamination with the affair. It was not until September that he returned to Roydon Hall. His brother Francis had been suspected of complicity in the rising but, with Sir Anthony St. Leger, Robert Burnham, Thomas Flood and John Maplisden, he was granted an indemnity by the House of Commons on 17 July 1648.

In her almanack Lady Twysden recorded for 30 January 1649 that the King was beheaded and that men said a wild duck flew by at the time. Twysden had no more hoped that the King would triumph over Parliament than he approved of Parliament's and the Army's triumph over the King. For him the proper constitution was a balance of power between King, Lords and Commons. Now the kingly part of the constitution was finally destroyed and there was no prospect that it would ever come in again. A return to a normal way of government was no longer to be hoped for, and a man could not now be blamed for making his submission to the powers that be; perhaps it was even his moral duty to do so; perhaps if, in an aloof way, he lent his collaboration to his erstwhile enemies he might be able to restrain their worse excesses and to lead public affairs again in the right direction. To remain in the wilderness could only lead to futility. Besides, without going so far as Cromwell in believing that every successful action was a sign of God's approval, the ordinarily reflective Christian could not help pondering on the way in which God's help seemed to have been withdrawn from the King's cause.

So Twysden set about his submission to the ruling powers as many of his former Kentish associates, including Richard

Spencer, had already done. In March 1649 the House of Commons published the terms on which delinquents should be permitted to compound. As a relief to 'tender consciences' such as Twysden's no longer was the compounder required to take the Covenant. Generally the fine was to be one-sixth of the total value of the estate. But when Twysden approached the Goldsmiths' Hall Committee he was met with the same answer as before—they had no authority to deal with him because his offence was committed before 20 May 1642. They could only advise the submission of a petition.

Not until 19 May could Twysden get his petition heard by the Commons. Both the Vanes, Sir Arthur Haselrig (the regicide), Lislebon Young and many others spoke on his behalf, and it was finally decided that the fine of £3,000 imposed on him several years earlier (and, of course, never paid) should be expunged, and that he should be allowed to compound at a tenth of the value of his estate, that is, two years' revenue. To his friends this seemed an almost lenient decision, one which would not have been possible had Weldon still been fulminating his charges in Kent. Twysden found it hard to reconcile himself to so heavy a fine, or indeed to any at all, for he still believed (and rightly) that he was legally innocent of any offence. But his friends' counsel prevailed, he negotiated with Goldsmiths' Hall, they assessed his fine at £1,500, and he managed to persuade them to reduce it to £1,340, half to be paid within fourteen days and the balance six weeks after the composition had been reported to the House. Those few words give an inadequate idea of the length and complexity of Twysden's negotiations but it would be tedious to describe them in their meticulous detail. He was not content to leave it at that, but in December asked for an abatement of £60 for quit-rents and annuities. The Committee replied that no abatement could be made, as it was contrary to the rules that they had made; but as Twysden complained, since the rules were never published how was a suitor to know what he should do? The Committee apparently felt that there was, in principle, some justice in the claim, for the following month they made an abatement of £40 without bothering to look at the papers or to check the amount of the claim. Twysden might be a nuisance but at least he was an honest man and could be trusted not to put in a fraudulent claim.

It was the beginning of 1650 before the business was finally settled. By then the Committee for Compositions had migrated from Goldsmiths' Hall to the House of Lords and after the final hearing Twysden and Mr. John Ash, the Chairman of the Committee, sat by the fire to warm themselves (the month was January) and fell to talking of Twysden's position. He was, he hoped, free of the imposition of the twentieth part which had been levied by Parliament—it was presumably covered by the composition? Ash, having looked at the orders made by the House of Commons, was able to give Twysden the comforting assurance that he wanted, and Reading, the learned lawyer who was of counsel for the Committee, confirmed Ash's interpretation of the law.

Twysden was therefore astounded, twenty months later, in September 1651 to receive an order from the Committee for the Advance of Money, etc. (the Haberdashers' Hall Committee) to appear before them on 17 October, to give satisfaction for the payment of the assessment of £600 which had been laid upon him for his twentieth part nearly nine years earlier on 29 November 1642. He managed to put off his appearance until 7 November and meanwhile consulted Mr. Ash, who did not seem to remember their earlier conversation. When he appeared at Haberdashers' Hall he begged the aid of Sir Michael Livesey and Augustine Skinner, both members of the Committee, but Livesey rather spoke against than for him, and what Twysden said on his own behalf was of little avail. In order to enjoy immunity from the imposition of the twentieth part, he ought, said the Committee, to have petitioned for permission to compound before 20 April 1649, but did not do so until the 20 May (ignoring the fact that the Goldsmiths' Hall Committee were at first unable to receive Twysden's petition because his offence occurred before May 1642); and moreover he ought to have paid the second instalment of his fine within three months of the first (in spite of the fact that the amount was not conclusively settled by the Committee until more than six months after the payment of the first instalment). However, the Committee reduced the assessment from £600 to £450, but this amount was to be paid in full within twenty-eight days.

The inequity of the committee's order stung Twysden. He thought of appealing to the House of Commons, but his friends advised that it would take five or six years, and that even then the outcome would give him no comfort. So he borrowed £200 from his brother Thomas and paid the first half of his assessment. The County Committee were indebted to Lady Twysden for £88 2*s.* 3*d.* the outstanding instalment of her fifth part, and as the County Committee's powers in the matter of sequestrations and the money in their hands had now been transferred to the Haberdashers' Hall Committee, it was obviously fair to set off this debt against the £225 which Twysden had still to pay. This was the view of the gentlemen who lately formed the County Committee for Sequestrations, and they willingly and courteously acceded to Twysden's request to certify the matter to Haberdashers' Hall. But the Haberdashers' Hall Committee, although they reduced the assessment from £450 to £400, were insistent that Twysden must first pay his debt in full and they would then pay what was owing to Lady Twysden. He paid his second instalment, being allowed £10 1*s.* 6*d.* for the chattels taken from the Redcross Street house, but although his kinsman Colonel Manwaring, a sound Parliamentarian, urged the matter on his behalf with the Committee, they decided that they could not repay him anything—it had happened before their time. It was a shabby, bureaucratic, decision.

'Monstrous' was a word which Twysden sometimes used to describe the treatment which he suffered at the hands of Parliament and its committees. Apart from Weldon, Sedley, and perhaps Livesey, these men were not moved by personal animosity; often Twysden goes out of his way to record that they were courteous and gentlemanly, and he even finds good things to say of Weldon. The difficulty was that the cumbrous and ill-articulated administrative machines of their creation had developed a momentum of their own, grinding out petty meannesses and injustices, and it required too great an effort on the part of men distracted and puzzled by the great problems of government that confronted them to intervene constantly to ensure that the Twysdens of the world were not oppressed.

The return to something like normality at Roydon Hall is indicated by an entry in Lady Twysden's diary for 25 February 1649: 'We began to keep house for ourselves at Peckham'. Since the sequestration the estate had been in the occupation of that faithful servant, George Stone. Now Twysden took over from him and within the next few months spent no less than £230 in buying cattle to restock the farm.

It seemed safe, too, to fetch Will home from France. It is easy to imagine the relief with which Lady Twysden wrote in her diary in April 1648: 'Will come safely to Rouen—I thank Christ.' On 8 September with his tutor Hamnet Ward, he came back to his home at East Peckham. For more than five years his parents had not seen him. He was a child of seven when he went away: he came back a lad of nearly thirteen. With what pleasure Lady Twysden must have recorded in her diary on 10 November: 'Bought Will a nag for £3 10*s*. 0*d*.—his first horse'. However, he was not long at East Peckham for he was sent off to school in Dorset with Dr. Ward before the year was out, whilst his parents returned to their London lodgings, dividing the following spring and summer between there and Roydon Hall.

During that spring there were more reunions. Lady Cholmley and her two daughters, and Twysden's brother John all came back to England. For a couple of years John made his home at Roydon Hall, where he could indulge his bent for chemical speculation and experiment with Master Johannes Hind who was full of such learning, although some things he was reluctant to talk about. It was known that he came from Mecklenburg, but even on his deathbed he would not reveal his true name, nor would he communicate his most important secret, the recipe for his famous red powder. John Twysden remembered that Hind had always wanted any adders found in the neighbourhood, without which, as he admitted, he could not make his powder. In spite of the fact that John Twysden was now a Doctor of Physic of the University of Angers, Hind would not give him the recipe which had been revealed to him under promise of secrecy. Finally Dr. Twysden discovered it for himself, and walking one day in a wood at East Peckham with Hind told him the results of his experiments. 'Dr. Twysden, God hath given you a great secret,' he replied: 'I am glad you have it without me. 'Tis yours, ye may give it to whom ye will, but 'tis not fit to be communicated.' The doctor followed Hind's advice and never made known his recipe, regrettably, perhaps, seeing that the powder was very effectual in diseases of the spleen, coughs, asthmas, worms, purulency of the chest, the plague, all manner of fevers, smallpox, measles, and catarrhs. In such discussion, and in speculation about producing the matter of the philosopher's stone by cleansing vitriol of all its impurities by frequent ablution and desiccations, the two scientists spent an agreeable couple of years.

In June 1649 Sir Hugh Cholmley returned to England, and went to live with his wife and family in Black and White Court in the Old Bailey. Although he had been in arms against Parliament and was a richer man than Twysden, his composition was set at only £450. The Committee for Compounding suspected that there was something fraudulent about the transfer of much of his property to trustees (of whom Twysden was one) for the benefit of his children, but the fact had to be accepted. He remained in London for two years until in 1651 Parliament, alarmed by the progress of the Stuart cause in Scotland, made an order that none who had been in the King's party should come within ten miles of London. He might have withdrawn to Yorkshire, but thinking that that might give rise to suspicion, he decided instead to join Twysden at East Peckham whilst his wife and children went to their own house at Whitby.

Apart from petitioning about his twentieth, Twysden was living quietly, getting the estate back into order, repairing here and renovating there, finding out which tenants were in arrear with their rent and reckoning with them, but above all devoting his leisure to reading and writing. Wotton, in his *Baronetage* said of him that at this time 'his greatest comfort was the conversing with the learned Fathers of the Primitive

Church, and the ancient laws and constitutions of his country—hoping for a time when both might be vindicated'. He had for years been working on his treatise on the government of England, although it was not to be finished until about 1655; in 1648 he published anonymously a pamphlet entitled *The Commoner's Liberty, or the Englishman's Birth-Right*; four years later there appeared *Historiae Anglicanae Scriptores X*, consisting of ten chronicles which were transcribed by his direction and published with a prefatory letter by him; he published a volume by his old friend Sir Robert Filmer on usury, under the title *Questio Quodlibetica*, in the same year. *An Historical Vindication of the Church of England in point of schism as it stands separated from the Roman and was reformed I Elizabeth* came out in 1657; *The Beginners of a Monastic Life* belongs to the same period, although it did not appear in print until 1698; and he was engaged upon *An Historical Narrative of the two Houses of Parliament and either of them, their committees' and agents' violent proceedings against Sir Roger Twysden, their imprisoning his person, sequestering his estate, cutting down his woods and timber to his almost undoing, and forcing him in the end to composition for his own.* He wrote it primarily for the benefit of his descendants, a cautionary tale of the calamities which follow when the old ways are departed from. No doubt the manuscript was also passed round amongst his friends and neighbours. Just two hundred years later it appeared for the first time in print.[1]

Even now what he believed to be the unlawful exactions of Parliament continued. A few years later there were the taxes to the Army. During 1651, the year of Charles's southward march through England to his defeat at the Battle of Worcester, Parliament's expenditure and consequently the taxes were abnormally high. It is impossible to be sure of the amount which Twysden paid or what proportion of his income the taxes represented, but it seems that in 1651 he paid something like £45 for his lands at East Peckham, Yalding, Wateringbury and Nettlestead, equivalent perhaps to 5–7 per cent. of his income. For the years 1655, 1656 and 1657 the payments did not amount to more than £8 or so each year. He compounded

[1] *Archaeologia Cantiana*, vols. I–IV (1858–61).

for excise on home-brewed beer at 24*s.* a year, and when an attempt was made at Christmas 1650 to increase the composition to 40*s.* he objected (to show the small quantity brewed) that he had three children and nine men in family, and (to show its poor quality) that it was not so good as 6*s.* beer in London. So he was allowed to continue at 24*s.* a year. The Army, in their exactions later, seem to have played a cat-and-mouse game. As the house of a delinquent Roydon Hall had been searched many times and all arms removed. But Twysden was then assessed as liable to supply arms for one horseman and had to buy new. These arms were then taken away by the Army, and he was again in default—this seems to have been the nature of their proceedings until the intervention of Monk in 1659 put an end to their practices and paved the way for the Restoration.

This, however, is getting things out of chronological order, and we must go back to 1651. On 15 March Johannes Hind died at Roydon Hall at the age of seventy-three, having lived in the Twysden household for thirty-two years. In spite of his skill in medical cures, he neglected to treat himself for a fall about three months earlier which was the probable cause of his death. At the age of forty-nine he had fallen in love with Mary Mills, another member of the Twysden household, but they were too religious to marry—nor was there ever the slightest suspicion of dishonesty between them. He was a devout Lutheran, but willingly communicated with Anglicans. Except for a few small monetary gifts to the poor, he left all his property in England to Mary Mills, including six or seven large gallipots containing powders. To Twysden he bequeathed a small gallipot of his cordial red powder, 'a select little one, purposely differing from the rest, I confess it much cured me of the grief I should have had for him'. It is an ambiguous remark, recorded in Twysden's private papers; did he mean that he was chagrined at so minute a legacy, or that the powder was particularly efficacious in restoring the spirit?

Twysden was soon to get caught up in graver events than the death of an old family servant. The situation in Scotland gave Parliament cause for alarm, and in April the former delinquents who had been released were taken into custody again, for the safety of the Commonwealth. At four o'clock in the morning of 26 April troopers came to Roydon Hall to search for arms and letters, as they said. They took away such arms as they could find and four or five letters which they deemed suspicious, together with Twysden and Cholmley, who were lodged as prisoners at Leeds Castle (near Maidstone), with Lord Aston, Sir Thomas Culpepper and others. A couple of days later John Twysden, who had been living with his brother since returning from France two years before, removed himself to Easton Maudit in Northamptonshire, to the home of his brother-in-law Sir Christopher Yelverton. Very soon Twysden was back at Roydon, for nothing could be found against him. Cholmley remained at Leeds and Lady Twysden visited him almost every week until he also was freed on 16 June. By the end of the month all of the prisoners had been released on entering into bonds to appear before the Council of State at ten days' notice, if summoned. Cholmley stayed on at Roydon Hall for another year. His wife and children made a ten-day journey from Whitby by sea and river to Gravesend and by road from Gravesend to East Peckham to join him. It was a cordial family gathering, but Cholmley insisted on contributing towards the housekeeping expenses—£12 a month for himself, his wife, children and three servants. In July 1652 he went back to Whitby to live a quiet and retired life. Even so, his household consisted of nearly thirty people.

Excluded from any share in county government, Twysden concerned himself with what was going on in the parish. When at Easter, 1653 Polhill, the Vicar, claimed the right to nominate one of the churchwardens, Twysden was one of the first to object that there was no such custom. The Vicar's nominee was an eminently fit person, but it would not do to accept him, otherwise a precedent would be established. Worrall, the previous Vicar, had tried hard to establish the right, but the parish had been too quick for him. Not that Twysden was on bad terms with the parson who had been instituted during his long absence from the parish; for many years he paid the Vicar an allowance of 10*s*. a year for clothing poor old William Dean, and Polhill schooled Twysden's two younger boys, Roger, who was now ten, and Charles, three years younger, for a modest charge of about £2 a year.

During the next few years death sadly diminished the Twysden circle. On 31 March 1654 the faithful George Stone died at the age of sixty-two in Twysden's house in Hadlow, which was still being repaired after the years of neglect. He had served the Twysdens well for thirty-five years and his staunch honesty and courage during Twysden's time of troubles had endeared him to his master and mistress.

Just a year later Twysden's sister Elizabeth, Lady Cholmley, died of a fever in London. Her husband was at Whitby at the time, and could be present neither at her death-bed nor at her funeral which took place at East Peckham on 20 April 1655. The cortège was met by Twysden and his brothers Thomas and Francis. She had always preferred Kent to Yorkshire and it was fitting that she should be buried near her father in the Twysden aisle of East Peckham Church. She resembled him in her hastiness of temper, and in her addiction to reading, especially history. Cholmley gave up his home in Yorkshire, and spent his remaining years in Kent, mainly with Thomas Twisden at Malling. He died two years later and was buried beside his wife.

Twysden and his wife continued to spend most of their time at Roydon Hall, with fairly frequent visits to the house which they now had in Dean's Yard, Westminster. On 9 March 1657 he writes to her in London from Roydon whither he had just returned that he is worried that she is unwell, and has put off other plans so that he may go up to her if necessary—'I do wonder how thou has taken cold again, I fear it was coming with me to the door.' She had been weak since the birth of her last child twelve years before and was conscious that her hold on life was uncertain. When, only a short time before her last illness, Twysden jestingly said to her 'If God rid me of this, for a second wife I will take no thought,' she had replied 'Mock not, it may be sooner than you think'. On 10 March a messenger hurried down from London with the news that Lady Twysden was failing. Her husband left Roydon at once, and was by her bedside at ten o'clock the same morning. She rallied a little, and together they received communion, after which she kissed the Minister and those about her. 'Then,' continues Twysden's own account 'growing nearer her end, desired to be laid to rest again, being heavy as nigher her time's end. About 3 of the clock she waked again, knew me. I kissed her and she me; but I could not well understand her speech, but, as I conceive, it was that she might die quietly, which she did, laying herself again to sleep; but never waked more in this world. When I kissed her, which was the last I ever did whilst she lived, she gave me many kisses together after her former manner so as I told her "Here is the old kiss still".' She smiled, as what she knew she used to do.'

She was buried at East Peckham. At her death Twysden took up his pen and made two memorial memoranda that correspond to two sides of his character; as a cautious estate-owner he recorded in his account-book that on 19 March he paid Mr. Polhill £1 for burying his wife, and on 22nd Elphy, the parish clerk, 10*s.* for making the grave and tolling the bell; as a devoted husband and a man of sensibility he wrote a memoir of Lady Twysden which so affected J. M. Kemble that, relevant or not, he introduced it into his Introduction to the edition of *Certain Considerations upon the Government of England* which he prepared for the Camden Society in 1849. The last paragraph will bear repetition:

> 'Her goodness I cannot express, her piety, mildness, temperance, not to be stirred, not at all passionate, sweetness of nature, judgment, justice, fellow-compassionateness, patience, humility, yet well understanding herself and her due, they who best knew her can only judge. Of her humbleness I shall give only one example: after some of her great journeys into Kent, which she undertook for my business, and so very wisely solicited, seeing her ill and great with child, I have sometimes said "What an unfortunate man am I that have brought a gentlewoman to such a deal of misery for my sake!" She would take me up, as intimating and saying she would endure much more for my sake. . . . She

was the saver of my estate. Never man had a better wife, never children a better mother.'

Still two more deaths have to be recorded to complete the pathetic tale of these few years. On 24 August 1658 Anne, the eldest of Twysden's daughters, who had celebrated her twenty-first birthday only a few months before, was married at East Peckham Church to John Porter, the son of Richard Porter of Lamberhurst. It was a quiet wedding; on the bride's side those present were only Twysden, her uncle Thomas Twisden and his wife, cousin Whetenhall and his wife, and a companion of his; on the groom's side there were six. Her marriage portion was £1,037 10*s.* 0*d.* which Twysden paid, in two instalments, not without difficulty. Until April 1659 she continued to live at her father's house, '*nihil solvendo*' as he notes. Then she went to join her husband at Lamberhurst, but soon they removed to a lodging in Westminster where, on 2 December 1659 a daughter, christened Isabella after her grandmother, was born. Six weeks later John Porter died, and on 8 March 1660 little Isabella succumbed, so he 'left no memorial remaining of him but the grief of his friends for his loss, which his poor wife takes very heavily'. She was only twenty-three; she lived on, a widow, for another sixty-nine years, long enough to see not only the end of the Stuarts and the beginning of the House of Hanover, but even to witness the accession of George II. She had grown up as a child in a period when government had scarcely found its way out of the Middle Ages, when the execution of a Strafford or a Laud seemed the only means of resolving serious disagreement; when she died the Act of Settlement had laid the foundation of our modern constitution, Walpole was in occupation of the office of Prime Minister, and the problem of religious toleration was being unheroically side-stepped by an annual Act of Indemnity to take the edge off the Test and Corporation Acts. This transformation within a lifetime may have lacked the element of glory but it can fairly be termed a revolution.

CHAPTER SEVEN

1660–1672

For Twysden sorrow for the death of his son-in-law and his grandchild was tempered by the constitutional changes which were already taking place. The prolongation by Parliament of its own existence had always been, in his eyes, one of the most extreme and terrible acts of abuse of power in the whole conflict, and the promptness with which, when the secluded members were recalled in March 1660, Parliament voted its own dissolution gave him intense satisfaction. That Charles II was permitted to return unconditionally was not, on the other hand, a cause of satisfaction, for Twysden was not the kind of man to be carried away by emotional excess for the Stuart cause and he had often stressed that he was far from wishing for the King's return as a conqueror or an absolute monarch. Although Charles passed within less than two hours' ride of East Peckham on his triumphal journey from Dover to London, Twysden does not record that he joined the crowds who gathered to greet their restored monarch, and it would have been altogether in character if he stayed quietly on his estate, conscientiously getting on with his duties there.

The prospect of obtaining compensation for the wrongs that they had undergone and the damage that their property had received at the hands of the Parliamentarians gave an added sweetness to the constitutional contentment with which the Royalists welcomed the Restoration. Twysden began to get together evidence of the losses which he had suffered because of the iniquitous conduct of his oppressors. From Lambarde Godfrey, formerly Sequestrator-General of Kent, he tried to get copies of the important letters of the Committee of the

Lords and Commons for Sequestrations. Perhaps it is not surprising that, writing on 14 June 1660, Godfrey has to report his inability to find them. The letters might have been useful to prove Twysden's losses, but he neither could, nor would, claim that he had been active on the King's behalf (after all, he had refused to pay ship-money and had been awkward about other abnormal royal impositions before the war) and probably he was disgusted, as other decent men were, by the many shameless deceits that were practised in the hope of getting reparation where none was justified. So Twysden did no more about putting in a claim. It was not that he did not need money but he was dubious both about the ethics of the thing, and perhaps even more about the prospects of success. His need for ready money he met by borrowing. His wife's sister, Frances Warham, lent him £500 on which, because she was poor, he allowed her more than 5 per cent. interest, and he borrowed a similar sum from his brother Thomas. Both debts were repaid within a couple of years.

Thomas's affairs continued to flourish, as did those of most lawyers, whose tenacity of professional life irrespective of who, if anyone, currently occupied the throne, was astonishing. Although he was supposed to have royalist sympathies, he was made a serjeant-at-law by the Lord Protector in 1654. The next year he got into trouble for his defence of Coney who refused to pay custom which Cromwell had imposed on the City of London without authority of Parliament and who was committed to prison for his refusal. Coney sued out a writ of *habeas corpus* and at the hearing Twisden 'insisted much on the taking away the Star Chamber and urged that subjects were not to be imprisoned nor their goods attached but in a legal way on trial by jury', a line of defence which was not to Cromwell's liking, so Twisden joined his client in prison 'for using words tending to sedition and the subversion of the present government'. Maynard and Wadham Windham, also of counsel for the defence, were committed to the Tower with Twisden but they all made a proper submission and after a fortnight in which they had an opportunity of reflecting upon the difference between the theory and practice of government they were released. It was a brief reverse in a steadily successful career, marked by the purchase of land in Kent, notably Bradbourne, in East Malling, which became the seat of the Twisden branch of the family for nearly 300 years. At the Restoration he surrendered the dignity of serjeant conferred on him by Cromwell and received it back a few days later from the hand of Charles II, who appointed him a Judge of the King's Bench, with the customary knighthood, on 22 July 1660. He was one of the judges at the arraignment of the regicides and later he tried John Bunyan. His reputation was that of a sound lawyer, but from the number of his judgements which are reported as beginning 'Twisden, *in furore*, observed', etc., it seems that he had inherited his father's impatience.

In a humbler sphere Twysden also was soon back amongst the judiciary. At the Maidstone Assizes on 11 September 1660 he was again sworn a Justice of the Peace and put into the commission of oyer and terminer. In the following month he was made a Deputy Lieutenant. These were not offices of profit—indeed he had to pay a fee of £5 on his Deputy Lieutenancy commission—but they were offices that combined dignity with power in the county. This was the true Restoration, not just the re-establishment of the King on his lawful throne but also the re-installation of the country gentry as governors of their counties, the restoration as it seemed to Twysden and his fellows of a properly ordered society. There were still taxes to be paid, never a pleasing fact, but at least now they were properly laid by King, Lords and Commons. Like other rich men in East Peckham and the neighbouring parishes Twysden was assessed both on his lands and his 'ability', or wealth, but he managed, as did the other Justices of the Peace, to avoid payments assessed on ability and not without reason as his debts at that time exceeded the value of his goods. It was not until some years later, at Rochester in 1669, that the Court decided that this was the correct interpretation of the law.

Even Nature seemed to take note of the fact that the royal family had been restored. On 3 June 1661, a great sturgeon that had made its way up the Medway, past numerous weirs and then up a little stream through the meadows, was taken at Hadlow. Nothing could have been more convenient, for the Duke and Duchess of York were at the increasingly fashionable Wells beyond Tunbridge, only seven or eight miles away, so Mr. Thomas Barton who managed to acquire the fish presented it to their Highnesses. Perhaps this was in near-compliance with the statute of Edward II that decreed sturgeon to belong to the sovereign; or perhaps Mr. Barton saw an opportunity of gaining the favour of the Duke. It was a nine-days wonder in Hadlow and East Peckham which even the sedate Twysden thought worth recording.

Much of his time was now taken up with the public affairs that fall to the lot of a conscientious Justice of the Peace and Deputy Lieutenant, and an account of them is given in a later chapter. But family affairs also engaged his attention.

First there was the question of the marriage of his two younger daughters, Isabella, born in 1637, and Frances who was three years her junior. He was willing to make the best provision that he could for them so that they might be able to make suitable matches, but Isabella did not choose to marry, or was not chosen; she died a spinster in 1725, four years before her elder sister, Anne, Porter's widow, with whom she probably shared a home. The younger daughter, Frances, it was arranged should marry Sir Peter Killigrew, baronet, of Arwenack in Cornwall, and the wedding took place in 1662. It caused Twysden to be busy much of the autumn with frequent visits to London. The main problem was to raise her marriage-portion of £1,500. He could not immediately lay his hands on so much money and it was some time before it could be paid in full, interest being due on the debt in the meantime. Presumably after her marriage Frances lived in her husband's county of Cornwall, 300 miles away from her family at Roydon Hall; at all events they now rarely saw her.

In 1665 Twysden was ill. It was a bad year for the plague, so bad in and around Maidstone that the autumn Assizes had to be put off from October until December. Whether it was the plague or some other illness which struck Twysden is not known. In March of that year there is a sudden deterioration in his handwriting; it becomes shaky, and entries in his notebooks are left incomplete. Writing on 13 March to his son Charles at Oxford he says: 'I have so very short breath as I can nothing walk as I was wont to do' (hardly surprising seeing that he was now nearly sixty-eight) 'so I see my time will not be long'. He recovered from the illness but took it as a warning to put his affairs in order. As a beginning, to make charitable provision for some of the poorer parishioners of East Peckham especially those who had been servants at Roydon Hall, he bought a little field called Duck's Meadow, on 29 April 1665 for £60, and the rent of £6. 10*s*. 0*d*. a year was thereafter distributed amongst the poor of the parish.

But it was for his children that Twysden was principally concerned. His heir, William, was almost thirty and still unmarried. By prudent management the property both at East Peckham and at Great Chart was being made to yield a rather larger income; two daughters had already received their marriage portions, leaving only Isabella as a contingent liability; the two younger sons must be provided for so as not to be a burden on their elder brother. Twysden's own wants were modest, and the estate could now support a married heir.

William married on 13 June 1665 Frances, the daughter of Josiah Crosse and his wife Frances, who was the daughter of Sir John Garrard of Lamer in Hertfordshire. They lived at Roydon Hall, and soon began to present Twysden with a succession of grandchildren though many, alas, died in infancy. The first child, born on 20 June 1666 was a boy, christened Roger, whose godparents were Twysden, Sir Thomas Twisden and his grandmother, Frances Crosse. The second child, a girl who was christened Frances, was born on 10 November 1667 and died the same day. A second son was born in March 1669, but he too did not survive his birthday. The second daughter, born in July 1670 for whom the name Frances again was chosen lived only three months. (Later, in 1673, the name was bestowed, for the third time, on a daughter, and she survived.) A fourth daughter, born in September 1671, was named Anne after her great-aunt Anne Porter who, with Lady Twysden, and Twysden himself, stood as sponsors. In his last years

Twysden had the satisfaction of seeing a grandson and a granddaughter helping to round-out the Roydon Hall family but the loss of the other three children must have saddened him. He would have been still more melancholy if he could have known that Roger would die at the age of nineteen and Anne at twenty-two; and that of all the seventeen children born to William and Francis, seven would die in infancy and only four live to middle age.

It was important that Twysden's other two sons Roger and Charles should have their own livelihoods and not be dependent on William; the estate would just support one family but not three. For Roger, born in 1642, Twysden purchased in 1665 an office as Cursitor, that is one of the clerks attached to the Chancery who had the duty (and privilege) of making and issuing writs for initiating suits at law. The cost of the purchase, probably in the neighbourhood of £1,000, was met from the proceeds of land in Yalding which Twysden had bought fifteen years earlier to make provision for Roger when he should grow up. When an office such as this was purchased as an investment the owner usually put in a deputy to do the work for him, his profit being the margin between the receipts and the salary which he allowed the deputy. Roger Twysden, however, seems to have exercised the office personally, at least for a time. In his will Twysden was able to record his satisfaction that Roger was in an office 'wherein I thank God he doth well'. He was called to the Bar at Lincoln's Inn in 1674 but died three years afterwards, when he seemed set for a promising career in the law.

Charles, the youngest son, was more of a problem. He had been born in 1645 in the midst of Twysden's troubles, his mother died when he was twelve, and his early upbringing and schooling took place in unsettled conditions; it would not be surprising if, the youngest of the family, he were spoiled by his parents and by Thomasine Warham who stepped into the role of mother to the lad when Lady Twysden died.

Charles matriculated at Christ Church, Oxford, in 1664 at the age of nineteen. By 1665 his father was already worrying about his career—worrying, too, about the cost of Oxford

(Charles's allowance of £60 a year never seems to be adequate —can it be done more cheaply at another college, he asks on behalf of Sir Thomas Twisden's wife, who is thinking of sending their Frank to Oxford); worrying about Charles's health when he seems to be falling into a melancholy—'Good boy, be merry and pluck up a good heart,' he encourages him; worrying about the company he keeps, adding the customary paternal advice to avoid plays and drinking in company.

A college fellowship was the first means of subsistence that Twysden thought of. 'I know in All Souls, of which I would fain have thee, nothing is to be done gratis and money is always the best friend', but when Twysden visited Oxford in July 1665 without seeing Charles or telling him of his visit, he found it was not so easy as he had hoped. None but gentlemen were admitted at All Souls, a quality which Charles undoubtedly possessed, but both there and at the other colleges the best procedure for acquiring a fellowship was hard for the visitor to discover. Charles, he thinks, would be well advised to make indirect rather than direct approaches.

Two years later Charles had still not settled on a career. Twysden writes to him on 29 April 1667 from East Peckham that he cannot expect to live at home as a dependant. If he cannot obtain a fellowship, perhaps he might become a Civil Lawyer[1] or a physician, 'two very gainful professions . . . though the Law be an honourable profession and much honour attends it, yet it is certainly a very laborious one'. The latter part of this advice Charles, perhaps, found discouraging. He did nothing, and in the summer of 1668 Twysden was in negotiation for a fellowship at Trinity Hall, Cambridge, which could be had for £150 down and was worth £40 a year. However, a Trinity Hall fellowship would not provide a subsistence, and it might be better to invest in a share of a Chancery office, which would bring in £80, or even £100 in a good year, but would cost so much that he would not be able to leave Charles

[1] Twysden may have hoped that Charles would emulate his namesake, Twysden's uncle, who after graduating as D.C.L. from Oxford, where he was Principal of New Inn Hall from 1618 to 1621, became a member of Doctors' Commons and afterwards Chancellor of the diocese of Lichfield and Coventry.

the £800 or £1,000 he had intended. With this income and his annuity he could live, unmarried, without being beholden to anyone.

Charles was unenthusiastic. If he cannot get a fellowship he must think of leaving the University, he tells his father; meanwhile, he needs money at once, or he will be dunned. On 17 August Twysden sends by the courier £10, all that he can lay his hands on, but Charles does not bother to acknowledge it, and a week later Twysden writes again, anxiously inquiring whether the money which he himself had been forced to borrow had safely arrived. He still proposes to go ahead with the purchase of a share in the Subpoena office, although it will mean borrowing £700 at 5 per cent. As for Isabella, 'I thank Christ, of a contented spirit loves her brother and to live with him and cares not for marriage in which truly she is the wiser, for she will never live so happily in it as she now doth.' Twysden must indeed have been relieved that his second daughter was prepared to live a spinster, for he would have been hard put to it to raise a marriage portion for her.

Early in 1669 he bought from Sir Walter Vane a fourth part of the Subpoena office for Charles. It cost £800 and was worth £90 to £120 a year. Answering one of Charles's periodical requests for money, on 8 February 1669 Twysden tells him that he cannot send him any for the very good reason that he himself is without ready money, but he will pay over to Charles £80 a year of the profits from the Chancery office, retaining the balance to pay the interest on the money which he had had to borrow for the purchase price. He thanks Charles for sending him two books, and would be glad to have more on the same subject (which is not specified) but sees no point in Charles's staying longer at Oxford. But in the following November Charles was still there, thinking of proceeding Master of Arts—'I do not know what good it can do you, being Master of Arts' writes his father. Charles was insistent, and finally on 6 December Twysden wearily gives in—'I will not contend about it', but to the perennial request for money firmly answers no. He remained in residence at Oxford, took the degree of M.A. in 1670, and soon afterwards embarked on an extended tour which took him as far afield as Turkey, the Holy Land and Egypt, and kept him out of England for four or five years.

By 1668 Twysden was contracting his activities. His Deputy Lieutenancy came to an end, somewhat unfortunately, as recounted in Chapter Nine, and he had for two or three years been handing over more and more of the management of the estate to his son William, to whom it had been transferred under the settlement on his marriage with Frances Crosse in 1665. Prudently he retained a fixed income of £200 charged on the property (Lear's mistake was not for him). He handed over to his son also a lawsuit, just as he had inherited one from his father, but this dispute was only with the Reverend Benjamin Cutter, Vicar of Wateringbury, about tithe. Finally the verdict was given in William's favour at Maidstone Assizes in July 1668, but it cost him 2*s*. a piece for the jurors and a gallon of sack for their morning draught.

Twysden continued to keep careful record of his financial transactions and even of the payment of tithes and quit-rents although he had passed the estate to William, but his handwriting was becoming minute, to be deciphered only by the myopic eye or with the aid of a magnifying glass, and little errors begin to appear—in 1667 he gives the year as 1567, for example. He was becoming forgetful, forgetful of the payments that he received from his son or that he ought to make to Isabella. Relations between the old man and his children were at times a little strained; it would be strange if it were not so. On 27 July 1670 William and his father had a reckoning, which showed that only £200 was due to Twysden; the entry was signed by William, but later Twysden returned to the book of accounts and privately added 'which I do not allow but it must be as he wills, it seems'. Isabella he allowed £20 a year, but in 1670 'she says I owe hys [*sic*] still £5', which he paid. They are the pathetic entries of an old man who is losing his grip on worldly affairs.

Conscientiously he tried to continue the notebook of interesting cases that came to his notice as a Justice of the Peace, but the events at the May 1671 Quarter Sessions were too much for him to record and he abandoned the attempt after writing a few lines. By October he was so much better that he was able to attend Quarter Sessions and give his opinion on the difficult question whether there was authority for making an allowance to an officer conveying rogues to the house of correction. On 3 November he was on his way to a magistrates' meeting at Town Malling when he was taken with a fit of apoplexy, the first that he had ever suffered. With difficulty he was taken into a near-by house, until he was sufficiently recovered that he could be brought home in his own coach, though still suffering frequent convulsive fits. He rallied, and his brother John Twysden wrote to William on 24 November 'if he scape this winter he may perhaps outlive some more'.

He did outlive the winter but it was his last. His illness he took as a warning from Heaven that his end was near, and now his only concern was to set his affairs and his thoughts in order. On 29 February 1672 he paid, and took a receipt for, 40*s.* which he had promised Sir Humphrey Miller in the way of charity to give towards the new market at Tonbridge, but worldly concerns no longer held his attention. He slowly grew weaker, and death came to him gently on 27 June 1672.

Prudent and provident to the last, Twysden had made his will two years before, whilst he was in good health, so that in his last days his mind might not be distracted by such considerations. The sensible, unspectacular testament, devoid of surprises, reflected his character. The estate of course devolved upon William, as the eldest son, whom Twysden besought to keep his allegiance to the King and not to buy church land (his enforced purchase under the Commonwealth of the lands which he held on lease from the Dean and Chapter of Canterbury continued to disturb him long after he had made restoration). Isabella's marriage portion was to be £1,500, and until it became payable she was to receive £50 a year so long as she lived with William; if she went to live with her sister Anne Porter her annual allowance was to be increased to £80. To Isabella and Anne jointly he bequeathed the use of the house in Dean's Yard, Westminster. Roger had already been provided for by the office of Cursitor, so his legacy was only £20.

Charles was bequeathed an annuity of £40, and Twysden expressed the hope that if anything went wrong with his share in the Subpoena office William would allow him £200, the difference between the cost of the office and the £1,000 which his father had intended him to have. Thomasine Warham, who had lived at Roydon Hall as a member of the household for more than thirty years, was left an annuity of £5 and William was charged to allow her to continue to live there with him. There were a few other small bequests, the usual direction for an inexpensive and modest funeral, and one cautionary provision: if there was any dispute about the will, it was to be settled by Judge Twisden, without any going to law.

As a final act of foresight he drafted the wording for his own memorial tablet to be put up in the Twysden chancel of East Peckham Church. He was not a man to leave things to chance or to take unnecessary risks.

PART TWO

CHAPTER EIGHT

The Landowner

OF ALL his responsibilities, as *paterfamilias*, as magistrate and deputy lieutenant, as member of Parliament, as constitutional historian and scholar, Twysden took none more seriously than those which fell to him as the owner of land. It was not in his nature to be careless in any of his doings, but where the conservation of the Twysden property was concerned he felt himself accountable to his conscience, to his successors and to the land itself, a sentiment which was the more acute because of his resolve not to leave the estate to his heir in the burdened condition in which he had received it from his father.

At his death in 1629 Sir William Twysden's debts amounted to £3,970. The largest creditor, for over £3,000, was his brother-in-law Sir Heneage Finch. Money had been borrowed to raise Elizabeth's portion when she married Sir Hugh Cholmley in 1622, but that loan was only of £200 (on which Sir William paid interest at 10 per cent. until it was reduced by statute to 8 per cent.) and most of the money borrowed was used to meet ordinary day-to-day expenses, not for capital investment such as dowries or the purchase of land or office; the £1,000 that the baronetcy cost brought no financial return. Sir William had for years been living beyond his income, more concerned about how much he could spend than how much he could accumulate or how his heir would grapple with the problems of an encumbered estate. When Twysden succeeded as heir he found that the annual payments of interest on outstanding debts came to £271. 12*s*. 0*d*., an amount that was equivalent to a quarter, or thereabouts, of the total income which the estate yielded. A further burden was the £100 a year allowance which Sir William bequeathed to his daughter Anne as a charge on the estate, and finally there was the larger, incalculable, burden of Lady Anne Twysden's expenses.

Twysden's first act as heir was to buy a book (methodically he records the price as 2*s.* 11*d.*) 'for writing things which may hereafter give light to those who shall succeed' in matters of the estate. The successful estate-owner must know what has been done before, what are the precedents, and oral tradition, useful though it sometimes may be, is unreliable. Unfortunately, Sir William—and it is as typical of his *insouciance* as the opposite practice is of Twysden's circumspection—kept no proper record of his affairs. The lack of a record might lead to double-payment: for example, Sir William had sold land in Ivy Lane for which, because it was held *in capite*, a licence was needed from the Crown, but he had failed to record that the licence had been obtained so Twysden was obliged to pay the fee of 30*s.* a second time. He duly records the transaction, and adds a word of advice to his heirs—always make a note in a book of the passing of such things and where they are recorded.

If Twysden had any illusions about that long-established institution, the Court of Wards and Liveries, they did not outlast the proceedings which followed his father's death. On the day after his death Thomas Twisden, on behalf of his brother, the heir, made tender of livery, and three months later a jury of fifteen men was empanelled at Maidstone to certify the death and succession. The costs of these proceedings amounted to £20. 6*s.*, the Escheator and the Feodary having been allowed double fees as was customary and wise 'because they can do men some courtesy in valuing their lands . . . the truth is they are so exorbitant in these courts, their fees are what they will ask'. One officer demanded, in addition to his normal fee, 40*s.* 'for hasting me, though he had done me no courtesy at all, and I was fain to give him to content him 20*s.* with which he was hardly satisfied'. At the conclusion of the business Twysden wrote down, for the benefit of his successors, some rules to be observed in suing out a livery; some are technical, others are counsels of expediency, such as always understate the value of your lands, let no Feodary or Escheator

Isabella Saunder, Lady Twysden

whatever see your evidences, and, above all, 'the best way and the only way to pass as lightly and as well in all things wherein the King hath his share is to bribe his officers'.

The fact that whilst most of the property was in Kent a part lay in another county, namely, the City of London, was an added complication in suing out livery. Obtaining probate of the will was, in comparison, fairly simple and expeditious.

Within Kent the Twysden property lay in three diverse parts of the County. First there was the house at Chelmington in Great Chart, which had been in the family since the early fifteenth century, forming the nucleus of an estate which, by the seventeenth, included also lands in the near-by parishes of Kingsnorth, Shadoxhurst, Woodchurch, Kenardington and Bethersden; secondly there were lands on Romney Marsh and Walland Marsh; thirdly there was Roydon Hall, which came in through the marriage of Twysden's great-grandfather with Elizabeth Roydon, and other land in East Peckham and the neighbouring parishes. In London Twysden owned the substantial house in Redcross Street which he sometimes occupied, as his father had done, and two or three smaller houses.

Twysden found himself the lord of four manors, Albans, Chart and Westburies in East Peckham and Wateringbury, and Cheesehouse in Bethersden. Westburies was a sub-manor of Swanscombe, owned by Sir Anthony Weldon, who in 1633 perturbed Twysden by bringing a lawsuit which reopened an awkward question, that had slept for fifty years, about the nature of his tenure. Weldon seems to have lost; it would not be surprising if Twysden succeeded on a technicality, and that this had something to do with Weldon's subsequent hostility towards him.

His lands were held of numerous manors—East Peckham, East Farleigh, Nettlestead, Cryall, Cranbury, Blackpit, Canon Court, Eastmere, and Hadlow Ward in West Kent; Great Chart, Wye, Tynton, Reculver, Westwell, Aldington, Snave alias Courtawike, Kenardington, and half a dozen others in East Kent. Such a multiplicity of tenures and tenancies made constant vigilance on his part essential if he was to ensure that none of his tenants evaded payments of their just dues, and none of the lords of whom he held land exacted payment of anything beyond their legal and provable rights. It was the sort of vigilance that he delighted to exercise.

When Twysden was permitted to compound in 1649 at one-tenth of the value of his estate, that is at two years' revenue, the fine was set at £1,500 on the basis of an annual income of £750. Twysden argued about an allowance for certain outgoings, such as quit-rents, but he accepted the valuation so obviously the valuers had done him a 'courtesy' by assessing his rents at less than the true figure. Earlier, in 1645, when his fine had been assessed at £3,000, his estate was said to be worth £2,000 a year but this was a vindictive assessment, probably influenced by the County Committee. For the purpose of assessing his twentieth the Committee for the Advance of Money took his estate to be worth £850 annually. The estate books, even though they are Twysden's, are not more exact or less ambiguous than most other seventeenth-century estate accounts, but it seems fairly certain that his rent-roll amounted to at least £1,000 a year, and at certain periods of his life to more than £1,200. The fields and pasture which he kept in hand at East Peckham were adequate to supply his household there and in London; the land on Romney Marsh, however, which was also in hand at Sir William's death, was used mainly for the market rearing of sheep and showed a profit of £250 to £350 each year until Twysden was forced to sell Honeychild Manor to pay the accumulated debts. The Chelmington estate was let. With an income of this order Twysden was not a rich man like his brother-in-law Cholmley, but it was almost exactly the figure which Chamberlayne in 1669 gave as the average income of 700 baronets, namely, £1,200 a year, and above the figure of £880 which Gregory King, twenty years later, estimated to be the average income of baronets.[1] On

[1] Here, for comparison, are a few other average incomes given by Gregory King: temporal lords £2,800; esquires £450; gentlemen £280; merchants and traders by sea £400; eminent clergymen £60; persons in science and liberal arts £60; labouring men £15; common soldiers £14; cottagers and paupers £6½. The average family income he estimated to be £32 a year (cited, *English Historical Documents, 1660–1714*, ed. A. Browning (1953), p. 516).

such a revenue Twysden could expect to keep on the house in London, to maintain and make modest improvements to the Roydon Hall estate, to play his proper part in the government of the county, to marry off his daughters suitably, and to provide comfortably if not generously for his sons. The time of troubles which would make these things difficult he could not foresee; the difficulty of which he was conscious was the burden of debt which he had inherited.

With debts amounting to nearly £4,000, Sir William left legacies totalling £550 to the younger sons, as well as the Walland Marsh lands, Anne's portion was to be £2,000, and £100 a year until she married, and the widow was to have all the money, goods, and stock in East Peckham and London. After anxious thought Twysden decided to embark on the, to him, hateful course of selling part of the property which earlier generations had so carefully aggregated. With every sign of reluctance and with an apologia recorded in the estate book to be read by future generations, he sold Honeychild manor in Romney Marsh to Sir John Sedley of Aylesford[1] for £5,000. Despite his protestations he was secretly glad to be rid of the land. His remaining 110 acres was more than enough for his own household needs, and Honeychild had several defects (which Sedley no doubt in time discovered): the sheep there got the scab, it was breeding, not feeding land, the scots were high, it had to be enclosed with posts and rails and timber was so scarce in the Marsh that fencing was very dear. In any case, with a selling price of £5,000, it looks as though the profits which Honeychild returned whilst the land was in the possession of Twysden and his father hardly exceeded the rent at which it might have been let.

During the forty or more years of Twysden's career as a landowner his rents varied little. Old-established quit-rents, usually fixed centuries before, of course varied not at all but they were a negligible part of his rent-roll. The houses in London if let at all were usually leased for only short periods with a consequent

[1] Not to be confused with his namesake and distant kinsman, Sir John Sedley of St. Clere, who later proved so unneighbourly a member of the County Committee.

variation in income from year to year, but after 1642 they were let together, except the one in Redcross Street, at a rent of £120 a year, which Twysden allowed his wife for the use of herself and the children. Between 1629 and 1669 there seems not to be a single instance in which the rent for land on the East Peckham estate was increased, although two small rents were reduced; in four cases, possibly a few more, the rents of lands in East Kent were increased, once by 25 per cent., but usually by no more than 5 to 10 per cent., and at least one rent was reduced. In far more cases where the history of a property can be traced throughout the forty years the rent was the same in 1669 as it was in 1629 although there might have been two or three changes of tenancy during that time. There is no evidence of rents rising because of a land-hunger.

The one possible exception to this general rule was the pasture at New Romney known as Great Leas. In area about sixty-one acres, it was let in 1631 on a ten-year lease at 25*s.* an acre, and in 1663 the same land appears to have been let at 45*s.* an acre, about eight or ten times as much as arable land might be expected to fetch in the seventeenth century. But everything about Romney Marsh, including the rents, is exceptional and it would be dangerous to assume a general trend on the basis of such abnormal evidence.

Very occasionally Twysden bargains, on a change of tenancy, for a part of the rent to be in kind—cheese, beeswax, a good sow fit for lard, the wool of a russet sheep. All these are East Kent tenancies and perhaps it was the inconvenience of transporting such things as beeswax from Great Chart or Bethersden that caused payments in kind sometimes to fall into arrear. The number of tenants who made serious default was not more than three or four throughout the forty years (the records do not cover the six years of sequestration, so we do not know how many tenants evaded their liabilities between 1643 and 1649), to which must be added the more numerous occasions when Twysden temporarily reduced or respited a rent because 'the times were hard' or 'the poor man broke his leg'. When Robert Fowler took over twenty-eight acres of land at Great Chart for which the previous tenant had paid

£8. 10*s*. 0*d*. a year Twysden agreed that if Fowler should protest upon his faith that he could not make so much the rent should be reduced to £8; as, indeed, it was. On another occasion Twysden sold standing timber to one of his old and trusted tenants for £16 on the understanding that, if the tenant should affirm, when he came to fell it, that it was not worth so much, the price should be abated by £2. Subsequently the tenant asked for the abatement, which Twysden granted him, but later still, finding the timber to be of greater value than he had thought, he repaid the £2. It is an illustration of the trust that existed between the landlord and his tenant; Twysden was a careful landlord, with a care that extended to tenant as well as tenement.

He had a proper appreciation of the value of a good tenant, and recorded encomium as well as bad debts in his estate-books. John Samson, who died at Plurenden in 1633, by industry, God's blessing and just dealing had increased his stock from £60 (with another £20 of his wife's) to £400 in ten years—'just, honest, true, hard yet not griping. . . . I fear I shall not suddenly (perhaps whilst I live) meet for everything with his fellow'. Between Twysden and Thomas Stephens, the tenant of the family house and lands at Chelmington, existed something much more cordial than a business relationship. When Twysden came back to Roydon Hall after his five years' exile in 1647, Stephens made him a present of a bay colt which Twysden affectionately called Bay Stephens, or Chelmington. Let him not be turned out of his tenancy or his rent raised is the tenor of the behest he recorded to guide his successor. In fact Stephens predeceased Twysden, who could find no tenant able or willing to take over all the properties which by then Stephens had accumulated, and it was some time before they could be let off, piecemeal, to new tenants—another opportunity for recording a piece of advice on estate matters for the benefit of his son and heir: for, 'though an honest man he hath undone me with his dying'. George Stone of Hadlow, to whose care Twysden committed his wife and children during his imprisonment, was another tenant and servant who was also a friend—'a true and honest man as I in my trouble had experience . . . by his death leaving me and all good men heartily sorry for him, if at least they knew he died'. True and honest tenants such as these are to be cherished, Twysden advises, and it is bad to break, for trivial reasons, with old and good tenants.

There is much advice offered, too, on prudent estate management, especially the management of woods. Here are a few items: oak should be planted at five bushels of acorns to the acre; timber should not be felled when the wind is in the east, for that causes it to be worm-eaten; it is not good husbandry to let wood stand unfelled too long, since with care nearly as much timber can be had from an acre at sixteen years as at twenty-five ('because so many lewd knaves will steal ladders, poles and such like'); let every owner keep in mind the dictum of Lord Burleigh, the Treasurer, that no man should cut down an oak of timber but he should sit in council before he did it to consider of its fitness; for every ten trees that are felled spare twenty; have a care to see that no tenant fells or damages timber contrary to his bargain; there is not a finer wood than the chequer, or cervise, tree, though maple is good for trenchers; finally, let oak, chestnut or beech, not coppice trees, be planted in a park for the mast will feed the deer and fallow deer will not harm the trees, although red deer will.

Of all his possessions, Twysden was especially proud of his woods. 'My son,' he writes, ' . . . there is not a more honorable thing than wood and timber in an estate and especially about your house and seat, so it is of great profit if well preserved. . . . It must be that you may take down 15 or 20 good oaks every year or such a house as this will fall for want of repair. . . . There is few men's estates in Kent whose woods lie better about their house than mine or whose wood is better, for it lives for the most on a good soil and fit for wood, not far from my house for carriage, and much of it is ash and willow, with a good quantity oak.' In spite of the mismanagement of the woods through ignorance or ill-will by the agents of the County Committee during his sequestration, he was selling timber in 1663 and again in 1668–9 to the Navy Commissioners at Chatham, 'the like of which' their agent reported 'is not to be found in any other part of the country'. The negotiations over price were lengthy, and the figure which Twysden finally agreed to accept was criticized by the Commissioners, who feared the Surveyor had given too much. The desperate state of government credit put the Commissioners in a weak position to bargain, and Twysden wisely insisted that he should have £620 in hand, as well as, for the balance, the personal bonds of the Commissioners' agents, not any official or royal bond which might afterwards be dishonoured.

Admirably provided though the estate was with timber, Twysden found when he took it over that there was inadequate meadow for winter-keep for cattle, and that the arable land was also insufficient. He therefore put under the plough two pieces of land that his father had recently added to the park, and for meadow he acquired in 1640 Downs Mead and Dorny Mead, in Yalding, of Robert Kenward. Twysden had other dealings with Kenward, and it was not until the conclusion of a long-drawn-out suit in 1656 that his ownership was finally established.

This protracted lawsuit came about because Kenward agreed that he would sell all of his lands and houses in Kent to Twysden, and that the conveyance should be by way of fine, in which his wife should join. However, the lady was not to be bullied or cajoled, pretending to be too ill to be troubled with such matters, and even after her husband was in his grave she remained obdurate, perhaps encouraged in that attitude by her second husband. It required years of patient litigation, and the aid of Chancery as well as of the Common Law Courts, to persuade her that she was well enough to complete the bargain.

During his first ten years as owner of the estate Twysden made several other purchases; at Great Chart two little holdings, Grayler's Corner and Randolph's Hill, and Curlings and Grinsteds in the adjacent parish of Kingsnorth, but it was in East Peckham that he was principally concerned to buy land that rounded off the Roydon Hall estate. His largest purchases, Newark and Longshots, lay on the west side of the Mereworth—Hale Street road, in Whetenhall's part of the parish. Economically, Longshots proved a poor bargain; it cost nearly £600 and Twysden could never let it for more than £24 a year. He bought it only 'for the convenient lying of it to my other grounds and the timber upon it'. The other additions to the estate were of less importance; a tenement at Snoll Hatch, a few small houses in Hadlow, two of which soon after were burnt down, and houses and orchards at Hale Street known as Feppes alias Mellars, Messengers and Hamfield. Later, in 1650, he took a release from his brother Francis of Blackpits at East Peckham for £140, in 1667 he purchased two more small parcels there called Middlefield Land and Annett Land for £66, and, in the last year of his life, he bought a 21-acre field for £240. Except possibly for Longshots his purchasing was cautious and prudent.

Part of the property which Twysden acquired from Kenward (and which incidentally made him tenant to Augustine Skinner, lord of the manor of Tutsham and Knight of the Shire) was purchased as an investment for Roger, soon after his birth. Twysden held the land for some twenty years and then selling it at a profit to his brother Thomas was able to provide for Roger by buying him the place in the Cursitor's office.

His only other purchase of importance Twysden made under duress. Several of the fields in Great Chart parish, lying between Chelmington and the church, were held on lease from the Dean and Chapter of Canterbury Cathedral. The practice of the Chapter was to grant a lease for a term of seven years, with a fine for its renewal which for the Chelmington lands was £31. One of Twysden's first acts after succeeding his father was to attempt to get a renewal for three lives, but he had to be content with renewal for seven years. And he could afford to be content; the rent which he paid the Dean and Chapter was £6. 10*s.* 8*d.* and the rents at which he sub-let the fields came to £38. When Parliament took over cathedral lands Twysden had no way of keeping possession of the fields except by buying the freehold. He was in a dilemma. He desperately wanted to keep the land because it formed part of the Chelmington property as it came to him and as he wanted to pass it on, as well as offering the only way of riding to church; on the other hand, for Parliament thus to deprive a religious foundation of its property was not only unlawful and inequitable but also verging on sacrilege, smacking too much of Henry VIII's expropriation of monastic lands, an action which Twysden, in common with many of his fellow Protestants, deplored. He decided to buy the land, having it conveyed into the names of Francis Twysden, Philip Bartholomew, and John Smallman, and in his estate-book in 1650 he entered an instruction to his heir: 'If ever the Church of Canterbury come to be restored, which God grant, I hope and desire my heir, with all willingness, return what was with violence by the horrid injustice of the Parliament torn from them lest it been indeed a canker to all the rest, and in the meantime I desire he will with the revenue of it at least and so much as was annually paid the Church, and somewhat more as ten pounds a year or thereabouts, remember some poor orthodoxal ministers or scholars.' Presumably Twysden observed his own behest but, if so, there was good reason why he kept no record of payments made by him for purposes which would certainly be regarded as additional evidence that he was a neuter, if not a malignant.

It was with relief that, after the Restoration, Twysden was able to restore the Great Chart property to the Dean and Chapter, but this did not inhibit him from bargaining toughly about the renewal of the lease in 1661-2—indeed his friend William Somner, the Chapter agent, warned him that his 'free' letter had so angered them that he would be well advised to avoid future strife, advice which he accepted. He renewed the lease again in 1669, reminding himself in his estate-book that he must do so again in 1676: an optimistic memorandum for a man then in his seventy-third year.

In addition to acquiring thus several small and a few fairly large pieces of land Twysden made some other minor improvements to the estate. In 1633-4 he rebuilt Buxford and Brest Mills at a cost of more than £200; according to Philipott he obtained from Charles a charter of free warren 'to reduce a certain proportion of ground into a park, which is that the house is surrounded with at present'[1] and the estate accounts

[1] T. Philipott, *Villare Cantianum* (2nd edn. 1776), p. 267.

show considerable expenditure on pale fencing; he levelled a plot of land to form a bowling-green; and he reconstructed the park pond and fish-stew. A year later he restocked the pond, Thomas Barton sending him 52 fine carp 'which were brought between water-grass often washed in a flasket, but 23 of them died'. In 1654 he purchased a bell to hang on top of the house for £4. 0*s*. 6*d*., and the following year entered into an agreement for making and burning a clamp of bricks in Dairyfield; it was expected that the earth there would make 100,000 very good crimson bricks. This suggests building operations on a large scale but unfortunately there is no record of what the bricks were used for, and no tangible evidence of Twysden's work has survived the extensive reconstruction of Roydon Hall in the nineteenth century.

One of the estate-books he devoted to a record of tithes, quit-rents, rates, and customary services, such as heriot. The amounts involved might be small, sometimes not more than a few pence, but they were all meticulously recorded lest, for want of evidence, more might be paid out or less received than was due. As an orthodox and conservative member of the Church of England, he accepts tithe as a legitimate and proper charge, no more wishing to deprive the Vicar of his just due than unjustly to burden his own estate by paying more than the exact legal sum. He was prepared to give Worrall, the Vicar of East Peckham, a gratuity of 40*s*., or some cordwood, because he was poor, provided that the Vicar solemnly promised not to make any record of it; not that Twysden objected to having his charities chronicled for the benefit of future generations, but he was insistent that there should be no record which could be cited against him as a precedent. In 1639 a dispute between Worrall and Twysden about tithes in East Peckham was referred to four Commissioners, who decided in Twysden's favour. Nevertheless, he paid all the costs, including the dinner for all the Commissioners and witnesses, 'for I would not let him pay for anything, though I never told him so'. To one of Twysden's temperament it was more important to spend £5. 19*s*. 0*d*. on establishing the principle than to pay a shilling or two a year in excess of the Vicar's just due of 30*s*.

Twysden acquired much recondite learning on the abstruse matter of tithes. It involved the kind of inquiry in which he delighted, the perusal of old records, the noting down of statements by old inhabitants, the establishing of old customs. He raised the question whether tithe was payable on land which had once belonged to a religious house, and although he agreed to go on making payment without prejudice, to get up the argument must have gratified his appetite as an historian. More important was the question of the northern limit of the Weald, within which woodland was not titheable. Lambarde, as 'a young novice and late adopted denizen', would not attempt to define its limits; 'a man may more reasonably maintain, that there is no Weald at all, than certainly pronounce either where it beginneth or maketh an end'. Nevertheless that there was a Weald, that it was to be distinguished from the Upland, and that men were conscious of the distinction was undoubted; amongst Twysden's papers is a note that about 1595 there was 'a football playing' and about 1610 'a cricketting' between the Weald and the Upland, and men do not begin to indulge in competitive sports in this way until they are aware of their differences.

It was all very well for a mere topographical writer such as Lambarde to ride off on a humorous conceit, but the landowner who was faced with the serious problem of either paying a demand for which there might be no justification in law, or withholding a payment which might be legally due, could not leave the matter there. In general Kentishmen took one of two positions: either that the Weald was bounded on its north side by the 'white hills', that is the North Downs, or that the 'red hills', the range running from Linton through Sutton Valence to Boughton Malherbe, marked its northern extremity. The first definition would bring in East Peckham and Wateringbury, the second would exclude them. The test case was Ovens, or Offams, Wood in Wateringbury. Twysden's father had refused to pay tithe when he felled the wood; his mother, moved by compassion for the Vicar's poverty, gave him a 22 shilling piece of gold as a gratuity—such charity was always dangerous because it might be construed as an admission of liability; finally in 1668 the dispute grew into an action at Maidstone Assizes between William Twysden, to whom Twysden had passed the estate, and Benjamin Cutter, the Vicar. Sir William Scroggs, who ten years afterwards became Lord Chief Justice of England,[1] was counsel for Twysden. He was warned by Twysden of the nature of the testimony that would be given, and advised particularly not to rely on Symonds' map—'it is certainly a most false and defective map'. The verdict, as already noted in Chapter Seven, was given in favour of William Twysden and for eighty years successive Vicars of Wateringbury let the matter rest. Then, in 1744, a Vicar more certain of the law or more willing to spend money on legal proceedings, brought another suit, recovered a verdict, and tithes for himself and his successors. The amount involved averaged perhaps a shilling a year, but it was the question of principle that mattered.

Romney Marsh, that fifth quarter of the world with its strange customs, almost inevitably had peculiar rules about tithe. This was another problem to which Twysden devoted himself *con amore* and many of his recondite notes on the subject are still extant. They were extensively borrowed, as his reputation for his learning about tithes spread through the county, and many times his advice was sought in some grave dispute between tithe-owner and tithe-payer. Profound learning about tithes was one of the several accomplishments which Twysden had in common with his friend Sir Henry Spelman.

But the customary payments and services which especially engaged Twysden's attention were those incident to manorial tenures. As lord of the manors of Albans, Chart, Westburies, and Cheesehouse he was vigilant to see that whenever one of his tenants died and the lord became entitled to a heriot in the

[1] Alleged, by Dugdale, to be the son 'of a one-eyed butcher, near Smithfield Bars, and his mother a big fat woman with a red face like an ale-wife'. According to Foss 'The last four of the chief justices of the King's Bench in the reign of Charles II—Scroggs, Pemberton, Saunders, and Jeffreys—may be cited as remarkable proofs of the general profligacy of the period, each having been elevated to his high position notwithstanding the notorious looseness of his early life. The obloquy which is attached to the name of Scroggs,' etc. (*The Judges of England* (1870), p. 597). He was an authority on manorial practice, and doubtless the best man for Twysden's action.

form of his best beast, there was no overlooking or evasion of the obligation for that might lead not only to immediate loss but also be evidence against the existence of the custom on all future occasions. There was nothing servile about the liability for heriot; when Francis, Earl of Westmorland, died in 1629 his heir gave Twysden satisfaction for three heriots, due to the manors of Albans, Chart, and Westburies. Twysden demanded heriot of the heir of his 'cousin' Thomas Whetenhall[1] for land in the manors of Albans and Chart (it came to 4*s.* 2*d.*), only four months after Whetenhall had demanded heriot, on Sir William Twysden's death in 1629, for land held of the manor of Eastmere. The seizure of the tenant's best beast was almost always a symbolical act, the lord of the manor accepting a money payment of an amount fixed by custom in lieu of the animal. A tenant who voluntarily came to Twysden to tender his heriot could often hope to get off lightly or, if he were poor, have his pig (for that was the best beast, perhaps the only beast of a small tenant) returned to him unconditionally. Occasionally there were defaulters, like Thomas Martin, tenant at 6*s.* a year of Messengers Croft who, turning from anabaptist to papist, made over all his effects to his son for fear of the law, and so, on his death in 1658, cheated Twysden of the heriot that should have been due.

As tenant he took the same strict view of heriot. He was willing to pay anything that was, and could be proved to be, legally due, but he was not prepared to make any payment, however small, and whoever the lord of the manor, unless there was precedent for it. He never took the view that the amount involved was too small to dispute. Twysden learned his lesson on his father's death. The King's bailiff seized the two best coach-horses as heriot for lands held of the manors of East Peckham and East Farleigh which belonged to the Crown, and Twysden compounded for £4, plus £1 for the bailiff, and a 3*s.* courtesy to his deputy. Later he found that this was more than need have been paid by custom; if his

[1] Whetenhall, a Roman Catholic, was interred privately without the minister, as appears from a marginal note in Twysden's own hand in the register of burials.

father had kept a note of these things, he implies, such overpayment could be avoided. In fact it was ten years before the Crown could produce a parchment by way of evidence to satisfy Twysden and before he made the final payment. A disagreement with 'cousin' Whetenhall whether heriot was payable on land held of the manor of Eastmere was settled 'to preserve love and neighbourhood' by calling in Sir Robert Honywood of Charing, who promised, on the word of a gentleman, to arbitrate indifferently between them. He awarded that, on this occasion, Whetenhall should keep the young mare which he had seized but that 'Sir Roger Twysden' should not be liable for heriot in future; 'and his heirs' was subsequently inserted after 'Twysden' and it is not hard to guess on whose insistence the words were added.

Almost immediately after the death of his father, Twysden was collecting evidence that High Leas and Low Leas which he held of the manor of Cryalls in Brenchley, were not heriotable. When the issue came before the Court Baron in 1632 he assisted the jury to give their verdict to that effect, which the Steward refused to accept, trying to persuade them to alter it by producing two unauthenticated little pieces of paper, and accused Twysden of having argued the jury into a view unfavourable to the lord of the manor. Twysden was obliged to admit that he had written the jury's finding himself ('because I was the best scribe, I think, for I would one of them should have done it, who refused') but he claimed that he wrote only at the behest of the others. The Steward, still refusing to accept the verdict, threatened to keep them all day, but finally Twysden, not wishing to appear contentious, as he says, proposed as a compromise that they should have further time to think about it. This further consideration seems to have taken about twenty-one years. In 1653 Twysden was summoned to appear at the Court Baron but, given only a day's notice, he refused to go. On 5 September 1654 he was summoned to a Court to be held on 20 October, but protested that he could not go 'in the dead of winter', the ways being hardly passable (it is about seven or eight miles)—he would have been prepared to go in the summer. Nevertheless, at the urgent request of the other tenants, he went. The homage, or jury, comprised five tenants, including Twysden, and he was able to persuade them as he had done in 1632 that there was no heriot custom, notwithstanding two rolls of 18 Elizabeth and 16 James to which he objected on many grounds. On this occasion the Steward accepted the verdict and Twysden had won his little battle against a threatened encroachment on the tenants' rights.

In similar disputes with the lords of other manors, Fromans and Cawston, who claimed heriot, by standing firm Twysden was able to resist their demands. For the benefit of his heirs he not only recorded these successes but also added, by way of advice, 'certain rules for those fear to have heriots seized at the death of any man':

1. If the cattle are kept in a stable or other building the bailiff cannot seize them.
2. It is not enough for the lord to prove that the custom of heriot obtains in the manor; he must prove that the custom applies to the very lands that are in question, and if tenants generally knew this the negligent keeping of court rolls would cause many lords to lose their heriots (but, since Twysdens are lords, as well as tenants, let this knowledge be kept secret).
3. Heriot is not payable on lands held for life.

In certain manors personal service as an officer of the Court Baron was required of the tenants. It was an obligation to be avoided, if possible. Sir William Twysden, at the time of his death, was serving for a year as Great Officer (or rent collector) of the manor of Aldington, an office in which Twysden succeeded him. He found it troublesome to collect the amounts said to be due; the records were badly kept, and some of the alleged debtors who had left were not certainly known ever to have had lands in the manor. He had to make good the defaults out of his own pocket, and apart from the inconvenience of having to serve the office it cost him £10.

More than twenty-five years later, in 1656, Twysden found, arriving late at a meeting of the Court of Aldington Manor, that the office of Collector for the Thirty-two Dens had been laid upon him. He protested, and demanded to know precisely the land in respect of which he was required to serve the office. Such a demand showed the precarious nature of the whole machinery of the court; the Steward and the homage were obliged to admit that they could not answer the question, and volunteered that if every tenant made the same demand half of them would escape. However, they admitted that unless they could specify which of the lands that Twysden held of the manor was so burdened he must go quit of the office. Each year for the next seven years the Court tried to force the unwanted office upon him but he held stiffly to his position. In 1662 Sir Edward Sydenham, the lord of the manor, told Twysden that the other tenants were now taking the same line so that he was losing his rents. So far as Twysden was concerned the affair came to an end the following year when, under protest, he paid 40*s*. towards the collection of the rents by another tenant, but he had won his point. It was another victory for the strict rule of law.

In another dispute the issue was whether the lord of the manor in the Weald was entitled to waste. The bailiff of the King's manor of East Farleigh told Twysden in 1635 that he proposed to fell Burrs Oak at Burrs Farm as he needed the timber to make a pound for the lordship. Twysden, who held Burrs Farm of the manor, claimed the oak as his with sufficient plausibility that the bailiff agreed to let it stand for the present, and meeting him in the Star Inn yard at Maidstone soon afterwards Twysden returned to the subject and was able to convince him of the custom that in the Weald the lord of the manor does not have waste; a rather bizarre venue, it may seem, for settling an important and difficult issue concerning the custom of the country, but it was not the first, nor the last, time that Kentish gentlemen would transact their business there.

Whenever there was a demand for a payment not clearly justified by custom, precedent, or statute, Twysden was moved to protest, no matter how small the sum. In 1633 there was a 15*s*. cess to Wateringbury Church—'an excessive great cess for us that are foreigners to pay who in reason ought to pay

Sr Anty, Welden.
From an Original Drawing in the
Collection of the Right Honble Lord
CARDIFF.
Pubd April 1st 1779. by Richd Godfrey No 120 Long Acre.

Sir Anthony Weldon

for no more than outside of the church'. He paid church and poor rates of 5*s.* 0*d.* on Dorny Mead in Yalding but had the amount reduced to 4*s.* 6*d.* because the area was, he alleged, only eighteen, not twenty acres. He resisted payment towards the repair of the highways in the parish of St. Giles-without-Cripplegate, because he paid towards them in the country; but the answer which 'satisfied them well' was that 'my father had never paid here'. In 1634 he resisted a 3*s.* demand by the Common Council for repairing the water course at Moorgate but, in the end, sinking his principles, paid because the amount was small and this was the last instalment.

In general the outgoings, whether they were quit-rents, tithes, church rate, poor rate, or taxes, were small and no serious burden (at least in twentieth-century terms) upon the estate. This was not true of certain years during the Commonwealth when the Parliamentary monthly assessment imposed a much heavier burden than ship-money had ever threatened, yet met with no general and overt opposition comparable to that which greeted Charles's attempts to raise money in an extraordinary way. Twysden records that in 1652–3, the outgoings for Dorny Mead at £5. 12*s.* 9*d.* (Parliamentary taxes £3. 12*s.* 0*d.*, poor rate 12*s.* 6*d.*, church rate 6*s.* 3*d.*, quit-rents 2*s.*, and tithe £1) amounted to almost one-third of the annual value of £18, but this was exceptional. In normal times his outgoings were probably no more than 6*d.* or 9*d.* in the pound of his income.

Twysden was as conscious and as certain as Hobbes or Locke of the rights of property. Long-standing obligations upon his estate he honoured; innovated impositions he hated and resisted. Ship-money or the taxes ordained by the Long Parliament were not simply an aspect of the wrongful exercise of power in the course of a political conflict; they were an attack upon all that men like Twysden believed to be their natural rights. 'The common sort of people,' he once wrote, 'are sensible of no loss of liberty so much as that which has joined with it a parting from money'. At whatever inconvenience to himself or embarrassment to his friends, he always stood foursquare upon his rights and liberties, not least where they concerned property.

CHAPTER NINE

The Public Man

As a young man of twenty-eight Twysden sat in Charles's first Parliament as burgess for Winchelsea. It opened on 18 June 1625 in inauspicious circumstances, for an extraordinarily rainy season was followed by an outbreak of plague of such exceptional virulence that after a few weeks it was thought advisable to transfer the Parliament to Oxford. Its business matched the circumstances in which it met: members were soon at odds amongst themselves over religious matters, the publication of Richard Montague's *A New Gag for an Old Goose*, in which the Synod of Dort was handled disrespectfully, being so obnoxious to the Puritan members that the author was summoned before the House of Commons and committed to custody, proceedings which the King felt it necessary to revoke. This was scarcely calculated to improve relations between King and Parliament which were already strained because of differences over foreign policy. The King and Buckingham were for war with Spain, but the Commons would vote only two subsidies, a quite inadequate amount for the prosecution of a land war, and moreover they proposed to vote tonnage and poundage, which since the reign of Edward IV had usually been granted to the King for life, for one year only. Because the Lords refused to concur the grant fell through altogether. It was at this point that Parliament was adjourned for three weeks and transferred to Oxford. Before it met again the news leaked out that Buckingham had promised Richelieu the loan of ships for use against the Huguenots of La Rochelle and that Charles's marriage treaty contained a secret undertaking that the penal laws against recusants should not be put into operation. Parliament, exasperated against Buckingham, was permitted twelve days of highly critical debate before it was dissolved.

Charles might be as incensed with his faithful Commons as they were with his favourite Buckingham, but his need for money overcame his resentment and the second Parliament of the new reign was summoned to meet on 6 February 1626. Twysden again represented the Ancient Town of Winchelsea. In the Commons the lead was quickly taken by that great orator Sir John Eliot who, with Sir Dudley Digges, managed on the Commons' behalf the impeachment of the Duke of Buckingham before the Lords, nominally for a variety of crimes but really for his bungling of the winter expedition to Cadiz. Twysden was by no means sure that this was not an encroachment on the true prerogative of the Crown. Where Twysden was doubtful Charles was certain, and he dissolved Parliament after four months, with the question of money still unsettled.

The next Parliament lasted longer, from March 1628 until March 1629, but Twysden was not a member of it, Winchelsea being represented by his father, Sir William Twysden. Thereafter, for eleven long years there was no opportunity for Knights of the Shire and burgesses to serve their communities in Parliament. With no Parliamentary duties to distract them, the gentry devoted themselves to governing their parishes and their counties. It was an activity much to Twysden's taste, in which he displayed a zeal and a competence that earned him the approbation of his fellows.

The result was that when, about Michaelmas, 1639, there began to be fresh talk of a Parliament and names were discussed in the county, Twysden's was one which came to men's minds. He was approached, but fearing the rebuff of a defeat or, in the alternative, the expense if he were elected, he gave a discouraging response. Some weeks later he met his neighbour and cousin, Sir Henry Vane, the Treasurer of His Majesty's household, who was making a visit to his house at Fairlawne, and learned that the Treasurer was minded to serve as Knight of the Shire for Kent in the expected Parliament, which was now the subject of talk wherever public men congregated.

There were various motives that might prompt men to stand for election to the new Parliament. Some were personal as, for example, Sir George Sondes, who, writing to Sir Thomas Walsingham, said, 'I am in a manner necessitated to it' [for those of us who have been Deputy Lieutenants] 'had need be present to justify ourselves the best we can when our actions are questioned as undoubtedly they will.[1] . . . Mr. Treasurer desires to be the other whom I conceive to be very deserving of it.' Twysden's interest in a Parliament was less personal, more general. There were numerous grievances to which he thought it needful for Parliament to attend. Laud's attempt to introduce order into the Church of England was work with which he could sympathize, not for doctrinal reasons (doctrinal disputation he regarded as proper to clerics, not to laymen) but because his was the sort of mind to which order was a *summum bonum*. However, the use of the Court of High Commission, the activities of the Star Chamber, and above all the ship-money demands, perturbed him in their threatened—and actual—infringements of the liberties of the subject. Such doubts and perplexities Twysden discussed with the Treasurer, who gave him the comforting assurance that those liberties should in no wise be diminished. So he promised to support and do his best to promote Vane's candidature, receiving in return the promise of a burgess's place which Vane, as a Privy Councillor, would have in his patronage. In the meantime there were many who were still canvassing the election of Twysden himself as Knight of the Shire. Writing on 20 December 1639 Sir Edward Dering assures him of strong support in East Kent, and continues 'You are better beloved than your modesty will suffer you to believe. If you be not fettered beyond all freedom, appear for yourself. If you love Mr. Treasurer persuade his dissistence. . . . If you be not sure of a burgess place you shall be guilty of a great fault not to own the country which seeks after you. If you desire to speak with me I shall come home on Christmas eve, and on Saturday following will attend you at Peckham.'

Twysden, replying on 24 December, confesses that he is engaged to the Treasurer but he has no burgess place in view—

[1] Sondes served the office of High Sheriff in 1636–7.

no doubt an accurate, if slightly disingenuous statement. The letter shows the friendship which still existed at this time between the two men and their common antiquarian interests: 'Where you speak of coming over hither (though with an if) on Saturday, I entreat you, if it please you, to do me that favour; or rather, because if it be on Saturday I fear you will be going on Monday, defer your journey till Monday, and stay to go on Saturday. We shall spend the time in reading, walking or somewhat else that will beguile it. . . . If you take so much pains as to visit your affectionate cousin, pray bring your history of William Thorne, and I will show you an old manuscript, some of the same abbey's [St. Augustine's] containing many pretty miscellaneas, writ about Edward III his time, out of which perhaps Thorne took some part of his history.'

When a few weeks later Twysden began more generally to solicit the support of the county on behalf of Vane, he found opposition to one who, as a courtier and close to the King in his counsels, must bear part of the blame for the universally hated ship-money. The only hope seemed to be to persuade all the other prospective candidates save one, Norton Knatchbull of Mersham-le-Hatch, to stand down in favour of Vane. Sir George Sondes and Sir Thomas Walsingham agreed to do so, although as late as the 6 March Sondes was writing to Sir Robert Darell reminding him of his promised assistance and 'confident that these rumours of my sitting down have not at all shaken you'. When Twysden spoke to Dering again both in the county and in London, Dering tried to persuade Twysden himself to stand, and finding he could not prevail upon him to do so, he began to hedge—he thought he might be regarded as committed to Walsingham (though he agreed Vane to be the fitter man), he did not want to give an answer until he had spoken at the Assizes to some other gentleman to whom he might possibly have entered into an engagement, and so on.

Vane requested Twysden to discover, at the winter Assizes, how the wind was blowing. He found the situation favourable and, in spite of some coolness on Dering's part, it seemed that Vane would be returned without opposition. Thus matters stood at the end of the first day of the Assizes, but overnight Dering spoke with Mr. George Strode of Westerham and Isaac Bargrave, the Dean of Canterbury, and next day, to the general astonishment, according to Twysden, Dering announced that he himself would stand. At once Vane withdrew, but urged Twysden to oppose Dering. Twysden's own account of the affair (*ex parte*, of course) records that he so far accepted the Treasurer's advice that he let his friends know that if he were called he would serve his county, that he did no canvassing, but that Dering on the other hand rode up and down, soliciting everyone.

Certainly Dering campaigned in a businesslike way, writing round to his friends for reports on their canvassing on his behalf. Lady Dering also sent letters to a number of acquaintances, soliciting their voices for Sir Edward. Sir John Sedley, of St. Clere, wrote Dering a characteristically malicious letter on 7 March denouncing Twysden, whom Vane had asked him to support, and retailing the gossip that Twysden 'hath endeavoured as far as may be to poison the good opinion the county hath of you, by possessing them how diligent and eager a servant you were for the court in the knighting moneys'. Evidently these attempts to sow discord between the two kinsmen came to Twysden's notice, for on 9 March he wrote to Dering, warning him of the displeasure he was likely to incur 'above', and doing his best to scotch the rumour that he had taxed Dering with Puritanism. Like everything that Twysden wrote it is modest and reasonable in tone, in marked contrast with Sedley's philippic:

'I am and always have been so desirous to do you service that I cannot but be sorry you show yourself at a time in which I cannot further your success. The truth is I took it very unkindly to see Sir Edward Dering from whom I hoped (and had good reason to do so) assistance, in the cause of a kinsman almost as near him as me, should be erected only to make a stop in the business, and was as sorry to see him for such a toy contract so potent enemies (which I was assured would follow) as for any other cause in it. But for that other imputation—Will you be for Sir Edward Dering? he is none of our Church—I will not go about to excuse it, much less defend it; if you have any opinion not of my wit, but that I have common sense, believe not I was nor am so foolish, or so little understanding of the word *Church* to think you of a differing one from me; neither upon summoning whatever has passed me, can I imagine on what it should arise, unless on the affirming of one you would never go up to the rails to receive the communion (which I do and justify the doing of) I did once say there was some other cause in you for refusing to do so, for all the world knew you were no Puritan: which I am confident you will not take ill, that some time have made a doubt to me whether a Puritan or a papist were nearer Heaven. Sir, I fear you will see they did not the least love you that at the Assizes wished you not then to begin. How it is taken above Mr. Dean has writ unto you. I wish it could lie in me to show (what just cause of exceptions so ever I have had) that I cannot be other than your kinsman that truly loves you, Roger Twysden.'[1]

When the poll was taken it was Twysden and Norton Knatchbull who were elected. The prospect of a Parliament was infinitely pleasing to them and their contemporaries. Here, at last, was a return to the old ways, at last harmony was to prevail again between a King careful for his people and subjects determined to render unto him all that loyalty and fealty demanded. Ship-money still rankled. As Theophilus Higgens of Hunton, one of Twysden's supporters, wrote to him on 30 March 1640, most men in the county conceded that in case of necessity the King might impose it, and he alone was the proper judge of the necessity. But there were four difficulties that troubled the Kentish freeholders: a necessity might be pretended against the accepted custom of the Kingdom, so it would be good if King and Parliament could agree upon a definition of necessity; money collected on the pretence of a

[1] Dering wrote his own account of the proceedings leading up to the election, a 68-page MS. which Sir Thomas Phillipps bought at the Dering Sale in June 1858. It became Phillipps MS. 16083, but it is not at the present time accessible.

necessity might be used for another purpose—if not needed for the announced purpose it should be used to abate the subsidies; ship-money might be increased at the King's pleasure until it became an insupportable burden; and lastly the farmers complained bitterly of inequalities in the imposition of the charge. These are the grievances for which Higgens looks to Parliament for a remedy, yet hopes 'you and all the other worshipful discreet gentlemen will sweeten all things to your power and not provoke His Majesty, that by fair treaty and entreaty things may be reduced to a good and peaceable conclusion. This is to be called The Happy or The Unhappy Parliament. . . .'

It was known as neither, but as the Short Parliament. Seldom can men's high hopes have been so soon disappointed. Parliament met on 13 April, quickly turned to a discussion of the subjects' grievances before considering the King's needs, and since it failed to deal with the only matter for which Charles had convened it, the voting of supplies, it was dissolved on 5 May, barely more than three weeks after it had so optimistically assembled.

Twysden returned home bitterly disappointed, as were all men of moderate views. He had felt certain that once the dialogue between King, Lords and Commons had begun custom and reason would prevail, that the calling together of Parliament was the way, indeed the only way, whereby the country could be extricated from the constitutional morass in which it was floundering. Now it was as though a life-line had been flung to a drowning man, only to be snatched away when it was almost in his grasp.

It was not long before Charles's need for money to purchase a Scottish peace compelled him to summon another Parliament in November 1640. Twysden characteristically observed the Kentish convention that a gentleman did not serve as Knight of the Shire in consecutive Parliaments[1] and was not a candidate although he was well supported, especially in the Weald, where he was 'voiced much' as John Player wrote to Sir

[1] It was a recent convention, not older than the sixth Parliament of Elizabeth.

Edward Dering. Dering himself stood again and again Twysden found himself taking the ungrateful decision that he could not support his kinsman, having committed himself elsewhere. On 24 October he wrote to Dering: 'I told you at Maidstone what barred me of running freely to serve you, neither is that stop taken off . . . you are, I hope, assured I wish Sir Edward Dering well, though I cannot give him assurance my own vote will be for him to whom I shall be ever a most affectionate friend and kinsman.'

Twysden does not say to whom he was bound (it was not to Sir John Culpepper; probably it was to Richard Browne) and the only evidence, if such it be, that he actively opposed Dering is another splenetic letter of 21 October from Sedley to Dering. Sedley warns Dering of plots against him, especially 'the malevolence of Sir Roger Twysden who turns all the teeth he hath though but few and those ill upon you by setting up old Browne in opposition when his good service the last Parliament had destroyed his own hopes. Yet his malice, or extreme officiousness to Mr. Treasurer Vane or both have so transported him that he solicits many by letters to Browne, with a servile importunity. . . .' He goes on to warn Dering of Norton Knatchbull's untrustworthiness, of the plots of the Barnham faction, and finally 'You must have a care also of [the] sheriff: you see how grossly he abused us all the last time by his partiality and you shall find him the same still, his converse being wholly with clowns and brutes.'[1] To one who wrote with such coarseness Twysden's niceness of style may well have seemed officious and servile. No doubt the dispute over the church pew rankled with Sedley, but perhaps even more than this it was a difference of temperament that separated the two men and accounted for the bitterness which Sedley evinced both now and, later, as a member of the County Committee.

However, in spite of Twysden's efforts to secure the return of Browne, on this occasion Dering was elected, with Sir John Culpepper, although later both were excluded and replaced by Augustine Skinner and John Boys. In 1641 Browne became

[1] David Polhill, esquire, was the Sheriff. He lived at Otford; perhaps it was his misfortune to have Sedley as a near neighbour.

the second member for New Romney, Norton Knatchbull being the other, and his attempts a few years later to further Twysden's cause in Parliament sprang from motives of gratitude for support in the election of 1640 as well as from ties of kinship.

Two elections in a year, and vigorously contested ones at that, were more than the Shire House at Penenden Heath could stand after its eleven years of neglect. Electors and their friends broke down the walls in order to put in their votes. The following spring the building had to be expensively repaired and the question arose whether it should be done by the Sheriff, with an allowance in his account to the Exchequer, or from the county stock—was it, in modern terminology, a central or a local charge? It was tempting to argue that it was the Sheriff's duty, but when precedents were quoted to show that previously the Shire House had been repaired at the expense of the county Twysden and his fellow magistrates had no hesitation in ordering that the cost should be met from the county stock.

Twenty years elapsed before the Shire House had to withstand the hurly-burly of another election or there was any question of Twysden serving again as Knight of the Shire. The Kentish members of the Convention Parliament of April 1660 were Sir John Tufton of The Mote and Sir Edward Dering (son of the former member). Encouraged by his friends and neighbours, Twysden stood as a candidate for the Parliament which was summoned for May 1661.

There were several matters which Twysden wanted Parliament to take into consideration. If the law against treason were applied in its full rigour to all the events of the Civil War forfeitures and other consequences would follow on a vast scale; ought not this to be looked into and 'have some moderation'? The powers of the Lords to judge a commoner were vague and uncertain: ought they not to be settled? Could the Commons' resolutions, the King and the Lords not participating, have the force of law? Finally, a reform which Twysden knew from unhappy personal experience was urgently needed, the fees and usages imposed upon those committed to prison were in need of regulation.

Twysden was undoubtedly more than willing to serve his county again but felt disinclined to canvass actively. His opponents, who included Tufton in spite of his having served in the previous Parliament, felt no such reluctance. Although at the outset Twysden had the larger following, efficient electioneering on the part of Tufton and Peyton turned the tables and they were elected. So Twysden missed what was to be his last chance of becoming a Knight of the Shire again.

Although Twysden was thus thrice a member of Parliament the three Parliaments to which he was returned lasted, in all, for no more than seven months. His membership of the Commons house brought him into contact with the great political figures at a time when the most important and fundamental political questions were being agitated. It was an experience that sharpened Twysden's interest in constitutional history, but in public affairs it was not as a Member of Parliament but as a governor of his parish and county that he made his mark.

Early on he was well aware of the casual and ineffective way in which the secular business of his own parish was being dealt with, and of the scant regard that was often had for the attempts to secure amendment—resented as outside interference—made from time to time by the Privy Council. In the summer of 1633 the Justices of the Peace, prodded by the Council, indulged in a short-lived burst of reforming activity. They required to be certified for every parish of the number of inns and taverns, the number of cottages built and inmates received during the last twenty years, the number of men and unmarried women, without means, living out of service, the number of apprentices and what masters had refused to be so burdened, what rogues and vagabonds had been punished according to law, whether ward was duly kept, how the surveyors of highways discharged their duties, and the constable was commanded to keep a book of all transgressors who were punished. But 'in East Peckham very little or no reformation was had'. Parish affairs were in the hands of uninformed and unenthusiastic officers supervised by the nearest Justices of the Peace. Where they were energetic the affairs of the parish might go well, but of the seventy or so justices who governed Kent some were hardly less casual and indolent than the constables and borsholders whose activities they were supposed to oversee.

Such was not Twysden. By 1636 he was in the commission of the peace, and he was as diligent in the office of magistrate as in the management of his own estate. In that year he began to keep a notebook of his proceedings (a practice which was advocated by Dalton, the helpful author of the magistrates' *vade mecum*, *The Country Justice*) and the detail with which it is written up perhaps betokens the enthusiasm that accompanies a new activity. It was in 1636 that the Lord Keeper caused an inquiry to be made through certain select Justices of the Peace how many justices whose names now stood in the commission of the peace were dead, how many justices dwelt in each hundred (an inappropriately framed question for Kent, with its abnormally large number of seventy or so hundreds), and what gentlemen of rank and quality (with an estimate of the value of their estates) might be put into the commission.

It was in character that Twysden took his duties, and no doubt himself, seriously. He already had a knowledge of the law and he made himself familiar with Dalton's work. By attending Assizes and Quarter Sessions he widened his circle of acquaintance and broadened his sphere of operations. His time was also taken up with meetings at the Swan Inn at Town Malling, where two, three or four of the justices for the south division of Aylesford Lathe were in the habit of holding their divisional sessions. Casual references provide the only information about the business transacted at the Swan, for no official record was kept of these divisional meetings.

Still less was there any official record of the business dispatched by the justice sitting alone, in his own parlour. Twysden's notebook shows the sort of case which, with a combination of law and common sense, he dealt with during the summer of 1636 without troubling his neighbour justices. In May, Jane Hernden, a married woman of Yalding, came to Twysden and complained about William Walter, a butcher; he called all the parties before him and made them friends, ordering Walter to pay Jane 2*s*. 6*d*., which he persuaded her to accept. But two months later the butcher was in trouble again, calling a lady of the parish by ungallant names, and Twysden gave a general warrant for him to be brought before a Justice of the Peace. At Brandbridge a squabble broke out over the flow of water to the mill, and the miller's man complained that Henry Parker and Robert Swan had beaten him so severely that he was almost dead when they left him; curiously enough he was reluctant to swear that he feared any further harm, so Twysden advised him to sue them in an action of battery. A known idle fellow was brought before Twysden on suspicion that the horse he was riding, two sackfuls of barley which he was carrying, and the sacks containing the barley were all stolen. He proved that the horse was his own, no one could prove that the barley was stolen, and it seemed to Twysden hard to commit him to prison for suspicion of a couple of sacks, but no one would bail him so off to gaol he went until he could be tried at the next Quarter Sessions. Thomas Turk, suspected of sheep-stealing was committed to the Assizes (where he was found guilty) being admitted to bail in the meantime. Twysden comments on the manner in which one justice frequently 'borrowed the hand' of another in releasing a felon upon bail; the statute required the bailing to be in the presence of two justices, but this was found to cause inconvenience so the practice was for one justice to grant bail and then send the suspect on to a fellow-justice to add his signature to the warrant—'a course not always to be followed' as the more meticulous Twysden notes.

But Twysden also could stretch the law in a good cause. John Johnson was brought before him for being seen with a gun and two dogs in the hedge where pheasants were sometimes found—and this during the time of divine service. Twysden intended to bind him over to his good behaviour, but the man so protested his innocence that Twysden contented himself with 'threatening' him—a nice example of 'Not guilty and don't do it again', but effective enough, no doubt, if dubiously lawful. Local bastardy cases illustrate once again the difficulty of proving paternity. A serving woman of Hadlow laid her bastard to William Salmon, and although when Twysden questioned her she admitted that the father was a youth, the son of her master, the unfortunate Salmon was ordered by the justices to allow her 18*d.* a week.

The justices had also to concern themselves with public health and public safety at a rudimentary level. In May 1636 so seriously was the plague raging in London that the Privy Council feared it would be spread by the extraordinary confluence of rogues and beggars in streets and highways, and ordered the justices to admonish the borsholders (as the tithingmen were called in Kent) to keep watch and ward, by day as well as by night, and take and punish unlawful vagrants. The times being unsettled, orders were also issued through the Deputy Lieutenants that the justices should ensure that the beacons were properly prepared and manned, ready to blaze forth their warning in time of danger. Some of the justices were doubtful about the propriety of their taking orders from the Deputy Lieutenants, but Twysden could quote precedents from his grandfather's papers to show that it had been done before (though then the Deputy Lieutenants had only *prayed* the justices, now they *prayed and required* them) and they agreed to pass on the instructions to the Constables.

As the justices were alert to ensure that there was no abuse of their rights, so the gentry in general were self-conscious about their privileges and dues. Their assertiveness is perhaps to be explained by an increasing tendency, explicitly and implicitly, to question their position. At the October 1641 Quarter Sessions the justices received a complaint from two gentlemen of Pluckley that in the Court Leet they had been chosen borsholders, and would have to obey the commands of the Constable, a man much inferior to them; it was, they alleged, 'by malice and faction of certain quantity of clowns' put upon them, and they begged to be discharged from the office. The justices sympathized, but did not think they had power to intervene although the gentlemen, in the end, did not serve the office. Nearly thirty years later, in 1670, a similar case arose at Aylesford where Edward Duke, grandchild to one who was both a knight and justice of the peace, was chosen by a jury of mean, inconsiderable men to serve as Constable with one who was no other than a cobbler. Duke came to Twysden, now an old man, who issued a warrant excusing Duke from the office. He spoke to the judge about it at the following Assizes, and the judge was more hesitant than Twysden about a justice's power to annul an election made in a Court Leet. As a younger man Twysden himself would have been more than hesitant, and the assumption is inevitable that old age and class consciousness combined to cause him on this occasion to act *per incuriam.*

During his six years or so as a justice before the Civil War Twysden interested himself particularly in the public finances. He was diligent in inquiry, zealous for economy, unremitting in his attempts to ensure that not a penny was spent avoidably; with these qualities he combined intelligence and conscientious devotion to public duty to such a degree that, in the twentieth century, he would inevitably have found himself filling the office of Chairman of the County Council Finance Committee.

Ship-money, as has already been said, was only one, although doubtless the most flagrant of the additional impositions with which the county was burdened. As part of the preparations for strengthening his navy the King bought 800 loads of timber in Surrey and Sussex, and in June 1636 ordered West Kent to meet a quarter of the cost of its carriage to Deptford. This perturbed Twysden and his fellow justices, for it had never been done before, and moreover whenever timber was purchased in Kent by the King the county had to meet the cost of its carriage, with no assistance from other counties. The justices agreed in October that these objections must be laid before the Privy Council.

Then there was the matter of the composition in lieu of the King's right of purveyance. Between 1637 and 1640 it went up by a groat in the shilling, an increase which led to many complaints and to discussion both in public and in private at the spring Assizes in 1641 about ways of getting it reduced. That would involve negotiation with the officers of the Greencloth but the officers were in a favourable position in any negotiation with the county gentry, for they knew the history of the composition and had access to the official records, whereas the gentlemen must rely on what they could remember or what their fathers had told them of earlier negotiations. So it was agreed that all the gentlemen, when they returned home, should search amongst their papers for any notes that they might have touching the subject, and come prepared at the next Quarter Sessions for further discussion, with a view to organizing a general meeting at the summer Assizes, and securing a reduction in the composition. Some said that the increase was due to the rise in the price of coal and wood since the basis of the composition was fixed in 1602; some looked to Parliament to remove the 'inconvenience'; but at the Assizes nothing effective was done to secure any alleviation, and the gentlemen began to look around for someone to receive and account for the composition during the following year, and their attention turned to Twysden. He was just such a sad and substantial man as the business required.

Twysden objected strenuously. Neither he nor his father had ever served the office, and with great earnestness he protested that he would not know what to do. What he did know, although this was not an argument that he advanced, was that men were increasingly reluctant to pay, that getting in the composition money would be a task as difficult as invidious, and that almost certainly the collector would have to make good from his own pocket deficiencies which would greatly exceed the £20 allowed him for his pains (with £5 for his man). Moreover the law took no account of the office of Treasurer or Collector of the Composition, and how could a man be compelled by law to perform an office which the law knew not? Notwithstanding these cogent objections Twysden was able to do no more than postpone the objectionable service. For this occasion Mr. Richard Lea of Rochester was constrained to serve, who even after much trouble could not collect all the money and was greatly out of pocket. But at the October 1641 Quarter Sessions Twysden was chosen to undertake the collection during the following year, with Sir William Boteler, Harry Dixon, and Augustine Skinner, the actual collection being delegated to Twysden. In fact by 1642 he was in no position to act as Collector or Treasurer, and in any case the composition between King and county which had existed since

1602 'broke' in 1641–2, either put an end to by the officers of the Greencloth or implicitly abandoned by the Kentish gentry.

Twysden was also appointed one of the Collectors of poll-money under the statute passed by the Long Parliament in 1641. The amount that was collected in his division, that is the south division of the Lathe of Aylesford, during the summer of 1641 was £872. 8*s*. 0*d*., in addition to the six subsidies raised between April and December which totalled about £1,370. During the first half of the following year the south division's share of the subsidy came to £796. 17*s*. 6*d*. and a similar amount was due in the autumn of 1642. The charge upon the county was apportioned between the Lathes according to a settled ratio, and within the Lathe of Aylesford the proportion taken by each of the three divisions was always the same, the north and east divisions both being responsible for five-sixteenths and the south for six-sixteenths. But Twysden was in prison before the second moiety of the 1642 subsidy could be collected, and his continued interest in public finance, now perforce become academic, is exemplified by the calculations he made in an attempt to estimate the total revenue from land in England. He put the figure at about £8 million, on the basis that a tax at £60,000 a month, or £720,000 a year, if it was generally at the rate of 2*s*. 0*d*. in the pound, as it was in Kent, represented a taxable value of £7,200,000; add something for the 2*d*. in the pound laid on the tenant and something more for land under-valued or not rated at all, and the answer is approximately £8 million. Confirmation of the estimate could be obtained by looking at the Kent assessment: a 12*d*. tax in Kent produced some £20,000, so the annual value of the land in the county must be about £400,000; Kent's proportion of imposition was usually one-twentieth of the figure for the whole kingdom, so this again would give a figure of about £8 million as the total revenue from land. (In terms of population Kent was over-assessed at a twentieth.)

Twysden was out of public life for eighteen years; wearisome years they must have been to one who saw strange convulsions in the government of country and county, much detestable innovation, and for long no certainty, scarcely any hope, of a return to established customs. That he remained secluded during the years of the Protectorate was partly a matter of choice. Others who had been sequestered returned to public life (the Earl of Thanet, a delinquent who fought with the King, was Sheriff of Kent in 1655), by 1649 Twysden's enemies in the County Committee were dead or disgraced, he stood well with his fellow-gentlemen, and he possessed the qualities that would have made him useful in the government of the county. But for Twysden there was an insurmountable objection to resuming life as a public man: it would have involved accepting a commission from a government whose authority had no lawful basis.

With the Restoration the foundation of legality was at once re-established, and Twysden soon resumed the responsibilities that befitted his station in life. His conduct in refusing to give aid and comfort to the revolutionary governments was thought worthy of approbation, and his son Roger would have been appointed to the Order of the Royal Oak if the King had not, wisely, decided against the introduction of an Order which must have perpetuated differences and divisions.

To reinsert a basis of legality into the constitution was one thing; to carry on the actual business of administration in parish and county, before all the necessary new commissions could be issued, was another. In the meantime there were no lawfully constituted Justices of the Peace; who, then, were to hear appeals from the overseers of the poor, how were the overseers to be discharged at the end of their year of office, and who was to 'allow' the parish poor rate? Such were the practical problems that troubled the gentry in the first few weeks after the Restoration. At East Peckham they were solved in a pragmatic way. The parish agreed to hold a meeting in the parish church on Sunday, 24 June, after divine service in the afternoon, when it was decided to appoint Richard Stanford and Henry Cheeseman as the new overseers, and that the old overseers, on making up their accounts and handing over the money in hand, should be discharged. A fortnight later the parish met again at church and decided to raise a rate of 4*d.* an acre, double the amount of the previous tax. It was not strictly lawful but the parish, thrown back on its own resources, was making sensible arrangements for the dispatch of its business until the machinery of government could be set in motion again.

There was a similar problem about the county tax. Twysden was asked to meet with other gentlemen in Maidstone on 26 June to decide what should be done. He called for Sir Thomas Style of Wateringbury on his way to Maidstone (was he perhaps feeling a little diffident, not having been to a meeting of the county for eighteen years, and anxious to have the fellowship and support of an old friend?) but Sir Thomas was entertaining company at dinner, and by the time they arrived at the meeting they found that it had been agreed to raise a tax, to cover three months, of 7½*d.* in the pound. Twysden was perturbed that it should be so much and asked why it was necessary to make any increase in the old rate of 6*d.* in the pound. The only answer that he got was that the charges could not be defrayed with a lower tax. A few days later Twysden was present at a meeting at Town Malling where the assessment of the tax on the south division of the Lathe of Aylesford was agreed upon.

Twysden and his neighbours did these things not by virtue of any office they previously held under Charles I, for all commissions lapsed with his death on 30 January 1649, but simply because the gentry were the 'natural' governors. Twysden's position was regularized when at Maidstone Assizes on 11 September 1660, he was again sworn a Justice of the Peace, and was restored to the commission of the peace and oyer and terminer.

No doubt because the novelty of the office had worn off, he did not keep a notebook of the trivial business which he dealt with out of sessions, as he had done so enthusiastically in 1636. It was now county business rather than parochial business that interested him. Just occasionally a case that came before him at a private sessions or meeting (it is significant that he is not clear whether these instances of the administration of justice should be called sessions, which denotes a certain regularity and formality, or merely meetings) caught his attention and seemed worth recording. One such case, at Malling in September 1662, is interesting because it shows a new and rational approach to the subject of witchcraft although such men as Sir Thomas Browne, Richard Baxter and Joseph Glanvill still held not to believe in witches to be almost tantamount to atheism. A Birling woman was accused of witchcraft, the principal witness, John Higgs, testifying that he knew by astronomy ('I conceive he should have said astrology' notes Twysden) that the woman had bewitched a neighbour who was sick, as she had formerly bewitched others who had fallen sick or whose possessions, through her machinations, had gone astray. Higgs came before the justices with a scheme and prognostications, but neither his English nor his Latin was orthodox. Twysden addressed him in Latin of which he found he did not know one word. It was also discovered that he was in the habit of taking fees, as much as £5 in one case, for removing spells, and that he had stood in the pillory at Rochester for his 'lewd carriages'. The result of the case was that the poor woman went free of the practices of which she was accused (and one can only hope that thereafter her neighbours' suspicions were abated) and Higgs was ordered to be whipped as a rogue and cheat and then transported back to Oxford, which he claimed to be his place of settlement.

Another troublesome case from the next parish of Leybourne came before Twysden in 1666. About twenty years earlier the Overseers had taken a tenancy of a house belonging to George Dennis and put an old man and his wife in it. The Overseers continued to pay rent for the house, but Dennis took back the little field attached to it, planted it up as a hop-garden, and built a couple of oasts. Recently the Overseers had placed in the house the wife of John Longley who had been pressed into the King's service, and she had her bed set up there. But Dennis pulled down her bed, threw bed and bedstead out of doors and thrust the poor woman out, although she was with child, so that she had to spend the night under a hedge. The Overseers appealed to Twysden. The case was at once simple and difficult: Dennis was in the wrong and Mrs. Longley must not be allowed to remain out of doors, but the question of breach of contract between Dennis as landlord and the Overseers as tenant was not one for a Justice of the Peace, and although if they had been persons of quality they might have been restored to possession under the Statutes of Forcible Entry of Henry VI and earlier reigns, that would have required the return of a jury and more trouble than the case justified. So, not without doubt about his powers to do so, Twysden threatened to bind over Dennis to his good behaviour. Legal or not, it was an effective remedy, for the parties composed their differences and no more was heard of them.

Twysden's knowledge of the law was rightly appreciated by his fellow-magistrates and his help was sought in cases of difficulty. There was one such in September 1664 arising from a quarrel between the men of Rochester and Strood and the oyster-fishers of Milton Regis about fishing rights in the Milton beds. At Canterbury Assizes in July 1663 Milton Regis got a verdict excluding the Rochester and Strood men, but they appealed and secured an Order of Council that they might continue to dredge and take oysters there until the question of the ownership of the fishery was finally decided at law, a proceeding that might take years. This decision led to a riot in which a Milton man was killed by a Strood man, against whom a verdict of wilful murder was found at the Coroner's inquest. He was committed to prison to await his trial, and the question which the Justices of the Peace, meeting twice specially at Maidstone, found it difficult to answer was whether they had power to bail one accused of murder. Coke and numerous statutes were referred to, but even in the face of such authority the doubt remained, and the accused was left in prison. Twysden was not satisfied, and felt that some declaration ought to be issued to resolve the doubt. In this case, he agreed, perhaps no great hardship was caused, but what of a woman, charged with doing away with a bastard child?—for that might be attended with such circumstances that it would be wrong for her to lie in prison. In spite of his devotion to legalism Twysden was a considerate man and, compared with many of his contemporaries, a humane one.

It was from a sense of humanity and duty that when the

October 1666 Quarter Sessions at Maidstone had to be postponed until December because of the plague in the town, Twysden was the one justice who, with the Recorder of Maidstone, attended to bail the prisoners, not thinking it right that they should languish in gaol for another two months, especially with the added risk of sickness. Amongst those committed for trial Twysden found one, a poor Italian, whose only offence was that as he was making his way home to his own country, he begged without a pass, contrary to the statute. Him Twysden freed altogether so that he might continue his interrupted homeward journey.

Twysden's long experience as a prisoner made him considerate towards those who were in gaol. He vigorously protested against the appointment as Keeper of the House of Correction of a drunken rascal who, for the space of two years, had let a room in his house as a meeting place for the Anabaptists, for he knew that he would fleece the poor men committed to his charge. At the same meeting of Quarter Sessions (April 1661) he took the initiative in putting a stop to the practice of the Clerk of the Peace who wanted to charge 4*s.* fee on every order for a pension granted to a maimed soldier. 'The King and the beggar,' quoted Twysden 'pay no fees'; but the Clerk thought that he was ill-used. Twysden had no intention of allowing county servants to increase their perquisites unlawfully, but equally he wished that they should be treated fairly. He was instrumental in getting an allowance of £10 in 1664 for the widow of the former gaoler, who had been put to unusual expense, having a very full gaol, in transporting his prisoners to Canterbury. The propriety of taking the £10 out of the money raised for maimed soldiers seems to have been questioned by no one, even though their pensions were at this time being reduced. Twysden's division always allowed the gaoler threepence a mile for conveying rogues to the House of Correction if the journey was more than three miles. Other justices, at the October 1671 Quarter Sessions, raised a doubt as to the justices' authority to do so, but Twysden firmly maintained that there was lawful authority for the practice. And he knew, from what had passed at Lambeth and elsewhere during the years of his own imprisonment, that the gaoler who failed to receive proper official fees would compensate himself at the expense of his wretched prisoners.

With his keen interest in public finance it was natural that, at the Restoration, he should promptly resume an active part in fiscal affairs both in his own Lathe of Aylesford and in the county at large. Many of the entries in his notebooks show that there was a woeful incompetence in the raising and collecting of the public revenues. On 10 October 1661 a special meeting of justices of Aylesford Lathe was held at Maidstone to receive a report from the Subcommissioners of the Excise but they came without their books, which were in London, could give no information and were unable to answer any questions put to them. All that could be done was to adjourn the meeting until 29 October when the justices of the Lathe met at Town Malling, but only one Subcommissioner then appeared and his deputy's books were so confused that they could make nothing of them. A further adjournment was necessary, the Subcommissioner promising to see that in the meantime the books were put into order, but when the justices met again a fortnight later the books were still in so absolute a muddle that the justices were constrained to reply to the Treasurer that they could give no advice about the possibility of improving the revenue from the Excise.

The collection of the Hearth Tax also gave rise to problems, some of them caused by the careless draughtmanship of the Act. It gave no powers to the Justices of the Peace out of their sessions to supervise the collection of the tax, but the local justices met first at Malling and then at Tonbridge in July 1662 to try to decide what ought to be done. They agreed upon an interpretation of the doubtful sections of the statute, but the Act continued to give trouble and the justices met at Malling several times during the ensuing eighteen months to consider other difficulties. They made small progress because of the 'perplexed ambiguity' of the statute. It required every householder to give an account in writing what hearths he had, and the borsholder was to endorse on the back the truth of the statement; how could the justices make the gentlemen in

London understand that scarcely one man in a parish, except the parson, could sign his name, let alone make out a bill of his hearths? Moreover the assessment was to be made on the medieval basis of boroughs and hundreds, not by parishes, the more convenient basis on which subsidies and fifteenths were raised.

There were frequent arguments, too, at the Assizes and elsewhere about the way in which the taxes and the Royal aid should be proportioned between the five Lathes and, within the Lathe of Aylesford, between the three divisions. Twysden was a great contender for the retention of the old way, but in 1666 a new apportionment was agreed upon, Twysden, to his subsequent chagrin, finally falling in with the views of the majority. When, in 1666, the question of apportionment arose over the £46 a week which was to be raised by West Kent for the relief of those parishes which had been seriously visited by the plague there were similar disagreements about the amount which each division of the Lathe of Aylesford should bear. The number of gentlemen engaged in, and the amount of time consumed by the argument seem quite disproportionate to the sums involved, which might be no more than 10*s*. or 20*s*. a week. It was the creation of a precedent, rather than the sum immediately in question, which was serious and was thought to justify such prolonged disputation.

The plague went on until well into 1667. Maidstone thought itself so hard hit as to qualify for county relief but the justices decided otherwise; the market had never been interrupted, and there had been no prohibition of butchers from serving the town, as there had been at Hawkhurst. Recording the justices' decision Twysden adds, with a proper appreciation of social gradations: 'Sir John Banks, newly made a baronet from a father [who] had been a shopman in the town and that now stood to be a burgess of the Parliament for that town made the motion, which perhaps made it succeed never the better with the Gentlemen.'

During the decade following the Restoration the business transacted at Quarter Sessions grew steadily as more and more duties were placed upon the justices, so that whereas when

Twysden was first in the commission the Sessions rarely lasted more than one day now they were rarely concluded in less than three. Twysden himself scarcely ever missed a meeting (from time to time the Sessions had to be cancelled because of the plague) and, even allowing for the fact that in his notes he would naturally remember particularly his own interventions and the occasions on which his brother magistrates sought his advice, it is evident that he was one of the prominent members of the Bench. Nevertheless, he never attained the honour of presiding as Chairman and giving the charge; others who were of better quality, or who were better qualified, such as his brother the Judge, did that.

Twysden's skill as a draughtsman was once again in demand. In 1660 the Duke of York, as Lord High Admiral, expressed his wish that men belonging to the Navy or the yards should be exempted from all public offices, as, he alleged, had been done theretofore. The precedents were much less definite than the Duke suggested. Twysden was able to produce some papers of his father's to show that the claim had been made, and challenged, in James's reign. In Rochester and Chatham the exemption of naval and dockyard men would throw a heavy burden on their fellow-townsmen, and the filling of the public offices might even prove impossible. When the Lord High Admiral's request came before Quarter Sessions in April 1662 discussion of it was adjourned until the gentlemen met again at the summer Assizes, and Twysden, with Mr. Wilkinson 'hammered out' a petition to the Judge of Assize, Sir Orlando Bridgman, begging him to intervene on behalf of the county with His Royal Highness. Twysden became the unofficial special agent of the county in pursuing the matter, both at Maidstone and in London, but Bridgman, the Lord Chancellor and the Duke did not share his assessment of the importance of the business and, after a good deal of importunity, the best answer he could get was that the county should proceed with moderation and equity—in other words the official direction would not be withdrawn, but the county could expect 'a winking at what we should do if occasion served'. It was much the same advice, almost in the same words, as a twentieth-century government department might give to a local authority raising an awkward issue.

The justices were concerned not only with seamen and others now in His Majesty's service, but also with alleviating the lot of poor, maimed soldiers who had suffered on his behalf. Their petitions, presented by their friends, were heard by the justices as they sat at dinner. Usually they were given 40*s.* a year, and 10*s.* or 20*s.* in hand, but some had £3 annually and one, a gentleman reduced to extreme necessity, was allowed £6. Twysden doubted whether the justices had power under the statute 43 Elizabeth c. 3 to award pensions in these cases, since the Act referred to those who 'were pressed and in pay for His Majesty's service' and the unfortunates who now petitioned fought voluntarily for the late King (and, indeed, for whom *were* those fighting who were wounded at Colchester?) not as pressed men. However, Twysden agreed that it was better to give some reward to such as had been for the King than to those, like Sir Michael Livesey's coachman, who had been against him. Cautiously, Twysden advised that the pensions should be limited to £2. 10*s.* a piece, lest the county stock would not hold out, but his advice was not heeded. Two years later, in 1664, the stock was so low that all pensions were reduced to 40*s.* (except the one pension of £6 to the person of better quality, which it was agreed to continue) and the parishes were so averse to increase their contributions that no new pensions could be granted until 1665.

Beside eleemosynary works of this kind, the justices in Quarter Sessions were called upon to determine, according to their collective knowledge and wisdom, numerous points of law, many of them so fundamental that it is surprising to find that, in the 1660's, they were still open questions (or at least were so to the Justices of the Peace in Kent). For example the Statute of Westminster I with its definition of felony as larceny *outre xii deniers* had been on the statute book for nearly 400 years but when the justices at Quarter Sessions in March 1668 were faced with the question whether larceny to the value of exactly twelve pence was felony or only petty larceny, it seemed that there was no authoritative answer. Twysden maintained that on a proper construction of the Statute it was no more than petty larceny, but the jury retired again, and obligingly found the stolen pair of sheets to be worth only eleven pence, not twelve pence, so the thief escaped with a whipping.

Nor were the justices by any means certain of the punishments that they could award at Quarter Sessions. The pillory was a known and well-established instrument of personal reform and public retribution; but was it in the armoury of the justices? Twysden raised the question with his fellow justices, expressing the view that they could condemn a man to stand in the pillory. Some of the others doubted it, for no statute gave them that power. Twysden adhered to his view, in which the Judge of Assize concurred, quoting an Essex or Hertfordshire precedent of 43 Elizabeth. Probably this was the law, but that there was so great uncertainty on such an elementary and everyday question comes as something of a surprise.

And what were they to do with a soldier travelling with a forged pass in which he had inserted the name of a non-existent Justice of the Peace? Could this be said to be counterfeiting the signature of a justice, contrary to the Statute 39 Elizabeth c. 17? Twysden was clearly of the opinion that it could not, for all that the man had done was to counterfeit the hand of a non-existent person, therefore no Justice of the Peace; and as on several other occasions he argued strongly that a penal statute (in which category he included any statute for levying a tax) should not be expounded by Equity, but must be interpreted strictly. It was not a currently acceptable argument and the doctrine of the strict interpretation of penal statutes is thought to have become generally received only in the eighteenth century.[1] The justices evaded their problem in this case, as they frequently did when difficult questions arose, by leaving the man to be tried by the Judge when he came to take the Assizes.

Then there were such awkward questions as whether a poor person who brewed beer and sold it at a horse-race or a cricketing was liable to pay Excise. Twysden argued that the Excise man could not exact money from such a one; the offence is

[1] See W. Friedmann, *Law in a Changing Society* (1959), p. 53.

keeping an alehouse without a licence, and the penalty a forfeiture of 20*s.* to the poor. To exact Excise as well would be an infringement of the maxim *Nemo bis punitur pro uno delicto*, and to the objection that Excise was not to be regarded as a punishment, Twysden retorted that it certainly was to the poor.

Settlement and bastardy cases provided numerous conundrums on which the gentlemen could exercise their wits. How, for example, were his responsibilities to be brought home to a Kentish man who crossed the county boundary to father a bastard in Surrey, and could a parishioner give evidence in a case concerning his own parish, or must it be excluded as testimony in his own cause? But if the parishioners were all excluded, how was evidence to be obtained, for no one except the parishioners were likely to know the facts? Such problems multiplied as fast as they were solved and kept the magistrates busy. In 1663 Twysden solemnly records: 'The sin of whoredom hath been always too common but since the taking away the Ecclesiastic Courts by the Long Parliament I think much more frequent than formerly'. Suitable research, if anyone felt inclined to undertake it, would probably show whether this really was so, or whether Twysden, in his mid-sixties and with memory setting into a pattern, was using a handy stick with which to beat the Long Parliament, an institution that he had no reason to love. He was certainly not the only one, then or since, to detect a contemporary decline in morals.

It would be tedious to prolong the recital of Quarter Sessions cases with which Twysden was concerned, though many of them raise interesting legal issues or throw light on the way in which statute and Common Law were mediated down to the ordinary people through their administration by the county gentry. One last example must suffice to show again that Twysden was not so devoted to an abstract legalism as to be indifferent to the human predicament of those who are the objects of the law. The gentlemen meeting at the Star Inn at Maidstone for the summer Assizes in 1661 considered the problem of a woman, living in the precinct of Rochester Castle, who had fallen into poverty; it not being known in what parish the Castle lay, by whom was she to be relieved?

Some thought that the hundred must do it, but that was shown to be wrong, so the gentlemen then agreed the obligation fell on the county. The county, expostulated Twysden, could act only at and through Quarter Sessions, and reduced to that course the poor woman might starve before she could be relieved. Perhaps she did; no more is recorded.

From the time that he was back in the Commission of the Peace Twysden was as assiduous attender at Assizes as he was at Quarter Sessions, exchanging views with the other justices and consulting, and also being consulted by, the Judge.

In the autumn of 1660 the magistrates were concerned with getting the machinery of administration, especially the collection of money, restarted. There was much talk, but little done, about the new Act for the disbandment of the Army; it involved the perennial problem of how to raise money from the county. Then there was the matter of the county's composition in lieu of purveyance. A fixed charge, provided it was of reasonable amount, was more convenient to the county than the exercise by the Crown of its prerogative of purveyance, but in 1641 the charge had become so burdensome that the composition had been discontinued. The settlement of a new figure with the officers of the Greencloth was bound to call for hard bargaining, and the Grand Jury with twelve justices, acting as 'the County' appointed a body of twelve gentlemen to negotiate for them, and Twysden's name is placed first in the list of negotiators. He evidently draughted, and with his neighbour Sir Thomas Style jointly signed, the letters to the Greencloth. It was a task after his own heart, but he could not persuade the officers to soften theirs, and his offer that the county should compound at £2,000 a year was rejected. However, the negotiations soon came to an end, for the statute that confirmed the suppression of the Court of Wards and Liveries also terminated, with compensation, the King's right of purveyance.

Twysden especially enjoyed his days at the Assizes for the opportunities they gave of learning in what directions the minds of the Court and Parliament were bending, of indulging in discussion of such controverted matters as the extent of the

King's prerogative (on which he disagreed with Sir Edward Filmer as years before he had differed from his father Sir Robert), and of hearing the inner reason for certain statutes and Orders in Council. The judge on circuit acted both as the government's apologist, and as collector of the views of the county.

Thus, at the summer Assizes in 1661, Sir Orlando Bridgman took Twysden aside and told him privately of the danger from the Dutch navy, that the King was spending £700,000 a year on his navy, that of the £70,000 given him for his coronation, the greater part had been spent on the navy, that nevertheless more money was urgently required—His Majesty would rather starve than take money by unjust ways, but earnestly did the Judge commend to him the gift granted to the King under the recent Act. Such was the persuasiveness of Bridgman's advocacy that Twysden—flattered, no doubt, by the thought that he had been singled out to receive this communication—was actually prepared to subscribe at once, but so was only one other, the rest of the gentlemen desiring to take time for consideration of the proposition. The Judge reproved them, saying that it would come to nothing if deferred, whereupon they agreed that none would ultimately give less that he now intended—and their present intentions they prudently did not disclose. The suggestion that His Majesty should take into account the taxes which the gentlemen had been obliged to contribute to Parliament before the Restoration was not well received, and the Judge thought inconsistent with the concept of a free gift. The honeymoon between Charles and the country gentry was already over.

Bridgman often came as the circuit judge. Two years later in July 1663 he spoke in his charge of the King's intent that all who failed to come to church, whether they were Papists, Presbyterians, Anabaptists, etc., should forfeit 12*d.* for every Sunday. He referred also to a Bill relating to the Sabbath which had been before Parliament but someone unknown had purloined it from the table in the upper chamber, so no further progress had been made with it. Had it passed, it would have required the strict observance of the Sabbath, with no games, at least during the time of divine service.[1] The next year Bridgman was again at Maidstone, expounding to the justices the new Conventicle Act and particularly the nature of a *notorious evidence of the fact* to which the Act referred. In 1665 his charge was largely given up to a discussion of the laws against recusants who would not come to church; the purpose of the laws, he emphasized, was reason of State not the compelling of consciences, and no doubt the justices returned to their parishes intending to administer the laws according to the nuances which they detected in the Judge's charge. The following year Bridgman was stricken with gout whilst he was on circuit in Sussex, so Sir Samuel Browne (the quondam chairman of the Committee for Sequestrations) alone came into Kent. His subject was not religious affairs but the King's urgent need for saltpetre, an essential ingredient in the making of gunpowder which was desperately needed for the wars against the Dutch. He produced an apologia for the recent commission which permitted the digging in outhouses—but not in dwelling-houses—for saltpetre, and even in outhouses no digging was to be undertaken but when the corn was out of the building. It was an old grievance: Weldon had said twenty years earlier that the saltpetre men were worse than ship-money.

The criminal cases which Twysden heard and noted down have the fascination of a twentieth-century Sunday newspaper combined with occasional historical significance. There was, for example, the man who only a few months after the Restoration publicly said that the King was a papist and went to mass twice a day, for which offence he was condemned to stand in the pillory at Maidstone on two market-days. Two years later Twysden reported to Bridgman, Lord Chief Justice, that he had sent to gaol one Lockyer who was suspected for being abroad in the night and writing much, and who had perpetrated the suggestions that the King would not live the month

[1] Each peer gave his oath that he had not removed it. There are hints that Charles knew what had happened, that it was less embarrassing to the King for the Bill to be 'lost' in this way than by the exercise of the royal veto. See D. Ogg, *England in the reign of Charles II* (1963 edn.), ii, p. 457.

out, that his bastard would reign only a little time, and that the bishops were a parcel of rogues; but these things he said when he was in drink and Twysden thought he looked more like a rogue than a traitor. However, in the uncertainties of the time the government was not disposed to tolerate much freedom of speech and at the Assizes in 1666 the pillory and imprisonment were awarded to one who spoke contemptuously of the King, expressing the hope that the Hollander would get the better of him, and that all the churches would be made into cow-houses and privies. An even more unpatriotic pair of rogues appeared at the Assizes in 1669 charged with selling the King's ordnance, with which they had been entrusted, at Ostend. They were convicted but being literate escaped with burning in the hand. (Mr. Boswell, a convicted felon, was even more fortunate, for he was not only literate but also a gentleman and was therefore excused even the burning in the hand.) In the trial of the purloiners of His Majesty's ordnance Twysden noticed a little by-comedy: a Jewish witness refused to be sworn on the New Testament but willingly took his oath upon a thicker book which he thought to be the Old Testament; Twysden observed that in fact it was the Book of Common Prayer and the Psalms.

To the inevitable list of sordid domestic murders and manslaughters Twysden was able to add one or two more exotic examples, where the actors were foreigners passing through the county to or from the Continent. A Knight of Malta and a French marquis indicted for killing a waterman of the long ferry between London and Gravesend (a scoundrel if ever there was one), and a Jew, probably from Turkey, and a young man arraigned for the murder of a Polonian prince were colourful variations on a drab theme. It was characteristic that when the interpretation of the statute 21 Jacobus I c. 27 (an Act to prevent the destroying and murthering of bastard children) came into question Twysden argued, carrying many with him, for the construction which was most merciful to the accused mother.

Two cases from Canterbury show that even eighty years after the advent of the Huguenots, they were not assimilated to the

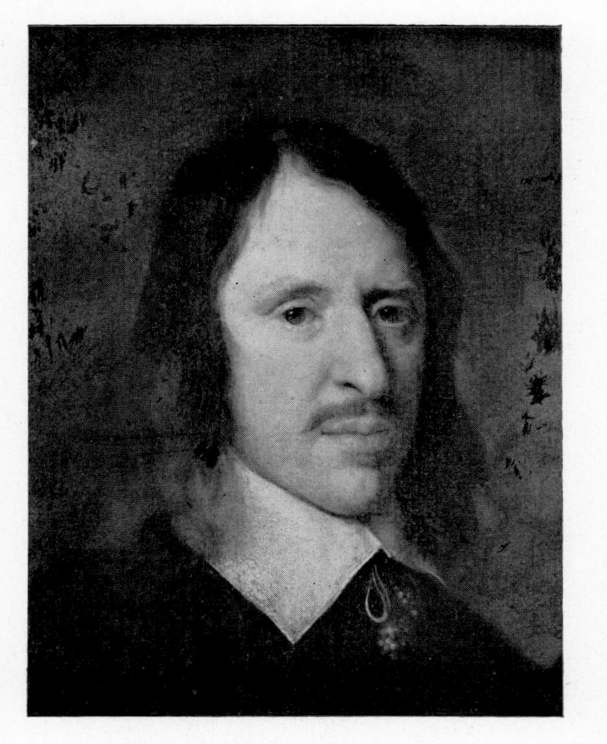

John Twysden, M.D., c. *1650*

Sir Thomas Twisden, 1st baronet of Bradbourne, c. *1670*

native community.[1] They claimed that since they kept themselves to themselves and looked after their own poor as they were required and empowered to do under an order of 1635, they should be exempt from the poor rate; the claim was disallowed by the Judge. More sinister was the indictment of two young Huguenots for the rape of a girl at Canterbury. The complainants were persons of mean quality—Anabaptists, Quakers, or such like—and by the conclusion of the trial it was clear that not only were the prisoners not guilty but also this was an attempt to blackmail two young men of excellent character but of alien origin. In an earlier trial for a similar offence the Judge, turning to Twysden, asked whether Kent justices usually bailed men accused of rape. Twysden replied yes, and thought it lawful, as the offence was but felony; the Judge agreed.

It is significant that the Judge addressed his question to Twysden. Almost from the time that he was first back in the Commission he was one of the two or three leading members of the county bench. When the circuit judges brought with them papers containing resolutions of all the judges on matters of practice and procedure, they were quite often handed over to Twysden after they had been read to the justices. His reputation as a careful man who kept his papers methodically must have commended him to the other justices as a suitable unofficial *custos*. Sometimes he sat next to the judge on the bench, and was able to proffer pieces of information or advice. With Bridgman he was on terms of friendship. It was Twysden's practice to present a calf to the judges when they came into the county, and even when the snow was so deep in March 1667 that he had to turn back after starting out for Sevenoaks (whither the Assizes had been transferred because of the plague in Maidstone) he still managed to send his customary gift. The plague continued throughout the year and Twysden was one of those whom Bridgman invited to meet him at Tunbridge Wells, where he was taking the waters, and advise him as to the wisdom of putting off the summer Assizes altogether. Twysden,

[1] In 1683 their expulsion was proposed after they had been presented as 'a nuisance' by the Grand Jury of the county (*Cal. S.P. Dom, 1683*, p. 103).

in turn, sought the advice of the Lord Keeper, as Bridgman now became, about the freeing of prisoners in the county gaol whose trial could not be held because the Quarter Sessions also were cancelled.

With Keiling, Chief Justice of the King's Bench, who was usually the circuit judge during Twysden's last few years, his relationship was different; gone was the old easy familiarity, bred of respect upon both sides. Of Keiling Foss says 'He retained the place [C.J.] during the remainder of his life, with little reputation as a lawyer, and frequently incurring censure by his want of temper and discretion.' He dispatched trials at a furious rate—sixty-five in three days at one Assizes—and at the spring and the summer Assizes in 1670 he got through the Crown business in less than a day. It was on the latter occasion that, from the bench and publicly, he reprimanded the Recorder of Canterbury, threatening to have an information against him in the King's Bench. He browbeat juries, would not even allow them to withdraw to consider their verdict, and in many cases told them how they were to find. Justices who, in the interests of their friends, sought to moderate his impetuosity, found the full heat of his lordship's anger turned upon them, as he bade them keep quiet. Morton, J., was another who had scant time for the interruptions of the local justices, and refused to allow Twysden to put a question to a prisoner—yet Twysden's commission, as he records, like the Judge's, was *ad audiendum et terminandum*. Morton was a testy man, and at the summer Assizes, 1670, he had an unedifying altercation with Sir William Leech who not only put up his foot on the bench to ease himself, being somewhat lame, but also ventured to question the Judge's ruling when he decided that a man committed by Sir William as an accessory must be acquitted when the principal was found not guilty. Twysden supported Leech's view. Morton did not conceal his contempt for the county justices—'these tedious old fools' he no doubt dubbed them in private, and perhaps not only in private. He was a hasty man, a man of action, a brave and much wounded soldier, the terror of highwaymen who secured not only the conviction but also the execution of the notorious Claude

Duval; he was uncharitable, but perhaps not entirely wrong in his assessment of some of the elderly justices.

But worthy, reliable, fair Twysden certainly was. It was those qualities that made him an eminently suitable Commissioner under the Act for Confirming and Restoring of Ministers of 1660. It was unthinkable that ministers who had been ejected by Parliament and the Puritans for their loyalty to King and Church should go without remedy whilst the men who had been inserted in their places continued to enjoy their livings; what is more surprising is that the spirit of the Act was not vindictive, and in its application a good deal of fair-mindedness and tolerance was often shown.

The first meeting which Twysden attended as a Commissioner under the Act was at Goudhurst on 6 December 1660 when he and the seven other justices who assembled there made an order restoring Mr. John Couch to the Rectory of Horsmonden, the Commissioners having no jurisdiction to deal with the allegation of simony against him, and ordered also the restoration of the Reverend James Wilcocks (a learned divine but a poor man and full of children) to the Vicarage of Goudhurst, occupied by the Reverend Edward Bright, described as a man of no great learning but a voluble preacher. Wilcocks had been ejected many years before. A petition against him from 'the parish' had been sent up to the House of Commons as early as March 1640 but it bore the signatures of only two parishioners and was rejected by the House. He remained uneasily in his living until, in the autumn of 1642, Colonel Robert Gibbons with his soldiers came into the church during the time of divine service, and called out to Wilcocks in the pulpit 'Sirrah, you that stand prating there, come down or I will shoot you down'. So he came down, and was carried off, a prisoner, to London. Bright made no attempt to dispute Wilcocks's title, but argued only over the amount which he must allow him for half the profits for the past year, and the fifths for the last ten years. The Commissioners had assessed the amount at £180, but privately advised Wilcocks to settle for £120. Bright at first demurred at giving anything, but afterwards he offered through Twysden to give £100. Twysden urged him to make it £120, but at the suggestion of Bright's counsel they agreed to split the difference and settle for £110, £10 to be paid the next morning, £50 at Christmas and £50 early in the New Year. Now it was Wilcocks's turn to be obdurate. He wanted the full amount immediately, and although all the Commissioners thought this unreasonable, he refused to move from his demand. It looked as though the agreement would collapse, when one of the Commissioners, John Horsmonden, offered to find £100 the next morning and to lend it free of interest so that the bargain could be concluded in a spirit of amity. Wilcocks did not long enjoy his restored Vicarage for he was dead within a few months.

A more difficult case concerned the Rectory of Trottiscliffe which eight Commissioners, of whom Twysden was one, heard at Wrotham on 21 December 1660. For a start one of the justices thought that they were entitled to act as judges of all scandals concerning ministers, including ignorance. Twysden and the others dissented: if the Bishop had ordained a man he must conclusively be assumed to have sufficient learning, and the Commissioners' jurisdiction, they maintained, extended only to the varieties of scandal named in the Act. ('Scandal' seems a scarcely appropriate word to describe the state of being under the age of twenty-four years, one of the grounds of disability specified in the Act.)

The Rectory of Trottiscliffe was in the gift of the Bishop of Rochester. This gave rise to argument as to who had the right to present during the vacancy of the See. A second difficulty was that whilst Woodward, the *de facto* incumbent, was admitted to be a man very infamous, his opponent, Head, appeared to have resigned the Rectory, although Twysden's view was that the piece of paper which was put in was an unsatisfactory and unconvincing document. But there was a third difficulty: Head now held a living in Essex; could he be restored to a second living to be held in plurality? The Act said that a minister who had been ejected from two or more livings should be restored to one of them, but no more. Head had not been ejected from two livings, but would it not be contrary to the spirit of the Act to restore him to the Rectory of Trottiscliffe whilst he held a living in Essex? It was too difficult for the Commissioners, so they decided to leave the reverend gentlemen to pursue their dispute in the ordinary courts, Twysden vainly commenting that the purpose of the Act was precisely to avoid the need for recourse to a suit at law.

In the autumn of the following year a group of Justices of the Peace, of whom Twysden again was one, called four ministers before them and admonished them for not using the Book of Common Prayer. The ministers pleaded the King's declaration of 25 October 1660 when he promised that none should be troubled for not using the Prayer Book until it had been reviewed and reformed, but that declaration, so Twysden thought, must have been intended for the easement of a parish where the majority of the parishioners were Presbyterians, not, as here, simply to allow the minister to flout the law. But indeed it was not easy to say exactly what was the King's policy over matters of religious toleration, and admonishing them only of the danger they courted, the Justices dismissed the four ministers whom, perhaps, they had been somewhat officious in summoning before them.

There were secular as well as ecclesiastical stables to be cleansed at the Restoration. The Act for the Well Governing and Regulating of Corporations, passed in 1661, empowered Commissioners appointed under the Great Seal to require all members of corporations to take an oath declaring their belief that it was not lawful upon any pretence to take up arms against the King and that the Solemn League and Covenant was an unlawful oath, of no binding force. Those who refused to take the oath tendered them by the Commissioners, or who were otherwise thought to be undesirable, were to be removed, and those who had been unlawfully removed were to be restored.

Unlike the Act for Confirming and Restoring Ministers, which constituted all the justices Commisioners under it, the administration of the Corporations Act was entrusted to select bodies of commissioners in each county. The corporations' representation in the Commons gave them political significance, and their purging and reform was therefore delegated to justices of standing whose discretion and judgement (prejudice, their opponents might have said) could be relied upon. Twysden was a Commissioner for Kent. On 12 August 1662 thirteen of the Commissioners met at Maidstone, and excluded from the Corporation two jurats and some common councillors. Heath, Attorney of the Duchy of Lancaster, a Commissioner, wanted to put out Lake, the Recorder, wishing to have the Recordership himself. Twysden objected, saying that Lake was a very fit man for the office and that, having been appointed since 24 December 1661, he was not removable. Heath lost his temper and hinted at collusion, but in the end they made up their quarrel and Lake was left in office. (It was with Lake that Twysden, a few years later, bailed the prisoners awaiting trial when the Assizes had to be postponed because of plague.)

The Commissioners thought that it would be of advantage to the King to have gentlemen as jurats of the town, and four gentlemen were found, qualified by residence in Maidstone, willing to serve. Here, however, a difficulty arose: if admitted now they would take precedence after the jurats already in office, but these jurats were not gentlemen. For gentlemen to come beneath those of lesser quality was inconceivable. The only solution was for all the jurats to resign, and for them all then to be re-admitted, the gentlemen first, the others afterwards. Thus the proper order would be preserved. Unfortunately the jurats were not prepared to co-operate in such a *pirouette*, the gentlemen were not willing to take second place, an impasse was reached, and the King had to do without the advantage of having gentlemen as members of Maidstone Corporation. The Privy Council, not knowing the niceties of the situation, suspected the gentlemen of deliberately seeking to evade the burdens of office.[1]

To Twysden these proceedings were distasteful. He disliked Heath's attempt to get the Recordership for himself, he did not care for the partiality shown by the Commissioners, he feared that their activities were more likely to breed discord

[1] See J. H. Sacret, 'The Restoration and Municipal Corporations', *English Historical Review*, xlv, p. 255.

than to produce concord, and the Act, apart from the usual ambiguities and infelicities of draughtsmanship, he felt to be arbitrary. He resolved to have no more to do with the business, and he kept to his resolution.

One other public office Twysden held, the most honourable of them all. On 16 July 1660 Heneage Finch, third Earl of Winchilsea, Lord Lieutenant of the County and Twysden's cousin, appointed him to be a Deputy Lieutenant. But by the time that Twysden had paid £5 as a fee on his commission, in October, Winchilsea had been sent on a mission to Constantinople and in his absence the Earl of Southampton was joined with him in the Lieutenancy. The exercise of the office thus fell into the hands of Southampton who, on 8 August, issued a fresh commission to Twysden under the Militia Act of that year. During these years the Duke of Richmond was intriguing for the Lieutenancy and although he lost time and occasion by marrying as his second wife the beautiful Mrs. Frances Stuart, to the anger of the King, he finally secured his desire in May 1668. He reappointed Twysden as one of his Deputy Lieutenants, but whereas in 1660 Twysden had without question given £5 as a fee to the Lieutenant's clerk, now he gave only twenty shillings; 'others gave more, forty, but I thought a pound enough, and as good as two'.

Twysden set about his duties as Deputy Lieutenant with exemplary thoroughness. He had inherited the books and papers which his grandfather had accumulated as Captain of the Light Horse of the Lathe of Aylesford in Elizabeth's reign, an office which was afterwards held by Sir William Twysden during the reign of James without, however, a comparable accretion of paper, and Twysden not only examined and copied out his grandfather's notes but also kept a notebook of his own.[1] He intended to write a history of the offices of Lord Lieutenant and Deputy Lieutenant, leaving thirty or so pages blank in his notebook for that purpose, but desiring to record events whilst they were fresh in his memory he pressed on with

[1] These note-books and papers have been published by the Kent Archaeological Society Records Branch as *The Twysden Lieutenancy Papers, 1583–1668*, ed. Gladys Scott Thomson (1926).

an account of the matters which followed the passing of the Statute 14 Carolus II, c. 3, and unfortunately never returned to the projected history.

The Act of 1662 is thirty-three sections in length, prolix, and detailed in its regulation of the militia, the arms to be provided, the training to be undertaken, the powers of Lieutenants, Deputies, Constables, etc., and the chargeability of those required to find horsemen and foot-soldiers. Twysden mastered the Act by making a skilful analysis of it. When problems arose, as inevitably they did, over the enforcement of the Act Twysden knew the law and was able to guide the discussions with his fellow Deputy Lieutenants. His interest was in the logistics of the Militia, not in its training as a military force; he was no soldier, and by now was an old man. He was learned on such questions as whether the clergy ought to be taxed by the Deputy Lieutenants or whether they should tax themselves as one of the three estates of the Kingdom, but when the Deputies all met in Maidstone in October 1665 to receive an account of what had been done under the Act, Twysden had to admit that the horse of the Lathe of Aylesford had not been mustered at all since the King's Restoration. He strongly resisted the suggestion that voluntary troops should be raised, for to do so would cast an aspersion on those who declined to volunteer; that man was *vir bonus qui consulta patrum qui leges iuraque servat*.

His insistence on proceeding according to due form of law got Twysden into trouble with some of the other Deputies. At the Quarter Sessions on 13 December 1665 Sir John Tufton asked him to sign a warrant fining one who had failed to serve the full period of mustering, but he neither told Twysden who the man was nor summoned him before them to give the culprit a chance of making his defence. Twysden refused. At this Tufton and Captain Ralph Buffkin were surprised and angry, but some of the other Deputies supported him.

The treat which the Duke of Richmond, as the new Lord Lieutenant, gave to his Deputies at Rochester on 21 May 1668 also found Twysden at variance with some of his colleagues. The question arose whether a man who owned estates in several parts of the county (as Twysden himself did) was to be charged for every estate or only for the division in which he lived. Twysden, with learned reasons, argued for the second interpretation of the law, but 'my Lord said he thought otherwise and would order it so; *satis cum imperio*'. The Duke further decided that he would like to see the militia men wearing uniform, his own men in yellow coats, the rest in red, and he asked his Deputies' assistance in compelling those who were under obligation to send horsemen or footmen to dress them according to his Lordship's desire. To this further obligation upon the subject, in no way warranted by the statute, Twysden would by no means agree.

A fortnight later there was a sequel to the argument which had taken place at Rochester. On the 2 June about midnight, Twysden being in bed and asleep, a messenger came from the Duke, blowing his post-horn and alarming the household. He brought for Twysden's signature eight warrants demanding payment towards the cost of coating the trained bands. Twysden begged to be excused; he pointed out that they were already subscribed by three Deputies and therefore bore an adequacy of signatures, he asked the Lord Lieutenant to remember the argument which had taken place at Rochester, and, in fine, with expressions of great respect for the Duke, he declined to be a party to a practice which, without authority of Act of Parliament, imposed a charge upon the subject. The following day the Duke wrote to Twysden from Maidstone: his Deputy's disobedience incensed him—'I am not Lawyer nor have I made it my business to be over inquisitive in what I do not understand'—and he cancelled Twysden's deputation forthwith. Writing some months later to his cousin Sir Heneage Finch, Twysden protests that he is not at all troubled at being put out of his Deputy's place; all that does worry him 'is that I hear he [*sc.* the Lord Lieutenant] says he did it by His Majesty's express command. I am not conscious to myself of any ill-deserving of the King, and to desire to conform myself to his laws I hope he will not interpret a cause of dislike, but I confess it makes me [think] I will never accept it again but upon his express command.' If this was intended as an oblique invitation to Finch, as Solicitor-General, to intervene with the King on Twysden's behalf it was apparently ignored.

However, the cancellation of his commission was not quite the end of the affair. On 29 July Captain Bickstaff issued an order for the trained bands of the Hundred of Littlefield to muster at Penenden Heath on 13 August, 'well mounted on serviceable horses . . . and well armed with back, breast, and pot, a carabine, case of pistols, and sword, with a convenient proportion of powder and bullets'. Twysden and his son were called upon to furnish two horses and two riders.[1] Thereupon he wrote to the Captain saying that neither his father, nor his grandfather nor his great-grandfather had ever supplied more than one; moreover, he remembered, as a former Deputy Lieutenant, that there were letters from the Privy Council of 5 August 1663 and from the King himself on 15 August 1665, requiring that the county should not be burdened with mustering in time of harvest; Twysden (out of the commission for only two months) protests that he does not know, of course, whether those orders have since been countermanded, but the implication is plain, that the Deputies were exceeding their authority, and that both Bickstaff and Twysden knew it.

The muster was not a success. Bickstaff issued further orders for a second performance on 25 August. Twysden and his son were again required to furnish two horses and two riders, and were posted as defaulters of one at the muster on 13 August. Not only had Twysden sent but one horse and one man; exception was taken to the condition of the man's carbine, which the Muster Master showed to the Lord Lieutenant and broke, to demonstrate its state.

To be posted as a defaulter and to have his property damaged in this way was more than Twysden could stand. He wrote again to Bickstaff protesting that he was no defaulter, his legal

[1] Horse were regarded as especially useful in resisting threatened invasion, and the Chatham disaster, when the Dutch entered the Medway and destroyed many of the King's ships, was still fresh in men's minds. Arlington's instructions to the Lords Lieutenant in 1667 urged them 'to make the greatest show you can in numbers . . . more especially of horse, even though it be of such as are otherwise wholly unfit' (*Cal. S.P. Dom. 1667*, p. 145).

obligation being one horse and one man, and demanding to know who had broken his carbine 'that I may either learn of him what clause in the Act enabled him to spoil my goods, or teach him he hath not power to do so'. As Twysden well knew, the Muster Master had no statutory authority for breaking the defective piece, and when Twysden brought his action of trespass for damage to his goods, the poor man could do nothing but confess a judgement.

This barrack-room law understandably exasperated the Duke of Richmond and his Deputies. With the support of ten of them he represented to the Privy Council the manner in which 'His Majesty's service relating to the Militia' was 'obstructed and discouraged by the ill example of Sir Roger Twysden, converting that interest which his public employment hath gained him in the county from the right use to a vain affection of popularity'. Twysden expected to be haled before the Council to answer for his alleged misdemeanours, a list of which was given him by his old friend Bridgman, now Lord Keeper. But though he spent the first half of December in London, awaiting a summons to attend upon the Council, none came, and he heard no more of his transgressions. The Duke of Albemarle tried to persuade him to take up his deputation again, and the Duke of Richmond used him civilly. But Twysden was not to be persuaded. He had never willingly broken the law, he said, and even so had been accused by the Lord Lieutenant; what indeed would his Lordship do if he really transgressed?

It was no 'vain affection of popularity' that motivated Twysden and the others knew it was not. He was old, set in his ways, stiff in his opinions, awkward, uncomplaisant, austere, but not a seeker after popular acclaim. He had too often seen the injustice, misery and bitterness that ensue when men begin to play fast and loose with the law to be willing to indulge in the game himself, and he was prepared to incur the opprobrium of even the most powerful of his fellow gentry in attempting to make sure that they observed the law as scrupulously as he himself did.

CHAPTER TEN

The Scholar

FROM HIS father Twysden inherited a library and a taste for books. His mother also was addicted to reading, and left him some papers of Edward III's reign that he was reluctant to lend even to his friend D'Ewes, so highly did he value them. Sir William's learning lay mainly in Hebrew, of which his son said he had an understanding that few could equal, and in the study of the Bible. To these he added such secular fields of interest as palmistry, physiognomy, and astrology—although to Sir William this last was based on Holy Writ. The difference between his father's interests and his own Twysden summed up in the sentence: 'He took more pleasure in reading the Bible than I should in some well written History'. For official records Twysden had respect, for the chroniclers he had positive affection, those, as he describes them '(whose memory for their industry and learning is ever dear unto me) that have with care transmitted to us what formerly passed'. He was a true bibliophile and tried, with some success, to communicate his enthusiasm for books to his son, for whose benefit (he then being two years old) Twysden recorded this memorandum in his notebook:

'I would not have them come after me sell any of my books, nay though they find I have two of one and the same sort assure himself there was somewhat why I kept them. Nay, if it so fortune I have the same edition twice, as certain works of Padre Paolo's[1] and other printed at Venice 1606 and 1607

[1] Twysden went to much trouble (as did Nathaniel Brent on behalf of James I) to secure a copy of Paolo's *History of the Council of Trent*, a book which gave offence in Rome. When Will Twysden was in Venice in 1632 he was urged by his brother to visit Fulgentio, a companion friar of Paolo,

during the time the Republic was interdicted by Paolo Vto, yet put them not away for they are such books as not to be got, at least of that edition, nor never will be printed again with equal authority by the approbation of the State, see the *Trattato dell' interdetto* printed at Venice anno 1606, not only by the allowance of the Republic but with the arms of that State, and I have two of them of that impression which I keep fearing I may lose one of them, or it might have some mischance, and one or more of another. Now for books that it may be my son cannot understand yet put them not away for some may come after us that will highly esteem them; my father was a great Hebrician and left many books of that tongue, which though I have little knowledge of yet I never parted with any of them, though I could have sold them well. So perhaps I have books of Italian, French, Spanish, and some manuscripts which my son will not regard, perhaps can not read, yet let them not be sold for perhaps his son may esteem them as much as I do. In short I would have my library for an Earthloom, or Heirloom as we call it, to the family of Twysdens for ever.'

These directions Twysden repeated in his will, by which he left his books to his eldest son William, requiring him to preserve them at Roydon Hall and not to alienate them. William followed his father's directions and his example; when he came to make his own will in 1694, he bequeathed to his eldest son Thomas all his books and library 'which I desire may never be sold but remain to my family'. Later the library began to disintegrate. In November 1716 Sir Thomas Sebright told Hearne 'that his library of Sir Roger Twysden contains a multitude of curious books, particularly such as relate to our English history and antiquities, in which Sir Roger was a great master'. Sir Thomas said that Sir Roger had written in many of them, 'which makes the books the more valuable'.[1] Hearne

now dead, and try to get from him more information about the Council; but Fulgentio was old, and though he received Will kindly he really remembered nothing. Twysden's copiously annotated copy of Paolo's work is now in the British Museum.

[1] Lord Acton thought Twysden's marginal notes in the *Historia del Concilio Tridentino* 'in part of real value'.

also records that some of Twysden's manuscripts and transcripts were believed to have been lost in his own lifetime, in 'the frequent removes which his family was forced to make in the time of the Civil Wars'. The library was finally broken up in the nineteenth century when Roydon Hall passed out of the family. Some of the books went to swell the great collections at Surrenden Dering, and when part of the Dering library came under the hammer in 1858—a sale to make the bibliophile's mouth water—thirty-eight of the 1592 items catalogued were noted as bearing Twysden's autograph or, often, manuscript notes. Most of the books which belonged to Twysden were concerned either with political or with ecclesiastical questions. The religious works show a tolerant choice: Cardinal Allen's *Defence of English Catholiques* is balanced by *A Short History of the Anabaptists of High and Low Germany*, for example. Amongst the more curious volumes is a copy, presented to Twysden by the author, of Manasseh Ben Israel's *Humble Address in behalf of the Jewish Nation* and *Vindiciae Judaeorum* published in 1656 in the attempt to enlist support for the Re-settlement of the Jews. Twysden's known tolerance and humanitarian attitude were presumably the qualities which Manasseh Ben Israel found attractive; there seems to be no evidence that he was especially interested in the Re-settlement.[1] Of the Twysden books in the Dering library one work only represents 'English Literature', and that is an effusion of Taylor, the water-poet, on *The Whole Life and Progress of Henry Walker the Ironmonger*.

Genealogy and heraldry were customary pursuits of the seventeenth-century gentleman who had historical proclivities. Twysden's tastes did not lie much in these by-ways, not to say culs-de-sac, of history, although he was on many occasions helpful to or helped by officers of the College of Arms with some of whom he was intimately acquainted. Thomas Philipott, the author of *Villare Cantianum*, who accompanied his father

[1] Dr. Cecil Roth thinks that Manasseh Ben Israel may have distributed copies of his book to several distinguished men (including Selden) as propaganda for his cause. But possibly, as a scholar, he visited Roydon to see the Hebraic collections made by Twysden's father and presented him with the *Humble Address* on that occasion.

John, Rouge Dragon, on his Visitation of Kent in 1619, described Twysden as 'both a gentleman and a scholar', one 'to whom for his learned conduct of these my imperfect labours through the gloomy and perplexed paths of antiquity, and the many difficulties that did assault me, I am signally obliged'. His father, Sir William, was on friendly terms with Selden, William Segar, Garter King-of-Arms, and William le Neve, who, with Sir Edward Dering, were to have witnessed, had not death supervened, the exemplication of twenty-three ancient deeds containing the name of Twysden which he caused to be prepared. Dering and Twysden were near contemporaries and shared a common interest in historical records. Together they gloated over the copy of Magna Charta which came into Dering's possession as Lieutenant of Dover Castle and which was one of many documents given by him to Sir Robert Cotton. As early as 1627 Dering obtained a warrant from the Council authorizing him to examine the public records, and no doubt he communicated some of his discoveries to Twysden in their frequent meetings. At the end of the letter of 24 December 1639, dealing with the coming election, Twysden presses Dering when he comes over to Roydon Hall to bring Thorne's History, that is Thorne's *Chronicles of St. Augustine's Abbey*, with him, and promises him that they will spend the time in reading or walking. It is a little surprising that Twysden was not invited to join that early society of antiquaries, *Antiquitas Rediviva*, which Dering, Sir Christopher Hatton, Sir Thomas Shirley and William Dugdale established in 1638, as, probably, the first example of co-operative historical research. Twysden was known to some, probably to all, of them and he could have become a useful member of the society. Possibly Dering, the author of this small and secret society, felt that one Kentish representative was enough.

Of Twysden's correspondence with foreign scholars such as Padre Fulgentio and Monsieur de Cordes practically nothing survives. It was the kind of correspondence that would certainly have aroused the suspicion of the troopers who searched his house in September 1642 and April 1643 and he feared that

Parliament would place the worst construction upon it. He had simply wished to get more information about the Council of Trent than was available in the libraries of England, but that meant communicating with those who, as foreigners and Roman Catholics, were doubly suspect.

It was his enforced stay in London, beginning in the summer of 1642, that gave Twysden both the motive and the opportunity for making a study of the public records. Whilst he was incarcerated at Lambeth he borrowed Sir Simonds D'Ewes manuscript *Parliamentary Proceedings 1558 to 1601*, taken from the Rolls of Parliament, and made a careful copy—581 closely written pages. (Seven years later D'Ewes was asking for the return of his 'Parliamentary Collections', probably this same manuscript.) Later, after he had been freed from prison but was required to remain in London, he spent a good deal of his time in perusing the records at the Tower of London which were kept under such conditions as to deter all but the most determined and persistent researchers. Some of the transcripts which he made at this time, e.g. Stowe MS 347 now in the British Museum, were written with obvious care and affection, and are quite exquisite. Amongst the documents he transcribed was the coronation service of the Kings of Scotland, copied from the very book that King Charles himself had in his own hand when he was crowned at Edinburgh in 1633. The book belonged to the Duke of Richmond, and Twysden borrowed it from the Duke's steward, William Hedges, who was a fellow-prisoner at Lambeth.

D'Ewes, Selden (described by D'Ewes as 'a man of deep learning and almost incomparable knowledge . . . exceedingly puffed up with the apprehension of his own abilities'), Spelman, Dugdale, Somner were a group of scholars each of whom Twysden could claim as a friend. It was to Selden that Twysden was indebted for advice about getting his sequestration removed and, a few years later, for advice of a more congenial nature, on the *Decem Scriptores* which Twysden was editing. He himself gave Dugdale advice about the second part of his *Monasticon*, promised to get him a sight of certain relevant rolls, and ended his letter 'whenever you have a mind to bestow

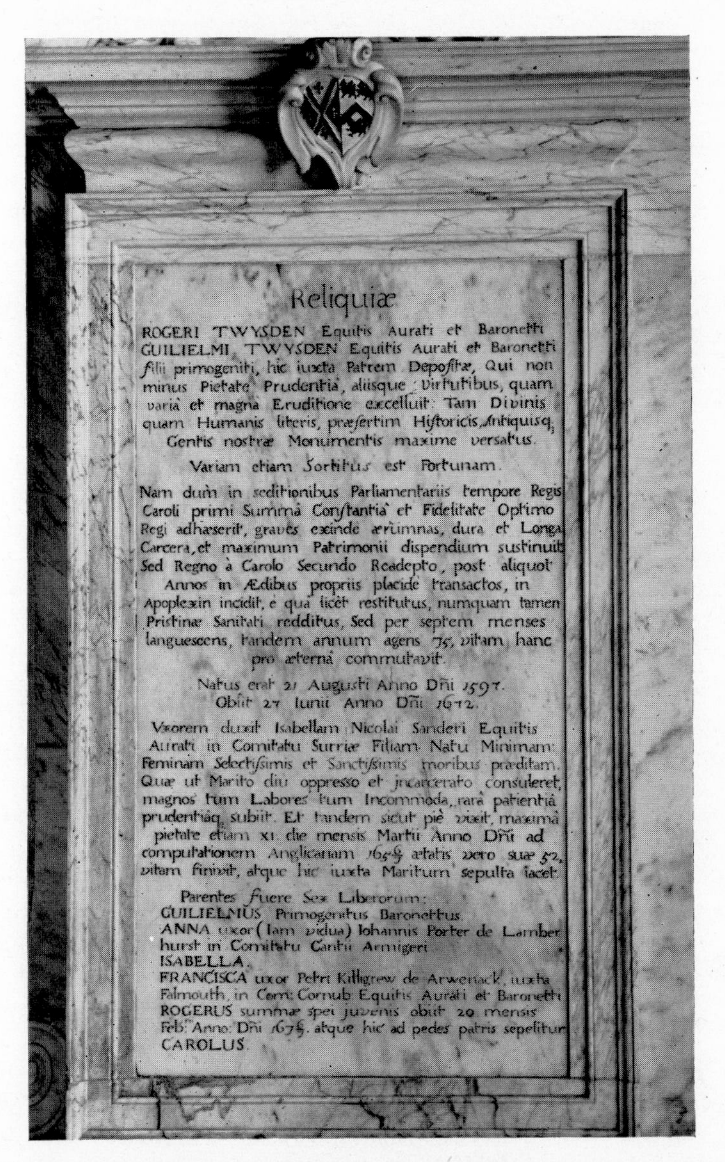

Reliquiæ
ROGERI TWYSDEN Equitis Aurati et Baronetti
GUILIELMI TWYSDEN Equitis Aurati et Baronetti
filii primogeniti, hic iuxta Patrem Depositæ, Qui non
minus Pietate Prudentia, aliisque Virtutibus, quam
varia et magna Eruditione excelluit: Tam Divinis
quam Humanis literis, præsertim Historicis, Antiquisq;
Gentis nostræ Monumentis maxime versatus.
Variam etiam Sortitus est Fortunam.
Nam dum in seditionibus Parliamentariis tempore Regis
Caroli primi Summa Constantia et Fidelitate Optimo
Regi adhæserit, graves exinde ærumnas, dura et Longa
Carcera, et maximum Patrimonii dispendium sustinuit
Sed Regno à Carolo Secundo Readepto, post aliquot
Annos in Ædibus propriis placide transactos, in
Apoplexin incidit, e qua licet restitutus, numquam tamen
Pristinæ Sanitati redditus, Sed per septem menses
languescens, tandem annum agens 75, vitam hanc
pro æterna commutavit.
Natus erat 21 Augusti Anno Dñi 1597.
Obiit 27 Iunii Anno Dñi 1672.
Vxorem duxit Isabellam Nicolai Sanderi Equitis
Aurati in Comitatu Surriæ Filiam Natu Minimam:
Feminam Selectissimis et Sanctissimis moribus præditam.
Quæ ut Marito diu oppresso et incarcerato consuleret,
magnos tum Labores tum Incommoda, rara patientia
prudentiaq; subiit. Et tandem sicut piè vixit, maxima
pietate etiam XI. die mensis Martii Anno Dñi ad
computationem Anglicanam 1656/7 ætatis vero suæ 52,
vitam finivit, atque hic iuxta Maritum sepulta iacet.
Parentes fuere Sex Liberorum:
GUILIELMUS Primogenitus Baronettus.
ANNA uxor (Iam vidua) Iohannis Porter de Lamber
hurst in Comitatu Cantii Armigeri
ISABELLA.
FRANCISCA uxor Petri Killigrew de Arwenack, iuxta
Falmouth, in Com: Cornub Equitis Aurati et Baronetti
ROGERUS summæ spei juvenis obiit 20 mensis
Feb: Anno: Dñi 1675/6. atque hic ad pedes patris sepelitur
CAROLUS.

Memorial to Sir Roger Twysden, 2nd baronet, in St. Michael's Church, East Peckham

a day or two to take the country air, you shall have at your disposal the horses of your most affectionate servant Roger Twysden'. Francis Junius, the philologist, who published an edition of Caedmon in 1655, was another scholar with whom he was in friendly correspondence.

With William Somner of Canterbury Twysden kept up a particularly close and friendly intercourse. They exchanged, as White Kennett wrote in his biography of Somner, 'many kind letters and intimate visits'. Somner sent Twysden notes and corrections to his edition of the *Laws of Henry I*, gave him an ancient cartulary of St. Augustine's Abbey ('now remaining with my very noble and learned friend Sir Roger Twysden' whether as a loan or a gift is not clear[1]), and provided an 'incomparable' glossary to accompany the *Decem Scriptores*. He was the greatest Anglo-Saxon scholar of the day, and Twysden was glad to contribute generously to the *Saxon Dictionary* which Somner published in 1659. Twysden was of superior social rank, but that did not prevent a warm friendship and mutual appreciation developing between the two men, whose experiences and intellectual inclinations were closely parallel. Both were opposed to dangerous innovations of the Puritans and of Parliament, Somner was put out of his office as Registrary of Canterbury Diocese as Twysden was put out of his estate by Parliament, and both had respect for and a delight in history. It was Somner who said that he had made it 'his constant endeavour that truth alone might flourish over falsehood, antiquity over novelty', but Twysden could fairly have described his own efforts in the same words.

It is difficult for the researcher of the twentieth century, with libraries (warmed and well lit), adequate catalogues, easy transport, photostatic copying, microfilms and the rest at his command to imagine the conditions under which the seventeenth-century scholar pursued his historical inquiries. The more ancient public records were at the Tower or Westminster

[1] Perhaps then, as now, too nice a distinction was not always drawn between possession of and property in a book; that at all events seems to be the inference to be deduced from a footnote to chapter V, 4 of *Certain Considerations upon the Government of England*: 'Historicus MSS. liber antiquus quem mihi dedit, vel saltem accommodavit, Dominus Georgius Newman.'

Abbey, the more recent, that is those dating from within the last century or so, were mainly in the hands of the office or court that created them. Professor Wernham ends an account of the whereabouts of the different classes of records in the sixteenth and seventeenth centuries by saying 'I hope this is a thoroughly confusing picture, for if it is, then it is an accurate likeness!'[1] Not only was access to the records physically difficult, but also was prohibitively expensive if fees were exacted according to the prescribed scales; fortunately, they were often waived and sometimes the keepers, being antiquaries themselves, transcribed the records in their charge and the transcripts passed into private hands where generally they were made available for the use of any reputable scholar.

The extent to which seventeenth-century gentlemen were prepared to place their libraries, both manuscripts and printed books, at the disposal of other scholars is cogent testimony to the existence of a sodality of learning. Twysden, as we have already seen, borrowed books from D'Ewes and consulted manuscripts from his library. He was acquainted with the contents of Sir Robert Cotton's collection which, it has recently been pointed out, was in fact if not in name a public library.[2] Others were equally accommodating: the Archbishop of Canterbury allowed Twysden to borrow Becket's epistles and keep them for some years—as Twysden says, one can never be sure precisely when one will need a book or manuscript, and a long loan is therefore essential; he had had the Becket letters in his possession for some five years before he was ready to make use of them. From the Dean and Prebends of Rochester he borrowed for some years the *Textus Roffensis* (containing, amongst other things, the laws of Aethelberht, and of Hlothhere and Eadric) which he returned to the Verger in November 1663 taking a receipt for it. At some period he seems to have had in his hands a manuscript memorandum of John Wycliffe

[1] R. B. Wernham, 'The Public Records in the Sixteenth and Seventeenth Centuries', in *English Historical Scholarship in the Sixteenth and Seventeenth Centuries* (1956), p. 14.

[2] F. Smith Fussner, *The Historical Revolution: English historical writing and thought, 1580–1640* (1962), p. 117.

which belonged to the library of James Ussher,[1] Archbishop of Armagh, and he borrowed manuscripts from Spelman and from Simonds D'Ewes.

The Universities were more cautious in lending their treasures. Benet (or Corpus Christi) College at Cambridge had a manuscript which Twysden would have liked to consult, but it was not forthcoming. He had the same unhelpful experience at Oxford: although he offered a bond of £40 for its return, Bodley's Librarian was not willing to let Walter Map's *De nugis curialium* go out of the library. To be able to use a book effectively, argued Twysden, you must have it in your possession and keep it for a good time so as to be able to work on it, compare it with other copies, and so on. At various times he read in the 'public library' at Oxford, but 'Your University' he wrote in 1669 to his son Charles then at Christ Church 'is so very curious they will not let a man that means them any good have the inspection of their books.' The disappearance of Duke Humphrey's collection within a hundred years of its donation to the University was justification enough for the Librarian's new solicitude for the books entrusted to his care, but the very fact that so reasonable a man as Twysden could regard the Library's refusal to lend a manuscript as unreasonable indicates a general state of library administration that was lax, yet congenial for the borrower.[2]

Twysden's own library at Roydon Hall contained a number of manuscripts, but unfortunately its contents are known only from chance references or opportune survivals. He had, in manuscript, Thorne's Chronicles of St. Augustine's Abbey, William of Newbury's Chronicles, the Letters of St. Anselm (perhaps borrowed from Cotton's library), Bede's *Ecclesiastical History*, William of Malmesbury's Chronicles, Ovid's

[1] Another member of Gray's Inn, having been admitted the year after Twysden, when he was already Bishop of Meath.

[2] Selden also found the Library disobliging in the matter of lending manuscripts, so abandoned his intention of giving his own library to the University of Oxford, leaving it instead to his executors to be disposed of according to their discretion. Fortunately they were discreet enough to give the library to the Bodleian (Hearne, *Letters written by eminent persons in the seventeenth and eighteenth centuries* (1813 edn.), p. 536).

Metamorphoses and *Epistles*, the *Decretum* of Gratian, the *Modus Tenendi Parliamentum*, *Officia Sanctorum*, and doubtless much else besides. Some of his manuscripts, and some of his books with learned and copious annotations, have found their way into the British Museum.[1] From time to time he made additions to the library; in 1628 he took the opportunity when he was in Edinburgh of purchasing books, and when his brother William was in France five years later Twysden asked him to buy some books, and sent him £5. Of purchases made in London there is no record but that they were many is scarcely to be doubted. Not only did he own books, but he read them, copying into his numerous common-place books passages or legal cases which he afterwards put to good use when he assumed the mantle of author ('notions in garrison, whence the owner may draw out an army into the field on competent warning' Fuller called such notes). Twysden did not write readily or spontaneously; he was a 'painful' author. Everything was carefully drafted, corrected and re-drafted, and his many notebooks now preserved at the British Museum, the Bodleian Library, Lambeth Palace Library, the Kent Archives Office, amongst the Kent Archaeological Society's collections and elsewhere show his ideas slowly developing from brief notes through essays to dissertations which afterwards were incorporated into his major works.

Twysden's first publication was an edition of the *Laws of Henry I*, transcribed from the Red Book of the Exchequer and never before printed, which appeared at Cambridge in 1644 as a supplement to a new edition of Bede's *Ecclesiastical History*. To it was also appended a new edition of Lambarde's *Laws of the Saxon Kings* (the *Archaeonomia* of 1568), Selden's version of the *Laws of William I* which Twysden was able to amplify from the Red Book, and a short Latin preface which Twysden himself wrote. The volume also contained a Saxon Glossary, not Twysden's work, which Somner observed to be faulty in many places. This work was the fruits of his enforced idleness in London during the first two years of the Civil War.

[1] At least ten ancient manuscripts now in the British Museum were once in Twysden's possession. See Appendix, p. 216.

His next publication was a thirty-two-page pamphlet which appeared, without author's or publisher's name, in 1648 under the title *The Commoner's Liberty: or the Englishman's Birthright.* It is an answer to the thesis propounded by the unpredictable William Prynne in *A Plea for the Lords*, published earlier in the same year, that the House of Lords had the power, in a legal way, to proceed against and punish a commoner. The House precipitated the dispute by its condemnation of Lilburne in 1646 and Maynard in 1647 (strange to think of the sober Twysden becoming an ally of the, literally, extraordinary Lilburne). That the Lords had jurisdiction over commoners 'the ignorant, sottish sectaries, Levellers, seduced by their blind guides Lilburne and Overton, peremptorily deny' says Prynne in his usual vigorous, unabashed manner 'the contrary whereof I shall infallibly make good to their perpetual shame and refutation'. He pours out a flood of authorities and references but carried away with the sheer joy of controversy his argument becomes incoherent, and in the end it is not certain exactly what question he is seeking to answer or what thesis he is propounding. Such was not Twysden's way of conducting a debate. Master Prynne he politely refers to as a great lawyer, but as for the 'ignorant, sottish sectaries' Twysden continues 'I must needs say (to answer once for all) that this is not a sincere way of treating the matter in question'. Then, in contrast with Prynne's rodomontade, 'Before I pass further, it will not be amiss to agree upon the question', which he then states simply and clearly, stripped of all the irrelevancies under which Prynne buries it. Point by point he rebuts Prynne, demonstrating that he also knows the precedents, that, moreover, he understands them, and that they do not support the proposition that the Lords have jurisdiction at first instance over a commoner. Finally he arrives at the question, if the peers try a commoner, what remedy has he? It might be argued that prohibition or supersedeas out of the King's Bench would be the proper remedy, but Twysden, doubting whether the King's Bench has jurisdiction over the High Court of Parliament, prefers to leave the question unanswered and concludes 'remembering that true advice of Master Prynne: *That who shall so suffer, shall have the comfort of a good conscience to support him;* and God, no doubt, will in his good time find some means to relieve him.' Twysden's own copy of the work, with copious marginal additions 'to be printed in the book itself, if ever it be reprinted' is now in the Bodleian Library. He returned to the subject in an exhaustive correspondence in 1668 with his cousin Sir Heneage Finch, Solicitor-General, afterwards Earl of Nottingham and Lord Chancellor. The controversy had arisen again in 1666 in the case of Skinner *v.* The East India Company, wherein the House of Lords assumed jurisdiction in a civil case and ordered the Company to pay £5,000 damages to Skinner, notwithstanding its plea that the matter was triable in the Common Law Courts and that the Lords had no authority to hear the action. The Company received the support of the Commons and a contention developed between the two Houses. The Solicitor-General, on such an issue of legal history, found it useful to have the views of Twysden, and they were furnished in good measure. The Lords' pretension is looked upon by some, wrote Twysden, 'as a burying of the regal power and liberty of the subject . . . for if they may originally judge a commoner and his rights, within a small time Westminster Hall may stand idle and they the only supreme judicatory of the nation'. And again, in a later letter, 'If the Lords get the point of a general jurisdiction over a commoner . . . we may, in a short time, talk of liberty but find none.' Finch urged the case against the Lords' claim and although it was not formally withdrawn, the Lords never again attempted to exercise original jurisdiction over a commoner.

This was the kind of inquiry in which Twysden delighted, the examination of some constitutional issue against the background of precedent. *The Commoner's Liberty* is a chip off the major work that he was engaged upon during the 1640's, *Certain Considerations upon the Government of England.* In the notebook, probably of 1640–1, which contains a first outline of the material later worked up into *Certain Considerations,* he wrote 'I have thought fit for my own satisfaction and remembrance to set down briefly some considerations touching the government of the Kingdom of England . . . though I know my own imperfections and wants to be such as I must do it very lamely, but this I assure myself, none shall ever mislike it because none shall ever see what I have set down'. But as the work proceeds, through various revisions, it becomes clear that Twysden was conscious of writing for an audience. His experiences of arbitrary and disordered government during the years which followed his first essay into the subject probably accounted for the increasingly public and polemical style. He had abundant, albeit involuntary leisure, and opportunity for searching the official records and using the transcripts of them made available to him by his friend Sir Simonds D'Ewes. For several years he was at work on the manuscript, making emendations mainly by way of addition, but also, in the case of some scholarly paragraphs, demonstrating Coke's failings as an historian, by excision. He had the manuscript fair-copied for circulation amongst his friends, but it did not appear in print until two hundred years later, when it was published by the Camden Society with an Introduction by J. M. Kemble in 1849.

Twysden had evidently read Filmer's *Patriarcha* (the printed edition of which was not published until 1680) and in *Certain Considerations* he examines and refutes some of Filmer's arguments that kings enjoy absolute power as the inheritors of the absolute power exercised by Adam. It is easy to show the vacuity of the argument, and Twysden does so more simply and common sensibly (and perhaps more effectively) than Locke in his *First Treatise of Government*. But he is not really concerned about questions of political philosophy, about the origin of government and the nature of political obligation. To Twysden it was self-evident that there must be government, that civilized life would be impossible, unimaginable, without it. What to him was of interest and importance was the way in which, and the conditions subject to which, political power was, and ought to be, exercised in contemporary England. The 'ought' he derived not from philosophical speculation but from England's history. It was this inquiry which caused him to embark on the first constitutional history of England.

In his first chapter, on the origin of government, Twysden

comes as near to an exposition of political philosophy as he ever gets. In his view of human nature he is nearer to Locke than to Hobbes: 'Experimental moderation amongst good men' he says 'advanced the first kings, not ambition', a statement which was surely intended as a rejection in terms of Hobbes' position. In Chapters 2 to 6 and 8 he deals with the monarchy in England, which he avers is limited yet, *pace* Filmer, is rightly called a monarchy. He traces the history of kingship in England, declining, with a caution greater than that shown by Coke, to go back to an earlier period than Saxon England. The Norman Conquest presented a difficulty to all those who wanted to prove a continuous line of development from the kings of the Heptarchy to the Stuarts, and the lawyers sought to diminish its importance by giving an artificial meaning to the word 'conquest'. Twysden faced the difficulty directly, and showed that William based his claim on right, not on force, that he was not received as absolute monarch but in some sense conditionally, and that in any event he could not be termed the 'conqueror' of his Norman followers, whose descendants formed part, but not a distinguishable part, of the English nation within a century or so after the year 1066.

Chapter 7 is an examination of the liberty of the subject, and of what it comprises. Liberty has been protected sometimes by force (Chapter 9), sometimes by other means, notably by the evolution of Parliament, to the history of which the last six chapters are devoted.

Twysden deals squarely with the question over which seventeenth-century men agonized, whether it is ever lawful to take up arms against the prince. He sought the answer in precedent, in authority as revealed by the Bible, and in common sense. Neither precedent nor the Scriptures, he believes, positively forbid the resort to force in every circumstance, but he concludes characteristically, with Machiavellian realism and prudence, that the people ought not to take up arms against the King because, by doing so, they are certain in the long run to hurt themselves. It is the worst sort of people, the extremists, that come to the top in any insurrection, the better sort suffer, and liberty instead of being enlarged is abridged. It is an unheroic and sensible conclusion, forced upon him not only by his reading of ancient and modern history, but also by his own experiences of the last few years. He would not have accepted the terms of the declaration against the legality of a resort to arms required to be made by parsons and teachers under the Act of Uniformity, 1662, and it may be that his unorthodoxy on this point was one of the reasons why *Certain Considerations* was not published during his lifetime. It was not a work that would have commended itself to those who were empowered to grant licences to publish under the Licensing Act of 1662 any more than it would have received the approbation of the Long Parliament.[1]

The last third of the book is devoted to a treatment of Parliament from the time of the Saxons up to the middle of the seventeenth century. Twysden was very conscious of the importance of Parliament in the constitution and is never in any danger of underestimating it *vis-à-vis* the powers of the Crown. At the same time he knew, from experience as well as from history, that an assembly can behave as tyrannically as a monarch, and the last chapter is significantly entitled 'What things Parliaments usually have not meddled with'. He regarded the constitution as properly providing a balance between Crown, Parliament and the judiciary, and in fact he comes near to enunciating the doctrine of the separation of the powers almost a hundred years before Montesquieu. In an early draft of the book there is an additional chapter 'Of the chief subverters of this government' by which he means flatterers of royalty, especially such as are privy counsellors, divines, and lawyers. It is a slight chapter, and Twysden was wise to suppress it.

Certain Considerations is not a profound work of original thought but it is a good journeyman-like constitutional history, so far as I know the first of its kind, and scholarly and honest

[1] In his will Twysden besought his heir 'to keep constantly his allegiance and his loyalty to his King . . . as I myself have done before him to endure what any usurping power shall force on him rather than swerve from his fidelity to his Prince . . .' but to remember that 'they serve him best who serve him according to his Laws'.

in the handling of evidence.[1] It has obvious limitations, as for example in its omission of any account of the development of the courts of law and of administration, but it is not the only constitutional history to be deficient in those particulars. The style befits the subject, and Twysden rarely strains after rhetorical effect. It is not, like some seventeenth-century treatises, dropsically out of proportion, and both for its intrinsic merits and as a pioneer work it deserves more notice than it seems to have received.

Several years later Twysden drew again on material which he had amassed in preparing *Certain Considerations* when, in 1666, he was corresponding with his cousin Sir Heneage Finch, Solicitor-General, about punishment for treason, particularly the forfeiture of the traitor's estate. Twysden cites numerous historical examples to show that forfeiture, which he regards as both impolitic and unjust, was not primordial in the law of England and that, contrary to the view propounded by Finch, our laws on treason are not mild compared with those of pre-Conquest England nor with those of other states, past or present, such as Germany, Persia, Polonia, Venice, Rome, Aragon, Biscany and Catalonia. Again, it is an impressive display of learning effectively used. He concludes the correspondence by adding that he had intended to say something about scandalous behaviour in the House of Commons 'in captivating men's votes by feasting, drinking, etc.', but he has said enough already and entreats Finch to burn the letter, an injunction which fortunately he disregarded. Finch, the 'Father of Equity' was a great lawyer and that he was anxious to have Twysden's opinion is convincing testimony of his reputation for scholarship amongst those of his contemporaries who were best able to judge of it.

In *An Historical Vindication of the Church of England in point of*

[1] Twysden knew, and valued, the works of Fortescue and Sir Thomas Smith, but neither of them can be regarded as a constitutional historian; still less can such writers as Coke and Prynne. Elsynge's *The Ancient Method and Manner of holding Parliaments in England* (which was not published until 1660, after Twysden had written *Certain Considerations*) touches on some of the same matters but is rather an exposition of contemporary practice than an historical treatise.

Schism as it stands separated from the Roman, and was reformed 1 Elizabeth, published in 1657 although probably written some years earlier, Twysden subjected the Reformation to the same cool historical examination that was applied in *Certain Considerations* to the constitution. His whole thesis is a refutation of Baronius's allegation that the Roman church prescribed as articles of faith none that had not been accepted by the primitive church and transmitted through the Fathers. It is not a work of theological disputation any more than *Certain Considerations* is a treatise on political philosophy. He says specifically that he will not argue 'the truth of any controversial tenet between us and the church of Rome' . . . 'I do not in this at all take upon me the disputation much less the theological determination of any controverted tenet (but leave that as the proper subject to divines), this being only an historical narration.' Nevertheless some of his private papers show that he was not indifferent to doctrinal questions. The commonplace book which he called 'Theologica' contains many of his own notes on controverted issues: do Roman Catholics in fact hold, as Protestants allege, that faith need not be kept with heretics? (perhaps not, is his conclusion, but the evidence shows that Protestants have cause to fear it is an opinion of some Papists) and on predestination, a doctrine which seemed to Twysden abhorrent, as it must to every humane man, he found comfort in the thought that Christ came to save the *world*, to succour *all* men, not only an *élite*.

At the outset of *An Historical Vindication* he declares that he is not prepared to defend the dissolution of the monasteries;[1] true they had strayed so far from their first institutions as to retain little save the name, but they had nourished men of piety and learning. It was the nature of the Pope's care of England which interested him most. He had no difficulty in showing, as a matter of history, that the pre-Augustinian Church in England was not regarded as subject to Rome, and whilst in Saxon and Norman England Rome and its Bishop

[1] Nor is he prepared to defend other actions of Henry VIII, such as burning Becket's bones, taking the treasure of his shrine, or beheading Fisher even though he had been found guilty of treason.

were highly regarded for their piety and learning, the reverence yielded to the Pope 'for more than a thousand years after Christ (was) . . . no other than the respect of love, not of duty; and Popes rather to *consulere* than to *imperare*'. The Pope's power over England being gained little by little and voluntarily submitted to (many historical instances are quoted to support these statements) must be *iure humana*. The Archbishop of Canterbury had no mediate spiritual superior (for such was not the Crown) but only Christ and God, and therefore the Church in England adhering thus to its ghostly superior could not be guilty of schism. The course of the Reformation under Henry VII, Edward VI, and Elizabeth is examined in detail, and shown to be justified by precedent. Contrary to his expressed intention, Twysden finds himself arguing on a doctrinal question, the doctrine of transubstantiation as propounded in the Elizabethan settlement. Finally he leaves it to divines, as a matter controversial but, he avers, in what Elizabeth and her Parliament did they 'had antiquity to justify their actions'.

This last phrase, which gives the key to Twysden's whole attitude to his subject, is an echo of the two texts printed on the title-page: 'Remember the days of old, consider the years of many generations. Ask thy father, and he will show thee; thy elders, and they will tell thee' (Deuteronomy xxxii, 7), and 'Ask for the old paths, where is the good way, and walk therein; and ye shall find rest for your souls' (Jeremiah vi, 16).

The Church in England, asserts Twysden, did not withdraw from the Roman Church. What happened was that the Church, in lawful synod, declared that certain opinions held by some in her communion were not articles of faith, and also redressed certain abuses; whereupon the Pope, without examining the rights of the case or the precedents, would needs interpret this as a departure from the Church. There was no encroachment by the Crown on the Papal primacy 'which (for ought I know) it might have acknowledged so far as is expressed or deduced from Holy Scripture, or laid down in the ancient sacred councils, or the constant writings of the ancient primitive Fathers'. It is we, of England, so Twysden maintains, who hold to the ancient faith; if the Roman Church can prove otherwise 'truly for my part I shall think fit to yield'.

It is a calm, urbane and learned piece of writing, in the tradition of Hooker and Fuller and with the charitable tolerance of the Church of England at its best.[1] Twysden never descends to abuse; he can pursue his argument without recourse to such sobriquets as the Whore of Babylon, and he not only rejects the equation of the Pope and Antichrist as offensive, but also as being inaccurate and plainly discrepant from the scriptural definition. On its own terms it is a convincing demonstration and Twysden quotes all his authorities so that if the reader doubts his statements he can verify them for himself. The Preface to the Reader ends with a touch of humour—if he dislikes the book 'his loss will not be great either in time or cost' (the book runs to only 199 pages octavo), and a modest declaration that the author is very willing to be convinced of his own errors, which is, I believe, more than a mere figure. A second edition of the book appeared in 1675, and it was thought of sufficient relevance to what Mark Pattison called the debate 'whether England was in a state of schism or no' to justify a third edition in 1847.

A year or so after the publication of the *Historical Vindication* in the early months of 1659, Twysden was engaged in a correspondence (now preserved partly at the British Museum, partly at the Kent County Archives Office, and partly at Lambeth Palace Library) with his distant cousin, Thomas Whetenhall, a Roman Catholic, who had been obliged to leave his home at East Peckham and was dwelling in London. They agreed that the three great subjects in issue between them were the scriptural canon, papal supremacy, and transubstantiation. The controversy was conducted with perfect good manners, but their methods of argument were different and there was never

[1] Twysden seems to have been on friendly terms with Herbert Thorndyke, Fellow of Trinity College, Cambridge (see the Latin poem addressed to him by 'H.Th.' now in the K.A.S. collections, 11.47/47 Z.2) of whom Mr. Ogg writes that he 'succeeded in evolving doctrines so oecumenic in character as to receive the commendation of Cardinal Newman' (*England in the reign of Charles II* (1963 ed.), i, p. 211). It is fairly safe to assume that the Cardinal would not altogether have disapproved of Twysden.

any hope that either would convert the other; Twysden relied on the citation of copious historical incidents, especially in relation to the Pope's supremacy, whereas Whetenhall bases himself on 'a truth so universally owned ought not to be disbelieved upon probabilities' and on 'the Church [which] is my security; and in grateful return for that happy tranquillity which I experience by relying on her' it is his duty to defend her. In transubstantiation and the canon of Scripture Twysden was handling matters where the empirical approach of the English common law was singularly inapt—at least, in his opponent's view, and probably in his own, also—but even there he displayed wide reading coupled with a critical attitude towards his authorities. The sects he does not seek to defend, but the Church of England is truly a Catholic Church, and Protestants ought not 'to be esteemed heretics to be proceeded against with more severity than against Turks and infidels. . . . God grant us that charity should be amongst Christians, and minds rather to seek truth than prevailing against each other.' Whetenhall courteously responded by begging that they should adjourn further examination of the controverted authorities 'till we meet once again in your closet, the properest place to examine books wherewith you are so excellently furnished'.

Certain Considerations and the *Historical Vindication of the Church of England* have been considered together because they are, whether intended to be so or not, companion pieces, the constitutional history of the body politic and of the body religious. A work which may also be taken with them is the preface which Twysden wrote to an edition published by him in 1653 of a treatise in manuscript of Sir Robert Filmer *Questio Quodlibetica; or a Discourse whether it may be lawful to take use for money*. The treatise was written by Filmer some thirty years earlier, and it had come into Twysden's hands at a time when he was perplexed about the morality of paying interest on the heavy debts which he inherited from his father. He was, he says, persuaded by some friends to publish Filmer's tract to the world. In an historian-like way Twysden's Preface examines the evidence and the authorities: 'Upon the whole matter I could not conclude, either by express words or necessary inference out of scripture, or the practice of the Primitive Church, either giving or taking interest for money lent, to be in its own nature amongst Christians sinful, so as no other circumstances made it so', and provided it is used with charity. 'Yet I do not take it upon me to determine it absolutely lawful, I leave that to some learned divine, only I have here historically related what I met with in the inquiry.' Filmer dealt with it more bluntly: 'This point of usury, as it is at this day controverted, is a mere popish question . . . [usury] is as lawful as any other contract or bargain, unless the laws of the land do prohibit or moderate it. . . . No commonwealth can or ever did stand without it.' And lest this seem merely the new mercantile spirit finding expression in Protestant doctrine, it is only fair to add that Filmer paid, but never took, interest on borrowed money.

The year before the publication of Filmer's tract Twysden put out, in 1652, a large work, the one for which he is probably best known, the *Historiae Anglicanae Scriptores Decem.* Cornelius Bee,[1] an industrious book-seller ('so industrious, as literally to answer his own name,' Somner said of him), tried to persuade Twysden about 1642 to edit and publish some of the various histories and chronicles 'most of them in a manner dissolved with the monasteries, wherein they laid and slept. Some of them had been raised from the dust by Joceline, Howard, Parker, Camden, Savile: but many were yet in chains of darkness which it would be justice and mercy to redeem, and expose to view.'

There were several respectable precedents for such a venture. In 1587 Commelinus published at Heidelberg a folio volume containing the chronicles of Geoffrey of Monmouth, Gildas, Bede, William of Newbury and John Froissard. Savile edited a collectanea consisting of William of Malmesbury, Henry of Huntingdon, Roger Hoveden, Ethelward and Ingulph which was published at London in 1596 and republished at Frankfurt five years later. Also published at Frankfurt in 1602 was another large folio volume, edited by Camden which included

[1] Bee's name appears on the title-page, but some copies bear also the name Lugd. Batav.

Asser, a life of William the Conqueror, Thomas Walsingham, Thomas de la More, William Gemiticensis and Giraldus Cambrensis. As long ago as 1571 Archbishop Parker had published Matthew Paris's *Chronica Majoram.* Selden edited the chronicles of Eadmer and published them, with his own 'Notae et Spicilegium' at London in 1623. But as Twysden and his friends knew, a vast number of chronicles had yet to be published, and until they were made accessible the history of England could not be written.

At first Twysden doubted his competence for such a task but he was encouraged in the enterprise by Archbishop Ussher and Selden, and finding that no one else came forward he finally resolved to undertake it. Through Selden he obtained six important manuscripts from the Cottonian Library and got them ready for the press. He employed a careful copyist, Ralph Jennings, who went to Cambridge to transcribe manuscripts, mainly at Corpus Christi College, and he persuaded Selden to write an introductory account of the ten chroniclers and Somner to provide a glossary, to which was appended the Old English alphabet for the benefit of those not accustomed to the language.[1] Twysden, in addition to examining the transcripts with the originals and preparing the book for the press, contributed a Preface in which he carefully described the provenance of the manuscripts used. The whole work is in Latin, a thick folio of more than 1600 pages. In it he found room for the chronicles and histories of Simeon of Durham, John of Hexham, Richard of Hexham, Ailred of Rievaulx, Ralph de Diceto, John Brompton of Joreval, Gervase Dorobornensis, Thomas Stubbs, William Thorn, and Henry Knighton.

The *Decem Scriptores* was well received, 'even the Puritans themselves . . . displayed something like a patriotic ardour in purchasing copies of this work as soon as it appeared',[2] and it remains as a conspicuous monument to his industry and

[1] A few years later Twysden bore a generous share of the costly edition of Somner's Saxon Dictionary (White Kennet's *Life of Somner*, in *Gavelkind* (2nd edn., 1726) 127). He also subscribed £10 towards the printing of the great Hebrew Bible, and got eleven others to do the same, collecting their contributions by instalments.

[2] Hearne, preface to *Otterbourne*, cited D. N. B.

scholarship, and to the co-operative effort of Twysden, Selden, Somner, Jennings and 'A.S.' who prepared the indexes. Twysden's care and accuracy are shown by the brevity of the addenda, corrigenda, and errata, running altogether to only three pages. Where they could he and Jennings collated different manuscripts of the chronicles, and published eleven pages of variant readings. The printer for his part was equally assiduous, casting a new fount of type and obtaining a fine paper for his book. By providing the quarry from which they could draw their material Twysden has deserved the gratitude of later historians of the Middle Ages, and his work has not been completely superseded by that of later editors, whose superior, in some respects, he remains.[1]

Towards the end of his life he was working on other manuscripts which he hoped to publish. Hearing that a rumour was passing around the University that he had further publication in mind he writes to Charles at Christ Church: 'Send me word how you come to know I am putting out of anything and what they say it is . . . truly if I had time, leisure and life I should set out some things that I do think not unfit to be published, but how thou shouldest know me to be about anything to be divulged I profess I do not a little admire.' There is no evident reason for this secrecy. The Archbishop of Canterbury had lent him Becket's letters, and these he proposed to print with Becket's life but it would make a small volume, as he wrote to his friend Dugdale on 7 April 1668 and to make it a 'just' volume he would like to include the Epistles of Anselm which he remembered to have seen in Cotton's Library; will Dugdale be so kind as to get the manuscript for him? The St. Anselm's Epistolae now in the British Museum (Stowe MSS. 33) which bears a note in Twysden's hand that it was examined by him and Charles Higins, the amanuensis, was presumably copied from the Cotton manuscript. However, difficulties supervened, Twysden was now over seventy, and the volume of Becket's letters and life and Anselm's letters never appeared.

Another of Twysden's works, *The Beginners of a Monastic Life*

[1] D. C. Douglas, *English Scholars 1660–1730* (2nd edn. 1951), pp. 220, 224, 225.

in Asia, Africa, and Europe, although dated 1661, did not appear in print until 1698, when it was published and bound in the same volume as Spelman's *The History and Fate of Sacrilege*. Spelman's book was written in 1632, and Wood says that it began to be printed in 1663 but stuck long in the press and the sheets printed off were lost in the Fire of London. Then one 'since become a prelate of our Church' forbade the printer to proceed, lest the work gave offence to the nobility and gentry. In it Spelman gives an account of the misfortunes which had overtaken those who had had dealings with religious lands following the Dissolution: since they included the ancestors of many of the nobility and gentry, there was reason for fearing that offence might be taken. Presumably it was because they both dealt with aspects of monastic houses that Spelman's and Twysden's works were ultimately published together. The manuscripts of the two works are now in the Bodleian Library bound up together in a collection of manuscripts sent by Dugdale to Thomas Barlow (MSS. Barlow 9).

The Beginners of a Monastic Life was almost certainly printed from the Bodleian manuscript, which is not in Twysden's own hand. It is obvious that the reference to Asia, Africa, and Europe in the title was a mistake on the part of the printer, who included in the title a few lines which were intended as a summarized list of contents. The book is, indeed, little concerned with Asia or Africa but is mainly about England, especially the authority of the Crown over the monasteries, and their withdrawal from the normal episcopal jurisdiction into the Pope's own hand. It shows Twysden's usual historical sense, but it is not an orderly and comprehensive treatment of the topic. On the last page of the manuscript appears a note 'Roger Twysden was author of this epistle' and the writing has the tone of a letter, not of a work intended for publication. The long and almost irrelevant digressions become explicable if it was an answer written by Twysden to a series of specific inquiries on, e.g. the antiquity of the prohibition on marriage, and variations in the tonsure. Both manuscript and the printed work break off in the middle of a sentence. A clue to the identity of the person to whom the letter was addressed is offered by the introductory words of the last paragraph, which are not related to what has gone before: 'Now I come to the Priory of Coventry . . .' From this it seems possible that Twysden's correspondent was William Dugdale, county historian of Warwickshire, and this possibility is made a high probability by the fact that the Bodleian manuscript was formerly in Dugdale's possession.

Dugdale and Twysden were on friendly terms and Twysden was no stranger to the Heralds Office, where Dugdale began as Rouge Croix Pursuivant and ended as Garter King-of-Arms. They had common interests, about which they were accustomed to correspond. In a long letter dated 11 November (1658) Twysden gave Dugdale some advice which now seems so obvious that it is hard to remember that, with Spelman, Twysden was a pioneer in bringing a scientific attitude to the examination of historical documents:

> 'I have sometimes told you I did wish in the preface to your second edition of *Monasticon* you would express somewhat as if you did not answer for the truth of every Bull or Charter you have related. . . . there never was greater forgers of Bulls and Charters than monks in former times were: I remember they of St. Augustine by Canterbury produced a bull, in lead, of their founder's, when no Pope used such a seal till 770. . . . But to come to the Book, page 16 is the Charter of King Edgar. I no way doubt his making such a charter . . . but, Sir, I shall desire you to consider whether it were the style of those times to write *Salve Romanae ecclesiae dignitate*, whether it doth agree with the other acts of that King. . . . Pages 66 and 67 you have a Bull of Pope Agatho, which Theodore approving writes himself *Romana legatione in has finas terrae destinatus*; certainly Theodore never used any such subscription. . . .' and so on.

In his own use of manuscripts Twysden noted carefully the probable date of the handwriting, and where it was contemporary with the events recorded he was prepared to give greater credence to the document. The methods he used are now the accepted methods of diplomatic, but in the seventeenth century they represented a new approach to the study of historical documents. Not many of his contemporaries read old manuscripts with the critical attention that he devoted to them; not many would have thought to write in the margin of a manuscript account of Edward I and Robert the Bruce which made reference to the Earl of Southampton the devastating comment: 'There was no Earl of Southampton in those days so this is merely fabulous'.[1]

Twysden has one other literary work to his credit:[2] *An Historical Narrative of the two Houses of Parliament and either of them, their committees' and agents' violent proceeding against Sir Roger Twysden their imprisoning his person, sequestering his estate, cutting down his woods and timber to his almost undoing, and forcing him in the end to composition for his own.* It was not published for two hundred years, until 1858–61, when the Reverend L. B. Larking, the founder and Honorary Secretary of the Kent Archaeological Society, who had married Frances Twysden of Roydon Hall, printed it in the first four volumes of *Archaeological Cantiana*. Although it is dated 11 December 1657, internal evidence suggests that it was mainly written some years earlier, about 1651 to 1653, with subsequent small alterations and additions. Twysden certainly wrote it with the intention that others should read it. The manuscript now in Lambeth Palace Library has a carefully written title-page with suitable quotations from Cicero and Tacitus. The reader is addressed directly—'I shall desire the reader impartially to consider,' 'You may ask me here', 'You may perhaps further inquire', 'Yet I think not unfit to tell the reader', and so on. The author is self-conscious about his digressions and occasionally offers conventional apologies for them. Perhaps he was writing in the main for his sons and their descendants. The

[1] Jean Mabillon's *De re diplomatica*, which raised the serious criticism of historical documents to the level of a science was published in 1681, thirty years or so after Twysden made these comments.

[2] He has been reputed to be the author of a manuscript treatise concerning Bishops being judges in Parliament in cases capital, but the manuscript, now in the Kent Archives Office (U. 48 Z/4) is not in his hand, and it asserts that anciently Lords and Commons sat together, a view which is specifically rejected in *Certain Considerations* (xi, 18). For these and other reasons, including stylistic, it seems very unlikely that Twysden was the author.

last paragraph is a heartfelt prayer that the country may be rescued from its burdens, that it may 'never see a perpetuity added to the two Houses of Parliament, nor committees to manage the justice of the Kingdom . . . admitting not the law for their rule: but the arbitrary, ambiguous, revocable, disputable Orders and Ordinances of one or two Houses, if not of their own framing. . . .' But, adds Twysden, this 'as things now stand, is rather to be prayed for than expected; neither can I find any way how it can be, but must remit all to the only wise God who . . . may be pleased to find some means of restoring everyone to their rights, the law to its vigour, by a just Protector of it'. Within a little more than two years after this was written a Stuart was back on the throne, and Twysden had to substitute King for Protector: so much for man's ability to foresee how events will develop.

'To be ignorant of evils to come and forgetful of evils past is a merciful provision in nature' said Sir Thomas Browne. Twysden's remembrance of evils past was keen and seems to be accurate. No doubt, like other men, he remembered his own side of the argument better than his opponents', and his account of his capture, in disguise, at Bromley is a little disingenuous—no man would wish to remember all the embarrasing details of that humiliating episode. Yet, although the *Narrative* is an *ex parte* memoir, it is supported by the evidence of public records and of the Roydon Hall and Chelmington estate books. It is an historical narrative, and Twysden had succeeded in preserving a rare degree of objectivity in that most difficult form of personal history, autobiography.

Objectivity, a consciously historical and scientific attitude towards the evidence, wide learning, and a becoming scepticism about his own conclusions stamp all Twysden's work. His reading was extensive: the Bible, of course, the Fathers, the classical authors, especially Aristotle (but not Plato), Xenophon, Caesar, Cicero, Dio Cassius, Juvenal, Livy, Lucan, Martial, Pliny, Plutarch, Seneca, Suetonius, Tacitus; Justinian's Code; Almainus, Aquinas, Barclay, Baronius, Bellarmine, Blesensis, Bodin, Cajetan, Castiglione, Comines, Gratian, Grotius, Luther, Mariana, Marsiglio, Pasquier,

Guilelmus Pictaviensis, John of Salisbury, Soave, du Tillet, de Thon, the Villani; the English Chroniclers, especially Brompton, Coggeshall, Diceto, Gervase Dorobornensis, Simeon Dunelm, Eadmer, Guilelmus Gemiticensis, Hall, Hoveden, Huntingdon, Ingulph, Knighton, Malmesbury, Newbury, Matthew Paris, Thorne, Stow, Polydor Virgil, Ordericus Vitalis, Matthew of Westminster, Walsingham and Florence of Worcester; Asser, Bede, Bilson, Bracton, Britton, Buchanan, Camden, Edmund Campion, Coke, Dyer, Ferne, Fleta, Fortescue, Fox, Plowden, Savile, Selden, Smith, Spelman, Stamford, Stapleton, Ussher, not to mention the Statutes, the Rolls of Parliament, the Commons' Journals and the Close Rolls—these are some of the works from which he quotes, but his reading was by no means limited to them. The surprising omission is *The Laws of Ecclesiastical Polity*. Such was Hooker's reputation in the seventeenth century and so similar were Twysden and Hooker in interests, outlook and temperament that one would have expected to find in Twysden's work numerous references to *The Laws of Ecclesiastical Polity*, whereas there appears not to be a single one. He had in his library *A Christian Letter of certain English protestants unto Richard Hooker requiring resolution in certain matters of doctrine in his Ecclesiastical Policy*, and it is very unlikely that he would have this without having Hooker's own work, which every man with any pretension to scholarship must have known.

Twysden's use of the Bible is far more sophisticated than was usual at the time. He never produces a text merely to belabour his opponent with it. The Old Testament he reads as an historian, and as the story of the Jewish people; he distinguishes between divine directions addressed to all men at all times and the particular rules laid down for the governance of the Jews. In the main he uses the Old Testament as a source of historical illustration in the same way as he uses Livy, Tacitus, Bede, or Matthew de Paris; he goes to it not for authority but to find out how human government has in fact been carried on.

Twysden learnt Anglo-Saxon at a time when few men had much knowledge of it. With him, as with Spelman and Somner, historical led to philological interests, for they saw that a knowledge of Anglo-Saxon was the essential key to the cryptic history of pre-Conquest England, and it was this little group of scholars that brought about what might fairly be called an English Language Renaissance. Of the three Somner was the greatest Anglo-Saxon scholar, but Twysden commanded a respectable knowledge of the language. He was ready in Greek and Latin, and besides knew French, Italian and Spanish, though he regretted his scanty Hebrew. For him a knowledge of these languages was essential so that he could read the records and literary works in the original. He was not content to take things at second-hand or to rely on other men's work. Dugdale offered to procure him the loan of an unspecified work from one whom Twysden describes (in 1658) as 'one of the great ornaments of the afflicted Church of England' but Twysden declined the offer: '. . . I am not so good at the Saxon as I wish I were, and I must tell you truly I have ever found myself unable to make use of other men's labours, for I must myself weigh every piece in an author, conferring one with another, or it doth me no good.' He was following the precept of Selden, who in his preface to Drayton's *Polyolbion* had written 'My thirst compelled me always to seek the fountains and, by that, if means grant it, judge the river's nature'.

He weighed his evidence cautiously, not accepting it merely because it was convenient nor distorting it to fit his argument. His approach, as he recognized, differed radically from that of Coke, and in several passages in *Certain Considerations upon the Government of England*, including the suppressed passages, he criticizes Coke's bad history. It was the difference between the lawyer who wanted to use history to create the present law and the historian who wanted to understand the past, to know what men had thought and said and done.

Twysden was fully aware of the difficulty of establishing historical truth. He was not conceited about his own achievement, expressed himself often as willing to be convinced of his error, and was prepared to leave a question open if he thought the evidence to answer it inadequate. One example will suffice to illustrate his attitude: after dealing with the difficult question of petitions in early Parliaments he concludes 'I confess I had in this rather hear the opinion of more learned men, and shall be ever ready to retract what I deliver as my own conceit upon better grounds, and, giving my reasons for what I hold, leave every one free to resolve upon better'.

Hearne, no negligible judge, spoke of 'the famous Sir Roger Twysden', and Professor Galbraith brackets him, with Selden and Spelman, as the 'three really big figures' in seventeenth-century historical scholarship.[1] In quality of scholarship, though not in quantity of output, Twysden deserves to be ranked with his two more famous contemporaries. To assess his achievement it is necessary to remember the state of historical writing in the seventeenth century. England had been rich in antiquaries and annalists, and Bacon's *History of the Reign of Henry VIII* and Ralegh's *History of the World* were great works. But, as Edmond Bolton said, our historical writings 'do seem to resemble some huge disproportionate Temple, whose architect was not his art's master'. Nothing quite like *Certain Considerations upon the Government of England* or *An Historical Vindication of the Church of England* had appeared before. With Spelman, Twysden showed how topical history should be written, how historical documents should be tested and interpreted, and how debate could be conducted with courtesy. He neither misused his materials nor abused his opponents, and there were few contemporary writers on controversial subjects of whom that could be said. In short, he was a scholar.

[1] V. H. Galbraith, in *English Historical Scholarship in the Sixteenth and Seventeenth Centuries* (1956), p. 118.

CHAPTER ELEVEN

The Man

TWYSDEN WROTE his own epitaph. We have Dr. Johnson's authority for it that in lapidary inscriptions a man is not upon oath, and it is a principle of the Common Law that a man is not obliged to incriminate himself. But when Twysden said of himself '*non minus pietate, prudentia, aliisque virtutibus, quam varia et magna eruditione excelluit; tam divinis quam humanis literis, praesertim historicis antique gentis nostrae monumentis maxime versatus*' he was not indulging in mere tombstone rhetoric.

Pietas is a quality which he constantly exhibited. By temperament as well by upbringing he belonged in religion to the *via media* of the Church of England as it had been established in Elizabeth's reign. Love of the Church and of antiquity for him, as for Camden and Spelman, Marsham and Dugdale, went hand in hand—naturally so, according to White Kennett, Bishop of Peterborough, for 'a good cause must appear best to those who look farthest back upon it'. With Hooker he believed that in those things which are matter of church polity, as opposed to matters of faith and salvation, a man should conform to the law duly made by the State in its secular aspect. When, in 1637 the communion table was moved to the east end of East Peckham Church and set up altar-wise, with seats against the wall for communicants, Twysden raised no objection and his only recorded comment concerned the manner of paying for the alteration. This was a matter indifferent, but when a witness said in his presence at the Assizes that her scandalous life here was no matter, for when she was gone from this life there was no other judgement to come, he was, literally, horrified. Where conscience was engaged he could become as obstinate as any

Puritan; as an example, although it would have been to his advantage to take the Covenant, he could not, in conscience, do it.

In religion, as in politics, he abhorred extreme positions and shunned doctrinal dispute. There was a streak of quietism in his character and had he been born three centuries earlier he might well have spent his life as one of those monkish chroniclers whose work he used so affectionately. The dissolution of the monasteries, in common with Leland, Camden, Spelman and Dugdale, he regretted: 'What can the ill be,' he asks 'to have places set apart, whither men either by Nature, Time or otherwise unfit for the world, may retire themselves in religious company, and think on Heaven and good learning'. This desire for a quiet life, to avoid the crude realities of the world of affairs, was one of the reasons why Twysden did not join the King at Oxford.[1] Had he done so Prince Rupert and the courtiers would have thought him, with his solid qualities of a Roman paterfamilias, a dull dog; and he would have thought them giddy and irreverent. Those who found themselves in opposition to Parliament were anything but a homogeneous group.

Prudentia is a necessary rather than an attractive quality, one which we know that we ought to admire and which we come to admire by ratiocination rather than spontaneously. Twysden had it in full measure. It guided him in all his affairs, whether on estate matters, historical or political questions, or parish and county government. Never, apparently, did he act rashly, save perhaps for the second excursion to the Assizes of 1642, and again in his last two or three years when the obstinacy of old age once or twice prompted him to a course of action that earlier he would have avoided as being unwise.

The prudence with which Twysden cared for his property was not just an emanation of selfish acquisitiveness. He saw himself as the trustee for one generation of the family estate, with moral obligations towards the property itself and towards

[1] 'He that is truly prudent,' Twysden cryptically confided to one of his common-place books 'cannot value his life less than his honour'. He valued both.

his descendants that assumed greater importance than its immediate enjoyment and exploitation. He never discusses the 'sacredness' of or the 'natural right' to property, partly because it was too obvious to need discussion, partly because such a discussion would belong to the realm of philosophy, which he eschews. But he was conscious of the connexion between the subject's right to property and his liberty. The expropriation of the religious houses troubled him as being wrong in itself and also a dangerous precedent: 'When the ice is once broken for either Prince or any else, by these extraordinary ways of assuming the estates of others (of what condition soever), it is hard to say where it will stop,' he wrote in 1641. Ten years later he knew from experience where it might lead to: the execution of the King, the despotic government of a self-perpetuating oligarchy, the clear stream of the law muddied and diverted out of its proper course, inequitable punishment, the arbitrary seizure of the subject's property. Liberty and property go together.

It was prudence that made Twysden anxious that a trial of strength between King and Parliament should be avoided since its inevitable consequence would be arbitrary government by the victor. The Kentish petition which landed him in such trouble urged a compromise between the two sides and that a good understanding be speedily renewed between them. He never wished, after war had been begun, that the King should come in as an absolute conqueror, and therefore as an absolute monarch, but that King and Parliament might each perform, and limit themselves to, those functions which England's constitutional history showed to belong to their respective spheres.

Modern writers have enabled us to see the new forces that were at work, the new trends that were developing in the seventeenth century. Not having had the advantage of reading their works, Twysden was unconscious of these metamorphoses. He looked for guidance to tradition and saw the future as a regular projection of the past. 'Ask for the old paths, where is the good way, and walk therein.' Even at his father's funeral he refused to allow the Vicar to take the black cloth over the hearse because it was not customary. His dispute with the Heralds also arising from the funeral was a dispute as to what was customary. His constant anxiety over heriot, as payer or receiver, was due to the fear that there might be a breach with what was customary, and therefore right. When he came to examine the great constitutional issues, he brought to them the same conservative attitude. Innovation must be avoided. The principle on which he acted, or more often resisted action, was that nothing should ever be done for the first time.

It is an attitude antipathetic to the radical, progressive, mind, one which can easily be caricatured. It stems from the fundamental notion of a system of divinely ordained order, the great chain of being with God at its head, the angels in their proper ranks subordinate to Him, then man, in all his hierarchical arrangement, followed by the birds, beasts and fishes, below them the plants and trees, and finally inanimate objects such as stones and metals. Let but one link be broken and the whole chain falls apart, chaos ensues. It is this same importance of order that Ulysses insists on in *Troilus and Cressida*:

> The heavens themselves, the planets and this centre,
> Observe degree, priority and place,
> Insisture, course, proportion, season, form,
> Office and custom, in all line of order;
> . . . O, when degree is shaked,
> Which is the ladder to all high designs,
> The enterprise is sick . . .
> Take but degree away, untune that string,
> And hark what discord follows!

Twysden was acutely conscious of the proper social order. He would not speak out of turn at Quarter Sessions or the Assizes, and to copy a letter or other document in which men are named in the wrong order of precedence is a matter for apology. He grew up in a society where men knew their place and in a family where proper order was insisted upon; for his mother, after all, was the daughter of a Countess.

Notwithstanding his respect for social order, he was, as his brother said, 'not to be awed by greatness'. He was as ready to oppose the Duke of Richmond, Lord Lieutenant, or the Assize Judge, as he had been to oppose the collectors of ship-money or Parliamentary impositions. Whenever it was proposed, and by whomever it was intended, to do something for which he believed that lawful authority (that is, authority based on good precedent) was lacking, he was to be found in opposition.

He showed equal independence of mind in his work as a scholar. Diligent inquiry, the amassing of all the evidence and its impartial examination must be followed by an independent judgement and that in turn by the action dictated by the proprieties of the case—'every man ought to satisfy himself and do accordingly' is the attitude of a sturdy liberty which is yet compatible with a modest diffidence and an acknowledgment that certainty is hard, perhaps impossible, to attain. Because no man can be sure that his opinion, beyond a peradventure, is the right one, tolerance is essential, especially in religious matters, for 'Men of great sincerity and judgement may differ in theological tenets'. Such an attitude marks the metamorphosis from the medieval to the modern spirit.

Yet in his devotion to precedent and his respect for history, Twysden exhibited the medievalism which was one of the contradictory features of the seventeenth-century common lawyer. He rejoiced when Charles summoned Parliament in 1640, for this was a return to the old paths, the good way, 'never imagining a Parliament would have took upon them the redressing things amiss . . . by a way not traced out to them by their ancestors'. In minor matters he was equally insistent that, both in form and in substance, the law should be meticulously observed. 'The due administration of justice' was dear to him, both the phrase and the thing. When a certain George Bristock set up a brewhouse in Tonbridge, claiming to have a patent from the Court giving him a monopoly of brewing in the town, only Twysden and one other justice, Henry Dixon, were prepared to proceed against him, and they did it not because their own private interests were threatened but because they contested the legality of his claim. It was the same with the small quit-rents and heriots; if they were legally due they must be paid even though as an act of grace they might be returned immediately. But once allow the smallest breach in the dyke of legality, and sooner or later the whole bank will crumble away.

Insistence on due process of law can degenerate into arid legalism, form for form's sake. Twysden sometimes got near it but on the whole was saved that besetting vice of lawyers by his sense of justice, honesty, and truthfulness. The inequity of Parliament's arbitrary proceedings outraged him. Equity required that both sides should be heard, yet the House of Commons constantly acted *ex parte*. The House might not have liked some of the petitions which were got up, but at least it should have allowed them to be presented and considered. To condemn a man unheard or to punish him for some act that is not a clearly proven breach of a known and certain law is tyranny. Dicey's doctrine of the Rule of Law would have commanded Twysden's unqualified assent. Penal statutes, he frequently argued, were to be given a narrow, not an extended construction; they should be precise, leave as little discretion as possible to the Court, and so limit the scope of arbitrary decision.

He made a conscientious attempt to judge fairly whenever in his writings he had occasion to pass judgement upon the conduct or character of his opponents. The scrupulosity with which he records the kindnesses which from time to time he received at their hands is one of the features that give credence to the *Historical Narrative*. He even found something good to say of Weldon: 'I can not deny him to have been a person had noble principles; yet shadowed with many vanities if not vices: a good friend where he took, no less an enemy . . . one, I dare say, did not in his heart approve the actions of the two Houses, yet the desire of rule brought him to run with the forwardest.' For years before the beginning of his troubles Twysden had known that Sir John Sedley was no friend of his, but refused to lend his support to an attempt to bring him before the Privy Council for using rash words to Sir Thomas Walsingham 'considering how unworthy it was to take upon me the Devil's office of an accuser'.[1] In the same spirit he refused to record in the *Historical Narrative* the names of the seven members of the County Committee who signed an especially iniquitous order for the felling of his timber. There is not a single recorded occasion of his making a spiteful or vicious remark orally or in writing.

A man who could show such charity towards his enemies was likely to be a kind friend, an affectionate husband, and a good father. Twysden was all three. He counted amongst his friends not only his gentleman neighbours and scholars who shared his taste for learning, but also old and trusted tenants between whom and their landlord existed a bond of mutual respect. In his domestic life he was the pattern of virtue. With his brothers and sisters and their wives and husbands he kept up a constantly repaired friendship. For his children he had a fatherly affection which stopped short of doting fondness. Neither within his family nor in the parish did he practise a thoughtless liberality, but there are many minor instances to show that he was often prompted by generous feelings. It was in character that he should involve the Vicar of East Peckham in a law-suit over tithes, and also in character that, having won the suit, he should pay the whole of the costs because the Vicar was poor, but without telling him in advance that he intended to do so. His notebooks record numerous small acts of almsgiving which must have been undertaken purely from charitable motives with no thought of popular approbation. By his will he left a 50*s*. rent-charge for the benefit of the poor of the parish but not to be used to relieve those on the rates, for that would be, indirectly, to benefit the rich. Caution and moderation did not desert him even when he was about acts of charity.

He was not a fluent speaker ('at his best he were never voluble,' his brother said) and delivered his thoughts more happily through his pen than with his tongue. Yet at times he

[1] The occasion was this. A proposal had been made that all Deputy Lieutenants in the County should be made Colonels. When Twysden, Sedley and Sir John Rivers were standing on the bench, Sir Thomas Walsingham came up to them. 'Sir John Sedley as it were calling to him, yet so as he could not hear him, cries out "Colonel Tom, Colonel Coxcomb, a company of Coxcomb Colonels" ', which words afterwards spread abroad.

could be somewhat hasty (he was of a sanguine complexion and rather short) but he was of 'an extremely sweet nature' so that his hastiness 'passed instantly without retaining the least resentment or so much as memory of his anger'.

Of his integrity no man ever made question and his contemporary reputation for accuracy, honesty and truthfulness has survived. He would stand upon his rights to the point of obstinacy but his mind was always accessible to reason. If ever there was an example of the law's 'reasonable man' it was Twysden. It was his misfortune to live at a time when the country was governed rather according to men's emotions than their reason: as, perhaps, it usually has been. Indeed, he was almost naïve in his belief that men would always act according to reason and to law, and that even in the midst of that misery, a civil war, those who were for the King would be safe—'there being nothing they could legally lose'.

The biography of a man so eminently worthy, so virtuous and so judiciously balanced, canno possess the excitement of the life of a Pepys, a Rupert or even a Peters. It is only too easy to bestow on such a one 'the spurns that patient merit of the unworthy takes', to write him off as being monumentally dull. He was not a complex character (Professor Notestein has drawn attention to the fact that even the privileged and fortunate men and women of the seventeenth century seem 'less complicated creatures than those of recent generations')[1] and he would, I suppose, offer little scope for the speculative operation of a psychoanalyst.[2] In his emotional and intellectual make-up there were no aberrant or inconsistent elements: he was all of a piece. Doubtless no one would choose him as a boon companion for a bout of conviviality, but his contemporaries were right to see that his virtues were positive and important ones. *Pietas, gravitas, prudentia:* they were the virtues of the Roman citizen when the Republic was at its height, and the virtues which are essential in the citizens of any free commonwealth if it is to survive.

[1] *The English People on the eve of Colonization* (1962 edn.), p. 34.

[2] He did keep accounts of certain legal proceedings, not all of them English, in which the evidence was of a kind more likely to amuse Chaucer than the Director of Public Prosecutions, but that hardly proves more than that his interests and appetites were normal.

Appendix: Manuscript Material used

British Museum

Add MSS.	34154	Rentals of manors belonging to the Twysden family, sixteenth and seventeenth centuries.
	34155	Survey of lands at East Peckham, 1630.
	34161	Letters from Twysden, mainly to his son, Charles.
	34162	Farm accounts, 1639–56.
	34163–5	Notebooks.
	34166	Accounts of Chelmington and Romney Marsh estates.
	34167	Payments of tithes, quit-rents, etc.
	34168	Receipts for rent, and note by Sir William Twysden of his father's death.
	34169–72	Diaries of Lady Twysden, 1645, 1647–9.
	34173	Family letters.
	34174	Miscellaneous papers, sixteenth to nineteenth centuries.
	34175	Miscellaneous estate papers.
	34176	Family papers.
	34177	Miscellaneous Twysden papers, sixteenth to nineteenth centuries.
	34178	Francis Warrall's Tithe-book.
	34558	Court book of the Manor of Albons alias Wymplingbury.
	5513	Catalogue of manuscripts relating to Kent (includes a list of MSS. at Roydon Hall: eighteenth century).
	22916 f. 6	Lady Twysden to Sir Simonds D'Ewes.
	24281–3	Cowell's *Interpreter*, with Twysden's notes.
	26785	Kentish correspondence, 1640–1 (printed as *Proceedings in Kent*, 1640, Camden Society, 1862).
Stowe	33	Transcript of *Anselmi Epistolae* made under Twysden's supervision.

Stowe	359	Extracts from Rolls of Parliament, 1 Richard III and 1 Henry VII, and Journals of the Lords and Commons, *regno* Elizabeth, transcribed by Twysden.
	184 and 743	contain letters about the 1640 Parliamentary elections.
Harley	6018	Cotton's library loan list.

The following British Museum manuscripts were formerly in Twysden's possession and some contain notes by him:

Stowe	49	J. de Voragne. Legenda Aurea.
	62	William of Newbury's Chronicle.
	96	Relazioni, etc., 1620–34 (a legacy from William Twysden)
	311–12	Dialogus de Scaccario
	329	Modus tenendi Parliamentum.
	346–53	Extracts from the Rolls of Parliament, from 1 Richard II to 39 Henry VI.
	378	Gratiani Decretum.
	857	Allegations and proofs as to watching duty on Denge Marsh.
Burney	3	Biblia Sacra olim Roberti Abbatis Augustini Cantuarensis.
	220	Ovid's Epistles.
	224	Ovid's Metamorphoses.
	297	Bede's Ecclesiastical History.
Egerton	2677	Missal.
Add MSS.	38139	William of Malmesbury's Historia.

Bodleian Library

MSS. Engl. Hist. C. 29. A chronological collection of historical notes, mainly extracts from the chronicles, made by Twysden.

MSS. Barlow 9. MS. of *The Beginners of a Monastic Life* (not in Twysden's hand).

MSS. Rawlinson K (Hearne) 124. Extracts from Twysden's *Remembrances*.

Twysden's MS. additions and corrections to *The Commoner's Liberty*.

Kent Archaeological Society's Collections (at the Kent County Archives Office)

U. 47/47 Z 1, 2 Miscellaneous papers collected by Twysden (including some of his MS. notes).

U. 47/47 O. 1 Notebook as a Justice of the Peace 1635–72.

Kent County Archives Office

U. 48 E. :	Lease to George Stone, 1643.
U. 48 F. 2, 3	Lady Anne Twysden's testamentary directions.
U. 48 O. 5, 1	Twysden's appointment as a Deputy Lieutenant, 1662.
U. 48 T.	Title deeds.
U. 48 Z. 1	Commonplace book.
U. 48 Z. 2, 3	Notebooks, containing some material afterwards used in *The Commoner's Liberty* and *Certain Considerations on Government.*
U. 49 A. 1	Account books, 1668–72.
U. 49 F. 19	Diary for 1638.
U. 49 O. 81	Book of receipts for hearth tax, etc.
U. 49 T.	Title deeds, and probates of wills.
U. 49 Z. 2	Notes by Francis Twysden, 1714.
U. 49 Z. 3/1–3	Notes and draft letters on treason and ecclesiastical matters.
U. 49 Z. 4/1, 2	MSS. relating to John Twysden.
U. 49 Z. 15	Holograph of *Certain Considerations on Government.*
U. 49 Z. 16	Transcripts made for Twysden from Cotton's library.
U. 49 Z. 18	Commonplace book, *Theologica.*
U. 49 Z. 19	Notebook of certain legal and historical terms.
U. 350	Dering MSS.
U. 386	Darell MSS.
Q/RT.	Hearth Tax assessment, 1664.

Lambeth Palace Library

An Historical Narrative of the two Houses of Parliament . . . proceeding against Sir Roger Twysden (printed in *Archaeologia Cantiana*, vols. I–IV).

Notebook as a County Magistrate, 1636.

Correspondence between Twysden and Whetenhall.

St. Michael's Church, East Peckham

Registers, 1558–1653 and 1653–1796.

Gray's Inn

Admissions book.

Maidstone Museum

A small collection of title deeds, estate papers and family papers.

Larking transcripts.

The Report of the Historical Manuscripts Commission on *The Manuscripts of A. G. Finch, Esquire, at Burley-on-the-Hill* (1913) contains summaries of correspondence between Twysden and Sir Heneage Finch in 1666–8.

Index